Microsoft

Microsoft
Power BI
Step by Step

Nuric Ugarte
José Rafael Escalante

Microsoft Power BI Step by Step
Published with the authorization of Microsoft Corporation by:
Pearson Education, Inc.

ISBN-13: 978-0-13-546832-6
ISBN-10: 0-13-546832-9

Library of Congress Control Number is on file.

2 2025

Trademarks
Microsoft and the trademarks listed at http://www.microsoft.com on the "Trademarks" web page are trademarks of the Microsoft group of companies. All other marks are property of their respective owners.

Portfolio Manager
Loretta Yates

Associate Editor
Shourav Bose

Development Editor
Songlin Qiu

Managing Editor
Sandra Schroeder

Senior Project Editor
Tonya Simpson

Copy Editor
Chuck Hutchinson

Indexer
Brad Herriman

Proofreader
Jennifer Hinchliffe

Technical Editor
Owen Auger

Cover Designer
Twist Creative, Seattle

Compositor
codeMantra

Contents

KD 11 17 2025 0441

4   Transforming data with Power Query **59**

7 Building your first report. **123**

8   Designing advanced visualizations. **153**

9   Enhancing reports. **175**

Acknowledgments

Nuric Ugarte

Writing this book has been both a challenge and a great privilege, and I am deeply grateful to the many people who made it possible.

First, I want to thank the Pearson team for trusting me with this project. Special thanks to Shourav Bose for his guidance throughout the process, to Tonya Simpson, Songlin Qiu, and our technical editor, Owen Auger, for their careful reviews and thoughtful feedback that made this book stronger and clearer at every stage.

I also want to acknowledge my co-author, José Rafael, who was the first person to introduce me to Power BI and my mentor during my early steps. Thank you for accepting the invitation to join this project; working together made the journey more enjoyable and enriching.

A heartfelt thank you to my family, especially my husband, Javier, and my son, Matías, for their love, patience, and support. Many evenings, weekends, and moments were given to this book, and I could not have done it without their encouragement and understanding.

This book is dedicated to everyone who believes in the power of data to transform decisions, organizations, and lives.

José Rafael Escalante

First of all, I want to thank Nuric for inviting me to be part of this project, and for her patience and trust during the moments when I doubted my ability to translate knowledge and professional experience into these pages.

To the entire Pearson team, and especially to Shourav Bose, Songlin Qiu, Owen Auger, and Tonya Simpson. This was my first editorial experience, and I deeply value the work you've done. The level of rigor and the many steps required to bring a technical book to life are truly impressive. My respect and gratitude to each of you.

To my family, my mother, Carmen, and my niece, Andrea, who witnessed the ups and downs throughout the months I spent writing, reflecting, and refining ideas to meet the teaching goals I had set. Thank you for being there.

About the authors

 **Nuric Ugarte** is a business intelligence consultant and Microsoft Certified Trainer (MCT) specializing in Microsoft Fabric and Power BI, with extensive experience delivering enterprise analytics solutions for major companies in the USA, Canada, and LATAM, working across a wide range of industries.

She regularly delivers workshops and training sessions on Microsoft Fabric and Power BI, empowering professionals and organizations to successfully adopt these technologies.

She is also active in the data community, contributing articles on a wide range of topics in Microsoft Fabric and Power BI, from data modeling and performance optimization to security, licensing, best practices, and certification preparation through her Gold Data blog.

Nuric served as a technical editor for *Exam Ref DP-600 Implementing Analytics Solutions Using Microsoft Fabric*, published by Pearson.

 **José Rafael Escalante** is a consultant and trainer specializing in data analytics and business visualization, with a proven track record in the strategic use of Microsoft Power BI. He was recognized as a Most Valuable Professional (MVP) in the Data Platform category, he has assisted organizations from different sectors in adopting business intelligence solutions, combining technical precision with pedagogical sensitivity.

His approach as an educator is reflected in a modular, clear, and empathetic narrative, aimed at facilitating understanding without sacrificing technical depth. Throughout his nearly decade-long career, he has developed semantic models, business reports, specialized articles, and educational video content, including online courses and a YouTube channel. He has also hosted a podcast and participated in technical community events, bringing complex concepts to a wide audience in an accessible and meaningful way.

Introduction

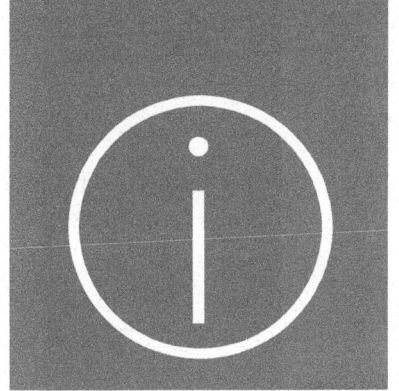

Microsoft Power BI is a leading business intelligence platform that enables individuals and organizations to transform raw data into actionable insights. With Power BI, you can connect to a wide variety of data sources, clean and transform the data, model it effectively, and create interactive reports and dashboards that communicate insights clearly. Power BI also integrates seamlessly with the Microsoft ecosystem, including Excel, Teams, PowerPoint, and now Copilot, making it a key tool for modern, data-driven decision-making.

This book is part of the *Step by Step* series, designed to guide you through the fundamentals of Power BI with clear explanations and practical, hands-on exercises. Whether you are new to data analysis or already familiar with Microsoft tools, this book provides the knowledge and skills you need to confidently use Power BI for your own projects.

Who this book is for

Microsoft Power BI Step by Step is written for beginning to intermediate users who want to learn how to analyze, visualize, and share data effectively. If you have experience with Excel or other Microsoft applications but are new to Power BI, this book will help you get started and progress to more advanced scenarios at your own pace.

This book is ideal for

- Business analysts and data analysts who need to transform and visualize data
- Excel power users who want to expand their skills into modern BI tools
- IT professionals and consultants who need to support business users with reporting
- Students, researchers, and small business owners who want to make data-driven decisions

At the same time, this book goes beyond the basics. In addition to covering the core skills every Power BI user needs, it includes a dedicated chapter on advanced topics and best practices, providing guidance on performance tuning, row-level security (RLS), and scalable design. In addition, a full chapter on Copilot in Power BI shows how AI can accelerate tasks such as preparing data, generating DAX formulas, and creating effective visualizations. These advanced sections ensure that you gain not only solid foundational skills but also practical knowledge to take your Power BI projects to the next level.

How this book is organized

This book is divided into 13 chapters:

- **Chapter 1, Introduction to Power BI,** provides an overview of the Power BI ecosystem, its main components, and its role in the business intelligence landscape.

- **Chapter 2, Setting up Power BI,** covers the installation and initial configuration of Power BI Desktop, including an introduction to the interface and essential settings.

- **Chapter 3, Importing data,** explores the Power Query Editor, shows how to connect to common data sources, explains storage modes, and describes privacy levels.

- **Chapter 4, Transforming data with Power Query,** focuses on cleaning and shaping data by defining data types, applying transformations, adjusting table structures, and combining queries to prepare reliable datasets for analysis.

- **Chapter 5, Creating a simple semantic model,** explains how to define relationships, manage filters and hierarchies, and customize the semantic model.

- **Chapter 6, Performing basic calculations with DAX,** introduces the DAX formula language and shows how to create simple measures and calculated columns.

- **Chapter 7, Building your first report,** explains how to create an interactive report by adding and customizing visuals, applying slicers and filters, and organizing the layout for clarity.

- **Chapter 8, Designing advanced visualizations,** explores complex visuals such as maps, scatter plots, decomposition trees, and small multiples.

- **Chapter 9, Enhancing reports,** covers techniques to improve design and interactivity, including themes, bookmarks, tooltips, and mobile layouts.

- **Chapter 10, Publishing and sharing reports,** explains how to publish reports to the Power BI Service, configure scheduled refreshes, and collaborate in workspaces.

- **Chapter 11, Creating dashboards,** shows how to combine content from multiple reports into dashboards, add comments, and configure data alerts.

- **Chapter 12, Applying advanced topics and best practices,** discusses row-level security (RLS), performance tuning, DAX optimization, and visualization best practices.

- **Chapter 13, Exploring Copilot in Power BI,** demonstrates how AI can assist in preparing data, generating DAX formulas, and recommending visuals both in Power BI Desktop and the Service.

The structure of these chapters allows you to learn the basics step by step if you are new to Power BI. If you are already familiar with data analysis, you can focus on the chapters that are most relevant to your needs. Each topic is self-contained, so you can follow the book from start to finish or jump directly to the skills you want to acquire.

At the end of each chapter, you will also find a series of practice tasks that allow you to apply the skills introduced in the chapter.

Download the practice files

Before you can complete the exercises in this book, you need to download the book's practice files to your computer. These practice files can be downloaded from the Downloads tab on the following page:

MicrosoftPressStore.com/powerbiSBS/downloads

> ⚠ IMPORTANT To complete the practice tasks in this book, you need to have Power BI Desktop installed on your computer. You can download it free from the Microsoft Store or from the official Power BI website.

The following table lists the practice files for this book.

Chapter	File
Chapter 3: Importing data	Financial Sample.xlsx
	Sales folder with five .CSV files.
Chapter 4: Transforming data with Power Query	Applying columnar transformations.xlsx
	Changing table structures.xlsx
	Combining and appending tables.xlsx
Chapter 5: Creating a simple semantic model	customer.csv
	date.csv
	product.csv
	sales.csv
	store.csv
Chapter 6: Performing basic calculations with DAX	DAX Practice file.pbix
Chapter 7: Building your first report	Report practice file.pbix
Chapter 9: Enhancing reports	Enhancing reports practice file.pbix

Get support and give feedback

The following sections provide information about getting help with this book and contacting us to provide feedback or report errors.

Errata

We've made every effort to ensure the accuracy of this book and its companion content. Any errors that have been reported since this book was published are listed at:

MicrosoftPressStore.com/powerbiSBS/errata

If you discover an error that is not already listed, please submit it to us at the same page.

For additional book support and information, please visit *MicrosoftPressStore.com/Support*.

Please note that product support for Microsoft software and hardware is not offered through the previous addresses. For help with Microsoft software or hardware, visit *support.microsoft.com*.

Introduction to Power BI

Practice files

There are no practice files for this chapter.

In the digital era, data is the most valuable asset of any organization. The ability to analyze it and transform it into useful information is key to strategic decision-making. This is where business intelligence (BI) tools come into play, and within this ecosystem, Power BI has become one of the most powerful and popular solutions.

Power BI is a platform developed by Microsoft that enables users to connect to data sources, transform and model that data, and create visually rich reports and dashboards. It empowers individuals and organizations to derive insights from their data and share those insights in compelling and interactive ways.

In this chapter, you'll explore the Power BI ecosystem and learn about its three core components:

- **Power BI Desktop:** Interface used to build data models and reports

- **Power BI Service:** Cloud-based platform for sharing and collaborating on reports

- **Power BI Mobile:** Mobile application that allows users to view, interact with, and share Power BI reports and dashboards on smartphones and tablets

In this chapter

- Understand how Power BI fits into the BI ecosystem

- Identify the main components of Power BI

- Recognize the key roles involved in working with Power BI

The chapter will also discuss the role of Power BI within the business intelligence ecosystem and what makes it a preferred tool for organizations of all sizes.

Understand how Power BI fits into the BI ecosystem

Business Intelligence (BI) refers to the set of technologies and strategies used to collect, transform, analyze, and visualize data to support business decision-making.

Traditionally, BI tools required complex infrastructure and a specialized team for their implementation and maintenance. However, the advent of modern tools such as Power BI has democratized access to data analysis, allowing users without deep technical knowledge to work with the information and gain valuable insights.

Let's examine a simple example. In a large company, critical historical data may be stored in fragmented systems or formats that are difficult to access or interpret. Business Intelligence tools like Power BI help transform that raw data into clear, actionable insights, enabling leaders to answer critical business questions with confidence.

Power BI didn't start as a standalone platform. It began as a set of add-ins for Microsoft Excel—PowerPivot, Power Query, and Power View. These tools laid the groundwork for the all-in-one solution that Power BI is today. If you're familiar with Excel, you'll likely find Power BI's experience intuitive and approachable.

Officially launched in 2015, Power BI quickly evolved into a robust BI platform that supports everything from data modeling to advanced analytics. Frequent updates, integration with Microsoft Azure, and support for artificial intelligence have made it one of the most popular BI tools in the industry.

Following are some of the reasons Power BI stands out:

- Power BI offers an intuitive, user-friendly interface that enables users to build reports and dashboards using drag-and-drop functionality, making the report creation process accessible even to nontechnical users.

1

- Power BI integrates seamlessly with other Microsoft products, such as Excel, SQL Server, Azure, Teams, SharePoint, and many more, allowing users to connect, share, and collaborate across the organization.

- Power BI has the flexibility to operate in both cloud (Power BI Service) and on-premise (Power BI Report Server) environments. It provides support for advanced analytics features, including artificial intelligence, machine learning, real-time streaming, and integration with Python and R.

Explore Power BI's role within Microsoft Fabric

Because you're reading this book, it is very likely that you are taking your first steps with Power BI. However, as you progress in your learning, you may at some point hear that Power BI is now part of a broader platform called Microsoft Fabric.

Power BI has evolved from being an independent service to becoming a key component within the Microsoft Fabric ecosystem, without losing its identity and functionality. Fabric includes services like Data Factory, Real-Time Intelligence, OneLake, and Microsoft Purview, which work alongside Power BI to provide a more scalable and intelligent analytics ecosystem.

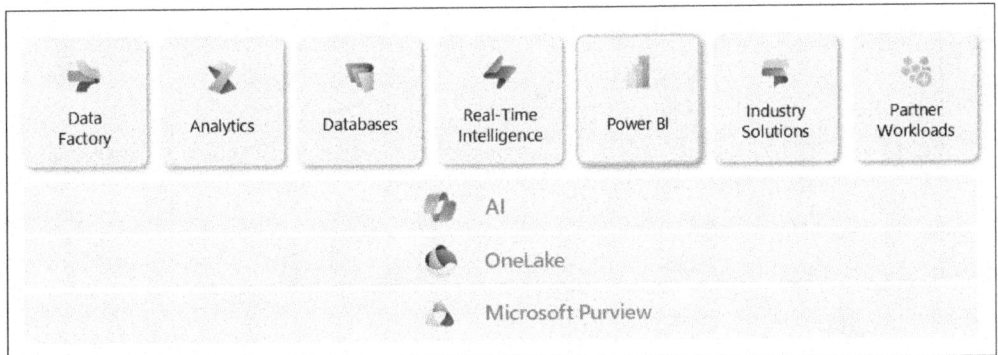

Microsoft Fabric platform components.

> ⚠ **IMPORTANT** You don't need to learn Fabric to use Power BI, but you do need to be aware that with this integration, Power BI benefits from an optimized ecosystem that allows you to connect, model, and visualize data in a more efficient and scalable way. Although Power BI still works independently, its integration with Fabric gives you access to advanced resources that enhance the way information is accessed and consumed.

What makes Power BI different from its competitors?

Power BI has established itself as one of the leading tools in the world of business intelligence, managing to stay in the leader's quadrant for several years alongside other big names such as Tableau and Qlik, standing out for its constant evolution and Microsoft's commitment to innovation and accessibility.

Gartner (June 2024)   **Gartner.**

Power BI in the Gartner Quadrant.

One of the most outstanding technical features of Power BI is its analysis engine, Analysis Services Tabular, considered one of the most powerful on the market. This engine, also used in large-scale business solutions, allows complex calculations to be performed quickly and efficiently, manages large volumes of data in memory, and offers optimal response times even in models with complex structures. This robust architecture allows Power BI to scale easily from personal solutions to full enterprise deployments.

Another major differentiator is that Power BI Desktop is completely free, allowing any user to start importing, transforming, modeling, and visualizing data without the need to purchase a paid license, democratizing access to business intelligence.

Furthermore, Power BI integrates natively with the Microsoft ecosystem, including tools such as Excel, Teams, SharePoint, OneDrive, Azure, and Microsoft 365, which facilitates its adoption and improves collaboration between teams within the same organization.

Identify the main components of Power BI

Power BI is made up of three main components: Power BI Desktop, Power BI Service, and Power BI Mobile, each with specific functions for the creation, publication, and visualization of reports.

Power BI Desktop: Building reports and models

Power BI Desktop is a free application that allows users to connect, transform, and model data, as well as create interactive reports. It is the main tool that analysts and developers use to build reports before publishing them in Power BI Service for distribution and collaboration.

Power BI Desktop provides a canvas where users can build visualizations, manage fields, apply filters, and customize the layout of a report.

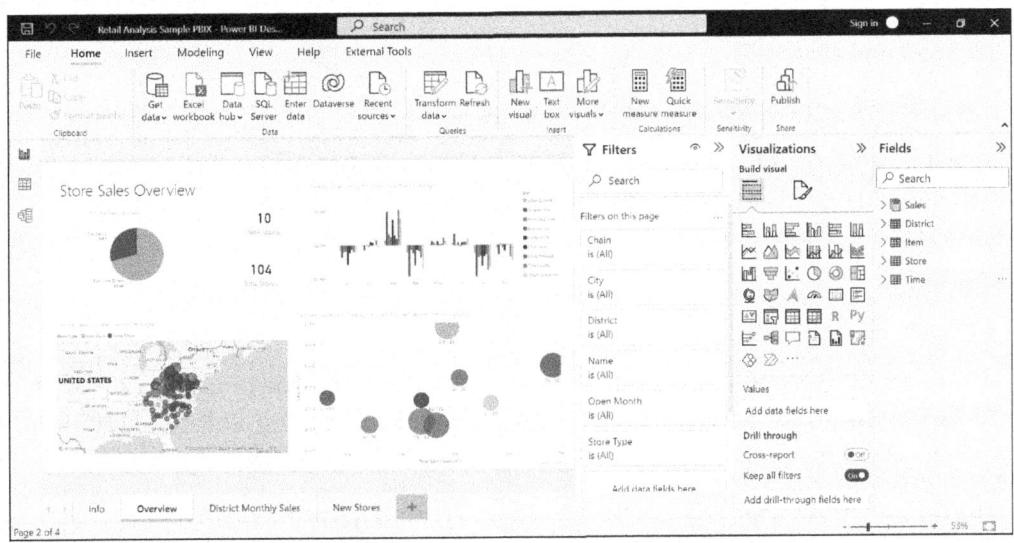

Power BI Desktop report design interface.

Main functions of Power BI Desktop

Power BI Desktop offers a comprehensive set of features that support every stage of the business intelligence workflow, from connecting to data sources to designing and publishing reports. Whether you're preparing data, modeling relationships, or building visualizations, these tools work together to help you create compelling and actionable insights. The following key functions are available in Power BI Desktop:

- Connect to multiple data sources such as Excel, SQL Server, APIs, and cloud databases, among others.
- Transform and clean data using Power Query.
- Create data models by establishing relationships between tables.
- Design interactive visualizations with charts, tables, maps, and custom objects.
- Write advanced calculations using Data Analysis Expressions (DAX).
- Publish reports to Power BI Service to share with other users.

Common users of Power BI Desktop

Professionals across different roles and industries use Power BI Desktop. Its intuitive interface and powerful capabilities make it accessible not only to technical users but also to business professionals who need to create data-driven reports. The following users commonly rely on Power BI Desktop in their daily work:

- Data analysts
- Report developers
- Business professionals who need to generate customized reports

Power BI Desktop is the starting point for any Power BI project because it allows you to build reports that can then be published in the cloud for distribution and collaborative analysis.

Power BI Service: Sharing and collaborating in the cloud

After a report has been designed in Power BI Desktop, it can be published in Power BI Service, Microsoft's cloud platform that allows for the sharing, collaboration, and management of reports online.

The Power BI Service home interface features a centralized dashboard that provides access to your recent reports, shared dashboards, workspaces, and recommended content.

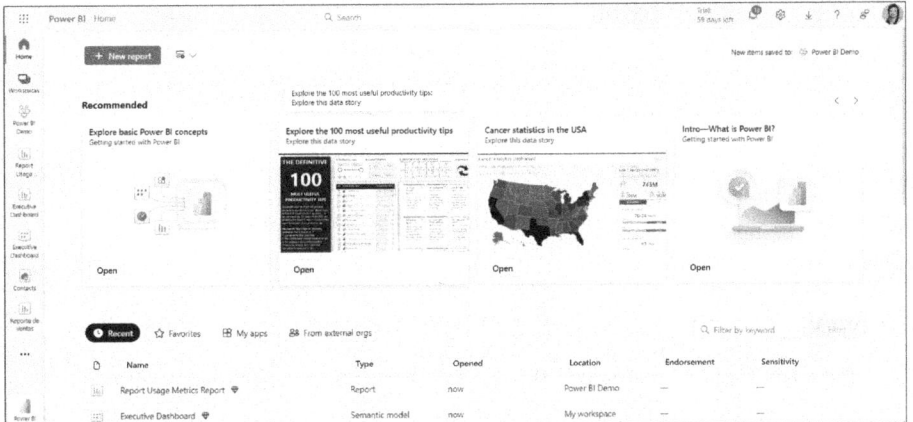

Power BI Service home interface.

Main functions of Power BI Service

After reports are created in Power BI Desktop, they are published to the Power BI Service. This cloud-based platform enables users to manage, share, and collaborate on reports and dashboards at scale. Power BI Service extends the capabilities of Power BI by providing tools for distribution, automation, and security. The following are some of its key functions:

- Publish and share reports and dashboards with other users within the organization.
- Provide team collaboration through shared workspaces and business applications (apps).
- Configure scheduled refreshes to automatically keep your data up-to-date without manual intervention.
- Offer security enforcement and access control using row-level security (RLS).
- Provide advanced analytics capabilities with artificial intelligence to detect trends and anomalies in data.

Who uses Power BI Service?

Power BI Service is designed to support a broad range of users across an organization, from decision-makers to technical teams. Its cloud-based environment makes it easy to access and share insights securely, enabling collaboration and data-driven decision-making at all levels. The following users typically benefit from the Power BI Service:

- Executives and managers (to view reports and dashboards)
- Data and IT teams (to manage security and access to information)
- Business analysts (to share insights with other departments)

Power BI service is available in various plans tailored to different user needs and organizational sizes:

- **Free:** For personal use with basic function

- **Pro:** For sharing and collaborating with other users

- **Premium:** For companies that need higher performance and advanced capabilities

Power BI Mobile: Access to data from any device

Power BI Mobile is Microsoft's application for iOS and Android. It enables users to access reports and dashboards hosted in Power BI Service directly from their mobile devices, allowing them to monitor and interact with data in real time from anywhere.

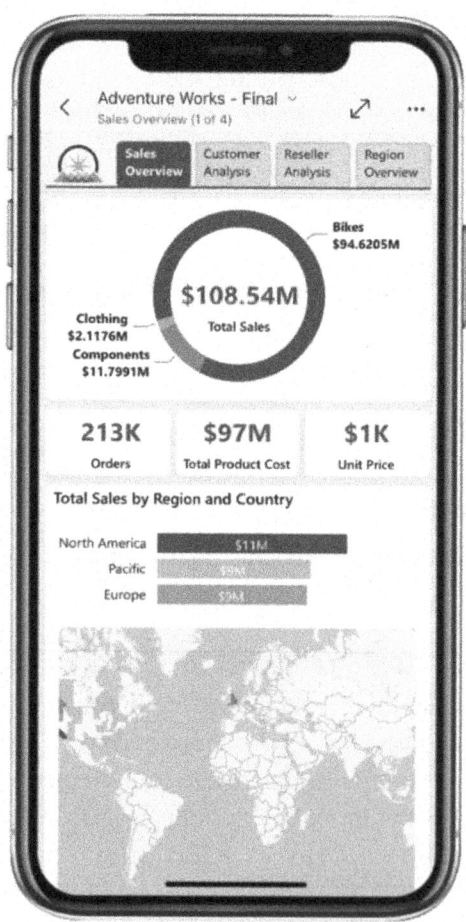

Power BI dashboard on a smartphone using the Power BI Mobile app.

Main functions of Power BI Mobile

Power BI Mobile extends the reach of Power BI by allowing users to stay connected to their data from anywhere. With native apps for smartphones and tablets, users can monitor key metrics, explore dashboards, and receive important alerts on the go. The following main features are available in Power BI Mobile:

- Access reports and dashboards in real time hosted in the Power BI Service.

- Interact with data through filters and touch exploration.

- Receive notifications and alerts about changes in key information.

- Scan QR codes to quickly access specific reports.

Who uses Power BI Mobile?

Power BI Mobile is especially useful for professionals who need access to critical business data while away from their desks. Whether checking performance metrics between meetings or staying informed during travel, users rely on the mobile app to make timely, data-driven decisions. The following are some of the most common users of Power BI Mobile:

- Executives and managers who need to monitor key metrics at any time

- Business and sales teams that require access to real-time information

- Users who want to receive alerts and notifications about changes in data

Power BI Mobile ensures that data is always available, regardless of the user's device or location.

Recognize the key roles involved in working with Power BI

In Power BI, several fundamental roles work together to transform data into useful information for decision-making. Although each organization can adapt them according to its structure, the most common profiles include the following:

- The *Power BI developer* is responsible for connecting data sources, transforming data using Power Query, designing the data model, and creating calculations using DAX. This role ensures that data models are scalable, efficient, and reusable across the organization.

- The *report creator* builds visually compelling dashboards aligned with the company's identity based on the models prepared by the developer. The focus is on visual design and presenting information in a clear, accessible way for the end user. In many cases, especially in small teams, the developer and the report creator may be the same person, which allows for greater integration between data modeling and final visualization.

- The *data analyst* is the one who explores the information in search of patterns and insights. This person often works with existing reports or creates analyses from shared datasets, without the need to model or transform data, but with a basic understanding of the structure. This work is key to supporting tactical and strategic decisions.

- The *end user* is the final consumer of reports and dashboards. This user interacts with the content by navigating, filtering, and drilling down into the data to inform decisions. The end user does not need technical knowledge but should be familiar with the Power BI interface to interact effectively with the information.

> ⚠ **IMPORTANT** Understanding these roles and how they work together is essential for the successful adoption of Power BI because it allows organizations to define appropriate access levels, responsibilities, and training plans for each profile, ensuring a sustainable and effective data strategy.

Skills review

In this chapter, you learned how to

- Explore the role of Power BI in the Business Intelligence (BI) ecosystem and how it empowers data-driven decision-making.

- Identify the main components of Power BI: Power BI Desktop, Service, and Mobile, and understand the function each one plays in the reporting lifecycle.

- Recognize the key user roles involved in working with Power BI, and understand how developers, report creators, analysts, and end users collaborate to build and consume insights.

Practice tasks

No practice files are necessary to complete the practice tasks in this chapter.

Understand how Power BI fits into the BI ecosystem

Review the following concepts discussed in this chapter to strengthen your understanding of Power BI's role in data-driven decision-making:

1. Think about how your organization currently manages and uses data for decision-making and how a tool like Power BI could improve data access or reporting.

2. Write a brief explanation of how Power BI fits within the broader BI ecosystem.

3. Reflect on why ease of use and Microsoft integration are considered key advantages of Power BI. Write a short paragraph summarizing these ideas.

4. Write a short explanation of what Microsoft Fabric is and how Power BI fits within its structure. Then describe two benefits of Power BI being part of the Fabric platform.

Identify the main components of Power BI

Power BI has three main components, each serving a specific role in the data workflow. Complete the following tasks to review their purpose and typical users:

1. Name the three main components of Power BI and briefly describe the function of each.

2. Match each type of user role (developer, report creator, data analyst, end user) with the most appropriate Power BI component these roles typically work with.

Recognize the key roles involved in working with Power BI

Power BI projects involve several key roles, each contributing to different stages of the data process. Use the following tasks to deepen your understanding of these roles and consider how your current or future responsibilities align with the Power BI workflow:

1. Create a table listing the four roles discussed (developer, report creator, data analyst, end user) and summarize the responsibilities of each in one sentence.

2. Reflect on which role you feel most aligned with at this stage of your learning and why.

Setting up Power BI

2

Practice files

No practice files are necessary to complete the practice tasks in this chapter.

In this chapter, you'll learn how to get started with Power BI Desktop, the main application used for creating reports and semantic models in Power BI. Power BI Desktop is a free Windows application that provides everything you need to design, build, and publish powerful data visualizations. It's the starting point for most Power BI projects and is used by analysts, developers, and business users alike.

This chapter will walk through the different ways to install Power BI Desktop, review the system requirements, and explore what happens the first time you launch the app. You'll also become familiar with the user interface and learn how to configure a few key settings to optimize your experience.

Install and set up Power BI Desktop

Before building your first report, you'll need to install Power BI Desktop. In this section, you'll learn the two installation methods, how to verify that your computer meets the system requirements, and what to expect the first time you launch the application.

In this chapter

- Install and set up Power BI Desktop
- Explore Power BI Desktop interface
- Configure Power BI Desktop settings

Power BI Desktop installation options

You can install Power BI Desktop in two ways:

1. Install from the Microsoft Store.

2. Download an executable file (.exe) from the Power BI website.

Both options will give you the latest version, but they work slightly differently and offer different advantages.

 IMPORTANT Power BI Desktop is updated every month, incorporating community feedback, new features, performance improvements, and visual enhancements.

Install from the Microsoft Store

The most recommended and easiest way to install Power BI Desktop is from Microsoft Store. You don't need administrator permissions, and updates are performed automatically, ensuring you always have the latest version.

To install

1. Open your browser and go to the Power BI Desktop page in the Microsoft Store.

2. Select **Install** to download and install the app.

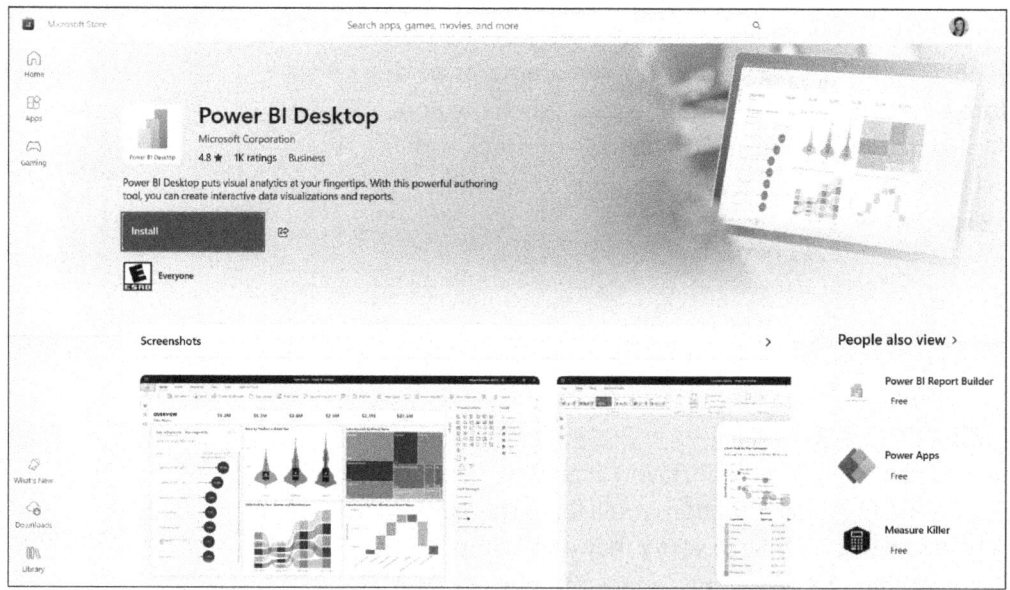

Install Power BI Desktop listing from Microsoft Store.

3. After it is installed, you can launch Power BI Desktop from the Start menu or directly from the Microsoft Store.

 TIP You can also access the Microsoft Store link from the Power BI service. Just select the **Download** icon in the upper-right corner; then select **Power BI Desktop**.

2

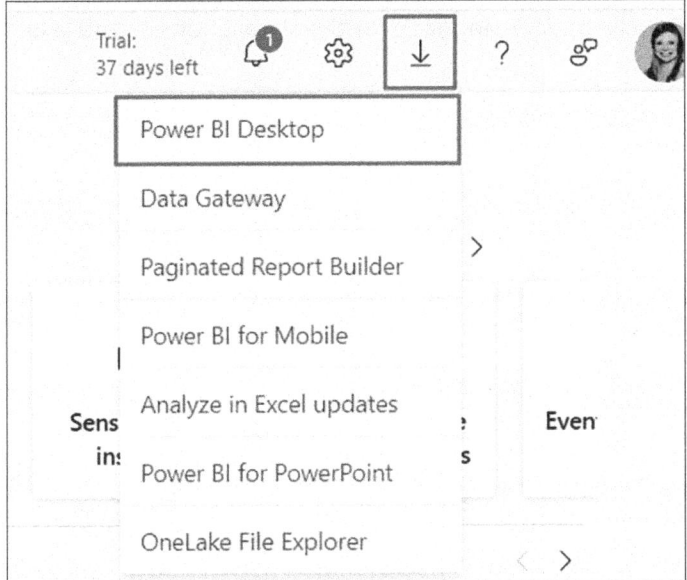

Accessing Microsoft Store from Power BI Service.

Installing from the Microsoft Store is the easiest and most convenient option. It provides automatic updates, does not require administrator rights, simplifies implementation across the organization, and reduces the download size by updating only the modified components. It also automatically detects your system language and applies it to both the interface and the data model.

 **TIP** Installing Power BI Desktop from the Microsoft Store doesn't copy user settings from the .exe version. You might have to reconnect to your recent data sources and reenter your credentials.

 TIP If you use SAP connectors, you might need to move driver files manually to C:\Windows\System32.

Download as an executable file

If you prefer not to use the Microsoft Store, you can download the .exe installer from the Power BI Download Center.

To install

1. Visit the Power BI Desktop Download Center page.

2. Use the dropdown list to choose the language for the installation file and select **Download**.

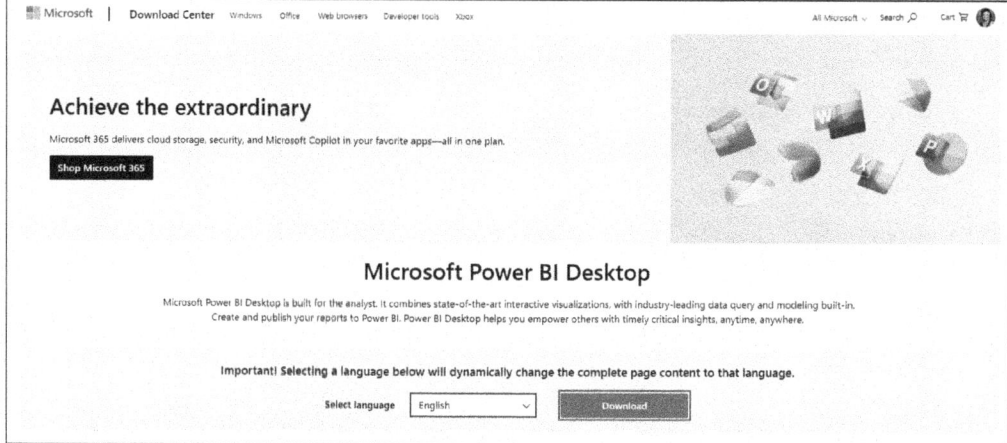

Download Power BI Desktop from the Microsoft Download Center.

3. Select the appropriate version and select **Download**.

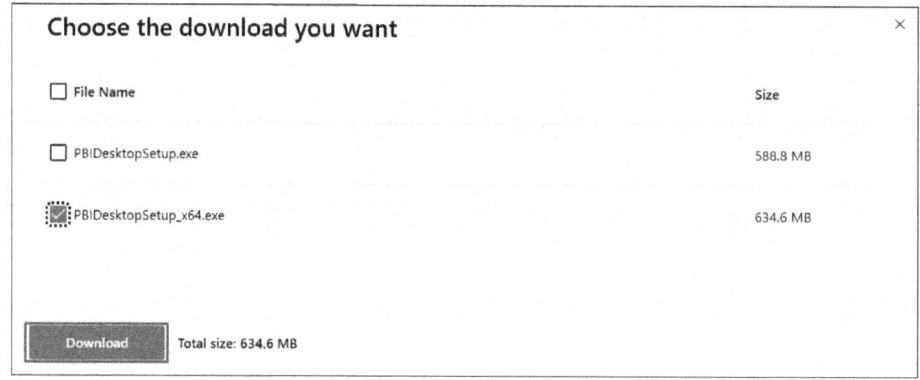

Power BI Desktop download options.

2

> ⚠ **IMPORTANT** Microsoft announced the end of support for the 32-bit version of Power BI Desktop on July 31, 2025. Only the 64-bit version is now available; it offers better performance and is compatible with most modern systems.

4. Once the download is complete, double-click the file to run the installer and click **Next**.

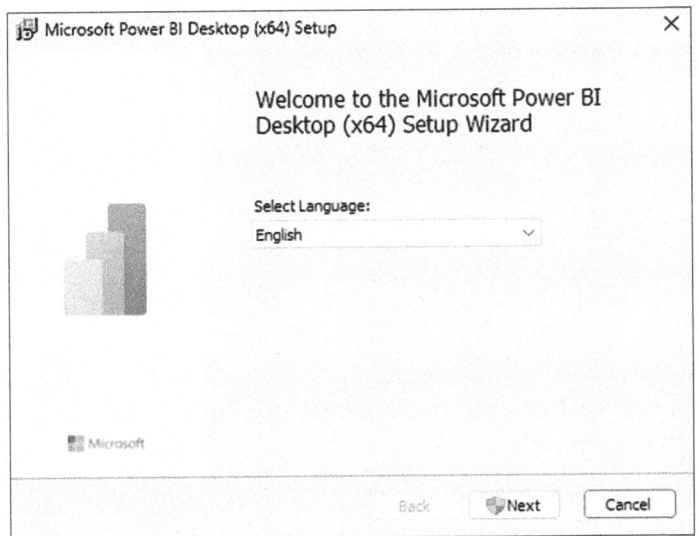

Power BI Desktop Setup wizard.

5. Windows will ask you to allow the app to make changes to your device. Click **Yes** to continue with the installation.

> ⚠ **IMPORTANT** You must have administrator privileges to complete this step.

6. You'll be asked to accept the Microsoft Software License Terms. Review the license agreement. To proceed, you must check the box **I accept the terms in the License Agreement** and then select **Next**.

7. Choose the Installation Folder and select **Next**.

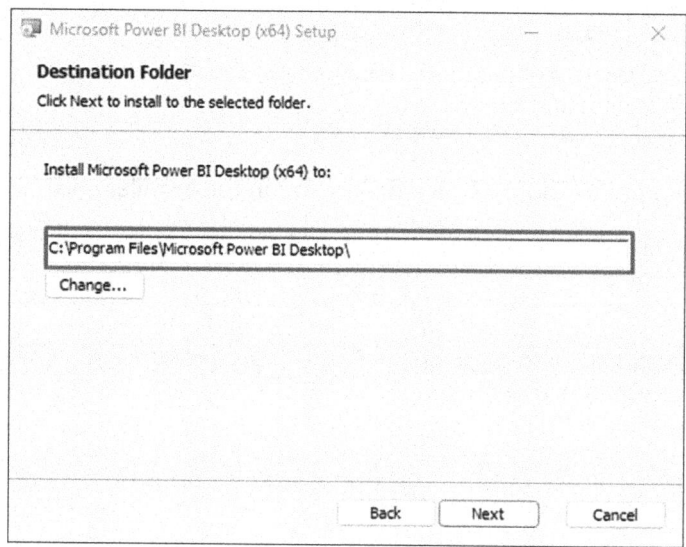

Destination Folder.

8. You'll see a summary screen confirming you're ready to install Power BI Desktop. Here, you can also choose whether to create a desktop shortcut (enabled by default). Select **Install** to begin the process.

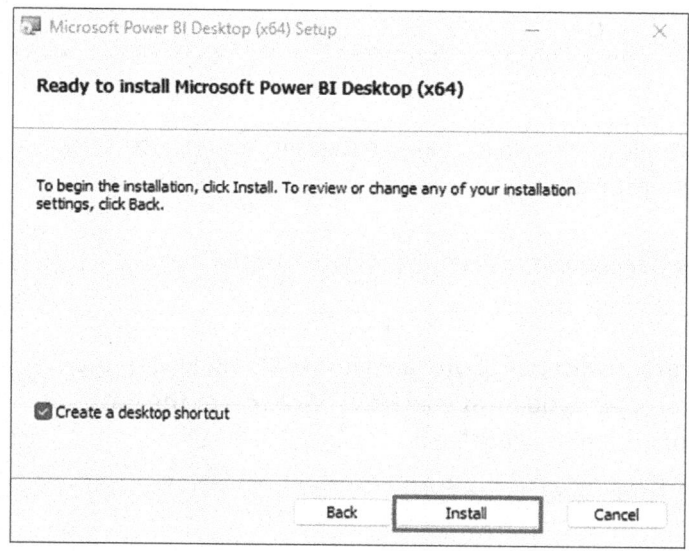

Installing Power BI Desktop.

IMPORTANT Do not install both the Microsoft Store version and the executable version at the same time. Uninstall one before switching to the other.

2

Downloading Power BI Desktop as an executable file offers greater flexibility and control, allows portable installations, and supports command-line deployment. This executable file can be reused on multiple computers. In addition, it can provide access to previous versions for compatibility or testing purposes, which is especially useful for advanced users or enterprise environments.

System requirements

Before installing, check that your PC meets the minimum requirements.

 IMPORTANT Power BI Desktop is no longer supported on Windows 8.1 or earlier.

Requirement	Details
Operating system	Windows 10, Windows Server 2016 or later
.NET	.NET 4.7.2 or later
Memory (RAM)	Minimum 2 GB, 4 GB or more recommended
Display resolution	At least 1440x900 (16:9); lower resolutions are not supported
CPU	1 GHz or faster, 64-bit processor or better recommended
WebView2 runtime	Required. If not installed, download from Microsoft Edge Developer page

IMPORTANT Power BI Desktop is available only for Windows. If you're using a Mac, you can access the Power BI Service through a web browser to view and interact with published reports. If you need to create or model data, you can run Power BI Desktop using a virtual machine or Windows emulator.

Start Power BI Desktop

IMPORTANT After you launch the installation package, Power BI Desktop installs as a standard Windows application that you can launch from the Start menu like any other app.

When you open Power BI Desktop for the first time, a welcome screen appears, designed to help you quickly begin your work. At the top, under the heading "Select a data source or start with a blank report," you'll see several common options such as starting with a Blank report or connecting to a OneLake catalog, an Excel workbook, a SQL Server, or even sample data. If you don't see the source you need, you can select **Get data from other sources** to access the full list of available connectors.

 SEE ALSO To learn how to connect to and import data from these sources, see Chapter 3, "Importing data."

Below that list, a Recommended section offers helpful resources to get you started, like tutorials or Power BI content that links to Microsoft learning material. At the bottom of the screen, the Recent and Shared with me tabs help you reopen reports you've worked on or that others have shared with you.

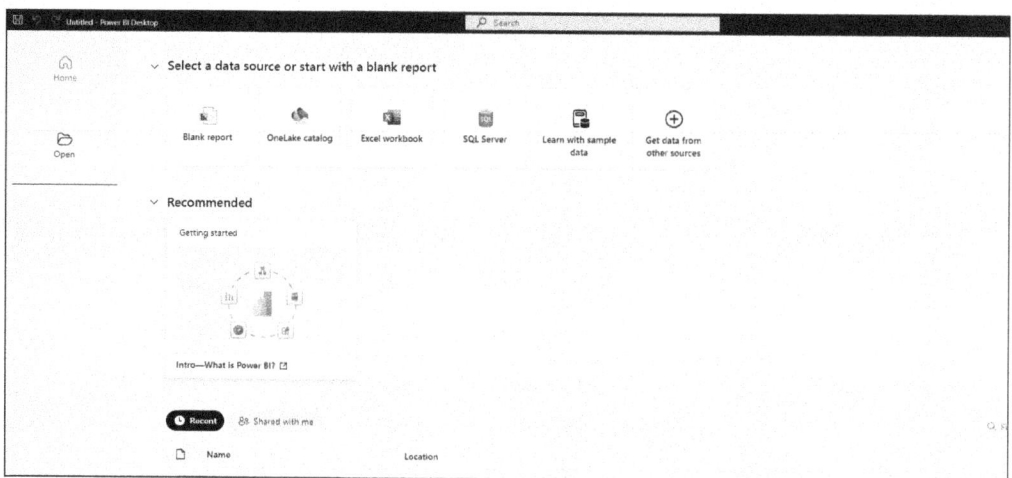

Start Power BI Desktop.

If this is a fresh install (not an upgrade), you may be asked to

- Sign in with a work or school account.
- Fill out a short form to proceed without signing in.

After that, you're ready to build and publish your first report.

Sign in to Power BI Desktop

You can use Power BI Desktop without signing in, even if you don't have a Power BI user license. However, the following features require that you sign in with a valid work or school account:

- Connect to online data sources (e.g., SharePoint Online, Microsoft Dataverse).
- Publish reports to the Power BI Service.
- Use tenant-specific features like organizational visuals.
- Apply sensitivity labels or access other premium capabilities.

 TIP If you're just learning or building reports locally, you can skip the sign-in process. But when you're ready to share, you'll need to be signed in.

To sign in

1. In the top-right corner of Power BI Desktop, select **Sign in**.
2. Enter your work or school email address.

 IMPORTANT Power BI does not support personal email accounts such as @gmail.com, @outlook.com, or @yahoo.com for sign-in. You must use a valid work or school account.

3. Complete the login process (typically through your organization's Microsoft 365 portal).
4. After you're signed in, you will see your profile picture or initials in the top-right corner of the window.

 TIP You can also sign out or switch accounts anytime by selecting your profile icon in the same location.

Explore Power BI Desktop interface

Power BI Desktop offers a clean and intuitive interface designed to guide you through the process of building reports.

Main elements of the Power BI Desktop interface

Power BI Desktop is organized into distinct interface elements that support the report creation process. Each part of the interface serves a specific function, whether for designing visuals, modeling data, or navigating your report. The following sections describe the key areas of the Power BI Desktop interface.

Canvas

The canvas is the central workspace in Power BI Desktop where you build and design your reports. It's a blank page where you drag fields, insert visuals, and arrange content to tell a story with your data. You can create multiple pages within a report, each with its own layout and visuals.

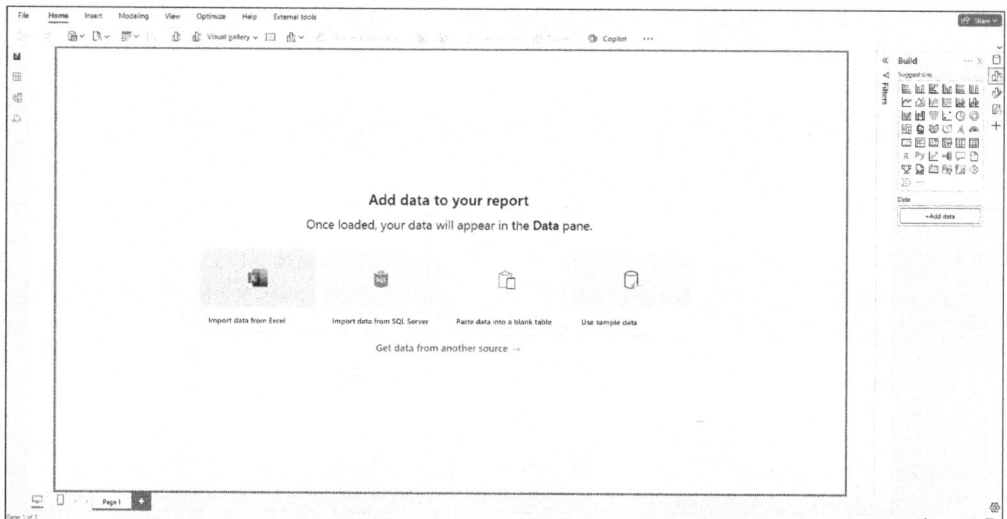

Report Canvas.

Ribbon

The ribbon is the toolbar located at the top of Power BI Desktop. Each tab is organized by function, making it easy to navigate and find the commands you need while building your reports. If you've used applications like Microsoft Excel or PowerPoint, the Power BI layout will feel familiar.

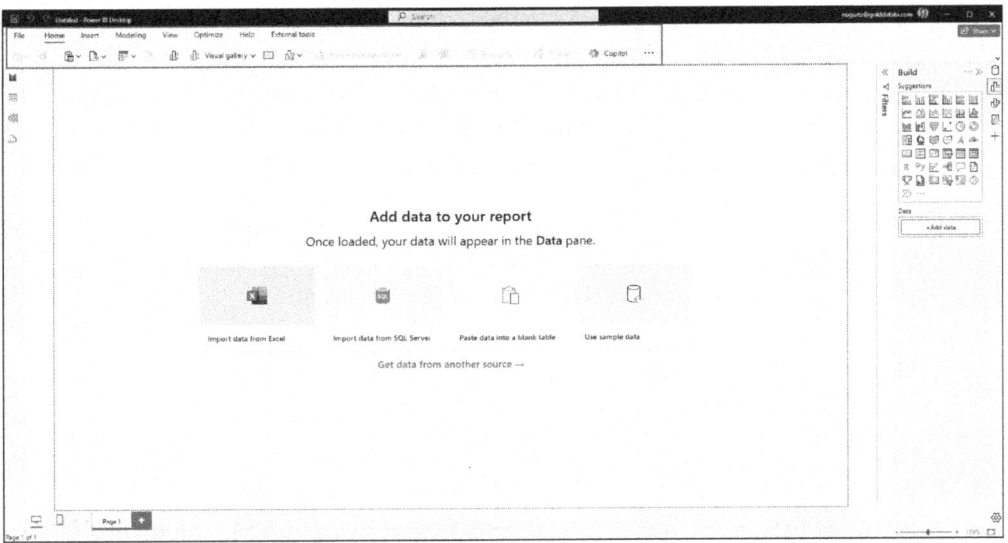

Power BI Desktop ribbon.

Let's explore each tab on the ribbon and its main features:

- **Home:** This tab is your starting point in Power BI Desktop. It includes the most used commands for managing your reports, data, and visuals. From here, you can connect to various data sources, refresh and transform data using the Power Query Editor, and publish reports to the Power BI Service. The tab also includes basic editing actions such as undo, redo, and copy/paste, as well as access to tools such as Copilot and the visual gallery.

- **Insert:** This tab allows you to add new elements to your report canvas, such as visuals, images, text boxes, and shapes. This tab also enables you to add buttons, such as navigation arrows, bookmarks, Q&A triggers, and slicer controls to enhance interactivity. Additionally, you can insert new report pages to better organize your report.

- **Modeling:** This tab is the place where you define the logic of your data model. You can create new tables, columns, and measures using Data Analysis Expressions (DAX), define relationships between tables, mark a table as a date table, and create parameters. This tab also includes security features, such as row-level security (RLS), to manage user-level access.

 TIP The Modeling tab becomes essential after your data is loaded and you're ready to structure it for analysis.

- **View:** This tab allows you customize the overall appearance and layout of your report. You can apply different themes for color consistency, use the Selection and Bookmarks panes to manage visibility and interactivity, and control the display of items like gridlines. Additionally, you can open the Performance Analyzer to evaluate how efficiently your report loads and runs.

- **Optimize:** This tab focuses on performance tuning and report efficiency. It provides tools to pause and refresh visuals, manage query reduction settings, apply or clear slicers, and run the Performance Analyzer.

 SEE ALSO For more details on performance tuning, see Chapter 12, "Applying advanced topics and best practices."

- **External Tools:** On this tab, you'll find tools like DAX Studio or Tabular Editor, which offer extended capabilities beyond Power BI Desktop's native functions. Experienced developers use these functions to perform detailed modeling, advanced DAX authoring, or version control.

- **Help:** This tab provides easy access to Power BI documentation, tutorials, and community support. From here, you can find learning resources, report issues, and explore updates or training materials.

Power BI Panels

Power BI Desktop includes several panels that help you manage your data, customize visuals, and control what is displayed in your reports. These panels are located on the right side of the interface and are essential for building and refining your report content.

- **Data Pane:** This pane shows all the data tables and fields you've loaded into your report. You can expand tables to see individual columns, measures, and hierarchies. Just drag and drop any field from here onto the canvas to use it in a visual. You can also right-click to rename, hide, or create new fields.

- **Build Pane:** This pane is essential for customizing how your data is displayed. Here you can choose the type of chart or visual you want to use, such as bar charts, pie charts, maps, cards, or tables. After selecting a visual, use the same pane to assign fields to different parts of the chart and format it with colors, labels, and more.

- **Filters Pane:** This pane enables you to control what data appears in your report. You can filter data at the visual, page, or report level. Just drag a field into the filter area and choose your filter options. This pane makes it easy to tailor the view for different users or use cases without changing the main visuals.

> **TIP** Although you can add slicers to the report for user interaction (we'll cover this topic later in Chapter 7, "Building Your First Report"), the Filters pane allows you to apply filters in the background. It's especially useful for applying filters that you don't need to see or interact with, such as hiding specific categories or limiting the report to a date range.

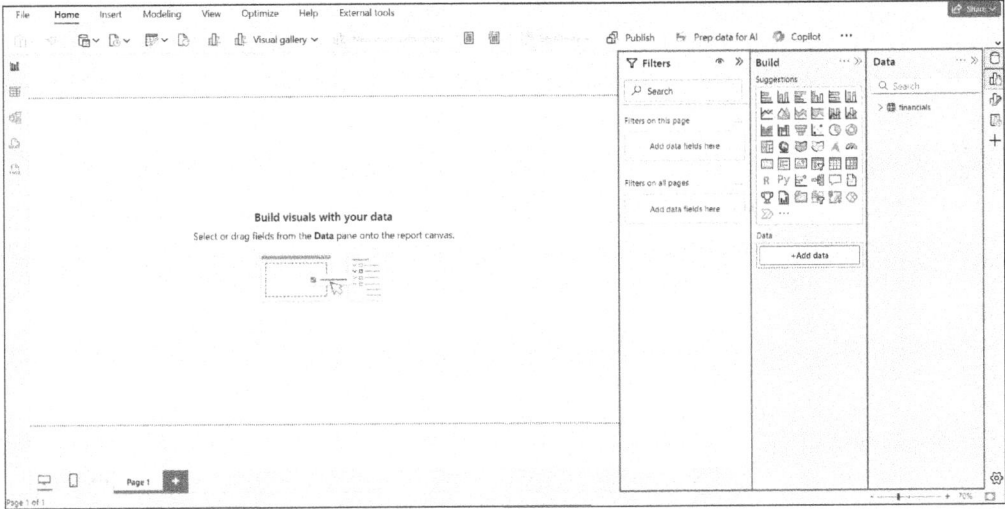

Power BI panels.

> **TIP** By default, Power BI Desktop displays the Filters, Build, and Data panes on the right side of the screen. Depending on the size of your screen or the selected visual, some panes may be collapsed or hidden. Select their icons to show or hide them as needed.

Pages Tab

The Pages tab, located at the bottom of the canvas, allows you to add and manage multiple report pages, just like slides in PowerPoint. Each page can show a different perspective of your data. You can rename pages, duplicate them, or rearrange their order to create a logical flow for your report.

Power BI Desktop Views

Power BI Desktop offers four main views, each designed for a specific part of the report creation process. You can switch between them using the icons on the left sidebar.

- **Report View:** This is the default view where you design your reports using visuals. You'll use this view most of the time to drag fields, add charts, and format your report layout.

- **Data View:** This view shows your data in table form, similar to Excel. It's useful for reviewing imported data, calculating columns, or verifying your transformations.

- **Model View:** This view allows you to create and manage relationships between tables. It's essential when you're working with multiple data sources or building a complex data model.

- **DAX Query View:** This advanced view lets you write and run DAX queries to explore or troubleshoot your data model. It's helpful for users with more technical needs or deeper analysis.

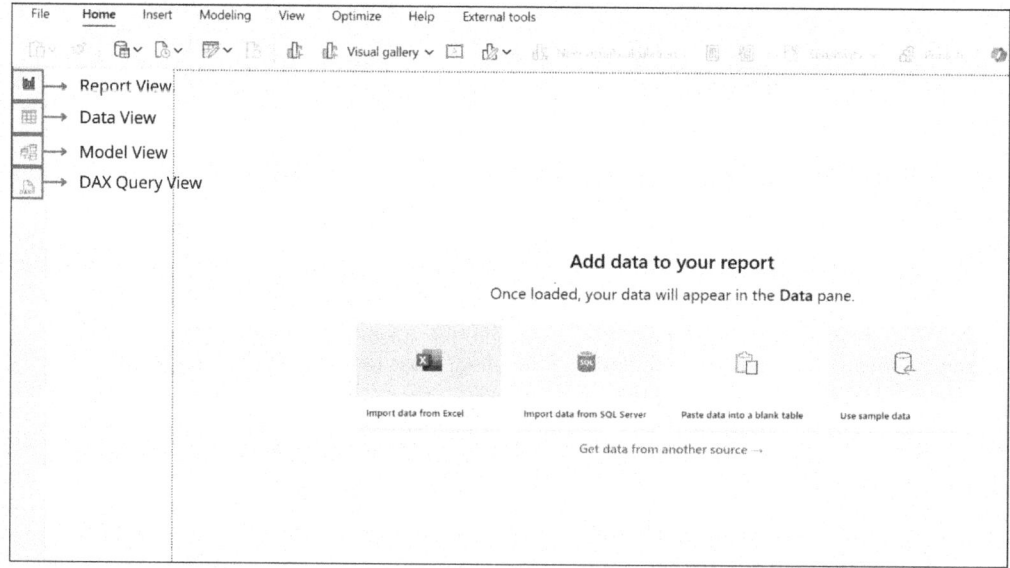

Power BI views.

Configure Power BI Desktop settings

Before you begin working on your first report, it's a good idea to review a few optional settings that can improve your experience with Power BI Desktop. You don't need to make changes right away, but knowing where to find these settings will be useful as you advance.

To access the settings, select **File > Options and settings > Options**.

The Options window organizes settings into two main categories in the left menu:

- **Global:** Applies to all files and Power BI Desktop in general

- **Current File:** Applies only to the report you are currently working on

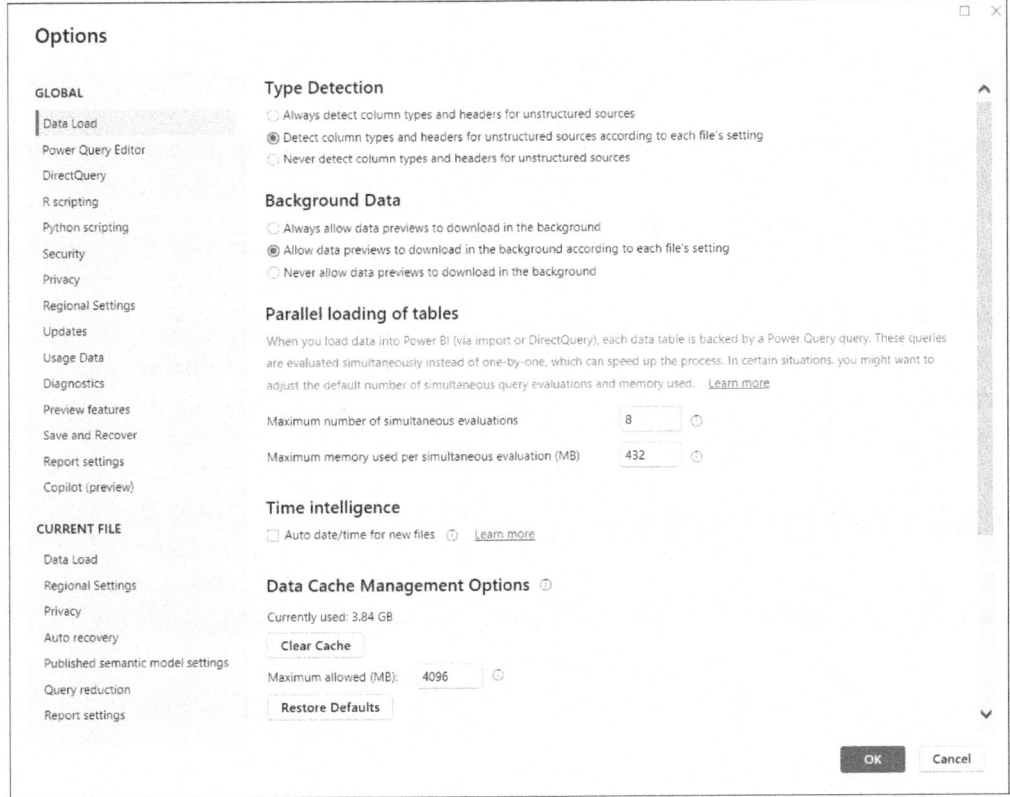

Power BI configuration.

Recommended setup options

To ensure a smoother and more personalized experience while working in Power BI Desktop, let's explore some recommended setup options that help optimize functionality, improve usability, and protect your work.

Enable preview features

Power BI frequently releases experimental features that you can try as they become officially available. To enable them, select **File > Options and settings > Options > Preview features** and check any features you'd like to activate.

 TIP You must restart Power BI Desktop to apply the changes.

Set regional settings

Under **Current File > Regional Settings**, you can specify your locale. This setting controls how dates, numbers, and currencies are displayed in your reports. Choose the region that matches your preferred formatting.

Enable autosave

To avoid losing your work, you can turn on Autosave. To do so, select **Current File > Save and enable autosave**. You can also configure how frequently Power BI saves your work automatically.

Check your Power BI Desktop version

To find out which version of Power BI Desktop you are using, select **Help > About > Version Information**. This information is helpful when you're troubleshooting or checking compatibility with certain features.

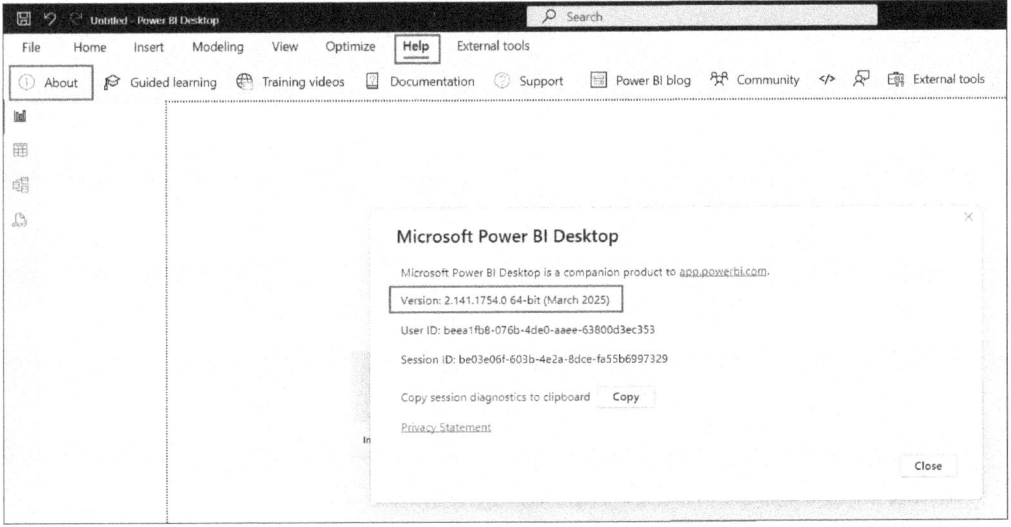

Power BI version.

Knowing your current version is especially useful when

- **Troubleshooting issues:** If you encounter unexpected behavior or errors, support resources often need to know your version number to assist you accurately.

- **Matching documentation:** Power BI updates monthly, and features may appear, change, or be deprecated. Verifying your version helps ensure you're following guidance that aligns with your software.

- **Collaborating with others:** Teams using different versions may notice inconsistencies in features or visual behavior, so aligning versions ensures a smoother workflow.

- **Accessing the latest features:** If you're missing a feature mentioned in this book or elsewhere, checking your version is the first step to confirming whether an update is needed.

> **TIP** Always use the latest version of Power BI Desktop to benefit from performance improvements, new features, and bug fixes. The Microsoft Store version updates automatically, but if you installed it via the executable file, you'll need to check for updates manually.

Skills review

In this chapter, you learned how to

- Install Power BI Desktop using either the Microsoft Store or the executable (.exe) installer from the Power BI website and understand the benefits and limitations of each installation method.

- Verify your system requirements to ensure your device is compatible with Power BI Desktop and supports optimal performance.

- Launch Power BI Desktop for the first time and sign in with a valid work or school account to access cloud-based features.

- Navigate the Power BI Desktop interface, including the report canvas, ribbon, views (Report, Data, Model, and DAX Query), and the Filters, Build, and Data panes to build, customize, and explore your reports effectively.

- Configure Power BI Desktop settings and check your Power BI version.

Practice tasks

No practice files are necessary to complete the practice tasks in this chapter.

Install and set up Power BI Desktop

Before you can start using Power BI, you'll need to install the application on your computer. Follow these steps to choose the right version and complete the setup process:

1. Choose and complete an installation method. Visit the Power BI website and decide whether to install the Microsoft Store version or download the executable file (.exe). Follow the steps outlined in this chapter to complete the installation on your device.

2. Check your version. After installing Power BI Desktop, select **Help** > **About** and note the version number currently installed.

Explore Power BI Desktop interface

After Power BI Desktop is installed, it's helpful to become familiar with its interface. The following steps will guide you through the key areas of the workspace so you can navigate it with confidence:

1. Launch Power BI Desktop. Open the **Start menu** and then select **Power BI Desktop**. Take a moment to examine the welcome screen and available data source options.

2. Familiarize yourself with the interface. Open Power BI Desktop and take a few minutes to explore the layout. Hover over different areas of the screen and identify the main elements of the interface, including the ribbon, the report canvas, and the Fields, Visualizations, and Filters panes on the right side.

3. On the left sidebar, locate the buttons that switch between Report, Data, Model, and DAX Query views.

Configure Power BI Desktop settings

To get the most out of Power BI Desktop, you may want to adjust certain settings. The following steps will help you personalize your experience and enable useful features:

1. Access the Options menu. Select **File** > **Options and settings** > **Options**.

2. Enable preview features (optional). Under Preview features, turn on any feature you'd like to explore. Remember to restart Power BI Desktop to apply the changes.

3. Review your regional settings. Under **Current File** > **Regional Settings**, select the appropriate locale for your reports.

4. Check autosave options. Under **Current File** > **Save**, ensure **autosave** is enabled and adjust the autosave frequency if needed.

Importing data

3

Practice files

You will need to use the practice files provided with this chapter to complete the practice tasks.

Importing data is the starting point for every Power BI project. Before building reports, you first need to bring data into Power BI Desktop. This process allows you to load data from different sources and combine it into a single workspace, ready for analysis and reporting.

Power BI supports a wide range of data sources, including local files, folders, Microsoft and third-party databases, as well as online services such as Azure, Microsoft Dynamics 365, Salesforce, and more. Whether you're working with an Excel spreadsheet, a SQL database, or a cloud-based service, Power BI makes it easy to connect to your data and start building insights.

In Power BI, the data import process starts with the Get Data experience. This interface offers a categorized list of connectors that help you navigate the different types of data you can import, including files, databases, and online services. After selecting a source, you can preview the data and choose to either load it directly into your report or open it in Power Query for further preparation.

In this chapter

- Explore Power Query Editor
- Connect to common data sources
- Select the appropriate storage mode
- Understand privacy levels

This chapter focuses on the data import process. You'll learn how to connect to common data sources such as Excel and CSV files, folders, SQL Server databases, and online services like SharePoint and webpages. You'll also explore the Power Query interface, where you can preview and prepare your data before loading it into your report. This foundational step prepares you for success in the next chapters, where you will dive deeper into transforming and modeling your data to ensure it meets your analysis needs.

Explore Power Query Editor

The Power Query Editor is the main workspace where you prepare your data before loading it into Power BI. You can connect to a wide range of data sources, preview the data, and apply hundreds of transformations to clean, combine, and shape your data for analysis.

Power Query has a user-friendly interface that helps you perform these tasks without writing any code. You simply interact with ribbons, menus, and buttons to apply changes such as filtering rows, renaming columns, or merging tables. These transformation capabilities work the same way, no matter what data source you're using.

As you apply transformation steps by interacting with the components of the Power Query interface, Power Query records each action and creates the M code required to do the transformation, so you don't need to write any code. Not having to write code makes your process flexible and repeatable because you can review, edit, reorder, or remove any step at any time.

 TIP Power Query uses the M language behind the scenes to apply your changes. You don't need to write code, but if you want to customize the logic, you can use the formula bar or open the Advanced Editor to view or modify the M code.

IMPORTANT Your data transformations do not affect the original source. Power Query works with a separate copy of your data, allowing you to explore and prepare it safely.

Discover Power Query interface

The Power Query Editor is organized into four main areas that help you work with your data:

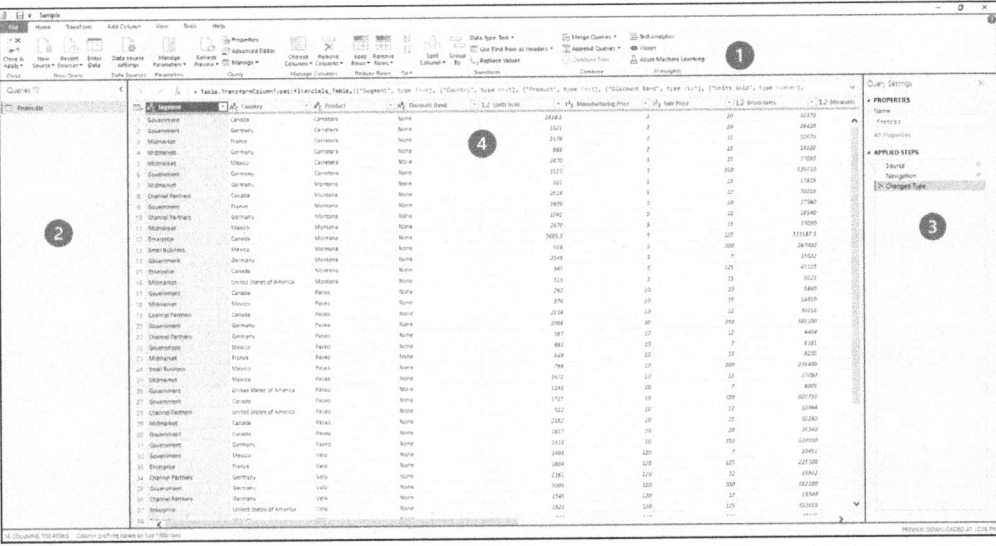

Power Query interface.

1. **Ribbon:** The ribbon provides quick access to the most data preparation options available in Power Query. It includes multiple tabs with buttons and options that help you clean and shape your data, such as removing columns or changing data types.

> **TIP** Depending on your screen size, Power Query may adjust the ribbon layout automatically. You can collapse or expand the ribbon to maximize your workspace.

2. **Queries Pane:** This pane shows all your queries (tables) you've loaded where you can

   - Select a query to view or edit it.

   - Rename, delete, duplicate, or reference queries.

   - Organize queries into folders (called groups) to keep related items together.

> **TIP** You can collapse or expand the Queries pane by selecting the arrow icon at the top-right corner of the pane. This capability helps you maximize space while working with your data.

3. **Query Settings:** This pane shows the Applied Steps list for the selected query, where every transformation you apply is recorded in order. You can select any step to review, edit, or delete it. Remember, the order of the steps matters because Power Query applies them in sequence.

 TIP If the Query Settings pane is not visible, go to the View tab on the ribbon and select **Query Settings** to show it again.

4. **Data Preview:** This area displays a preview of the data for your query, where you can see your data as you apply transformations, allowing you to explore your table and check how each step affects your data.

 TIP You can resize columns and scroll horizontally in the data preview to explore wide tables more easily.

Get Data in Power BI

The first step in any Power BI project is to bring in data from one or more sources. Power BI Desktop makes this process easy with the *Get Data* feature, which allows you to connect to more than 100 types of data sources, including files, databases, cloud services, APIs, and more.

The Get Data dialog organizes data connectors into the following categories to help you easily find the source you need:

- **All:** Displays the complete list of connectors from all categories in one place.
- **File:** Includes sources such as Excel, CSV, JSON, and XML.
- **Database:** Covers relational and nonrelational databases, such as SQL Server, Oracle, MySQL, and PostgreSQL.
- **Microsoft Fabric:** Provides connectors to Microsoft Fabric services, including OneLake and Lakehouse.
- **Power Platform:** Offers connections to Power BI datasets, Dataflows, and Dataverse.
- **Azure:** Includes connectors to Azure services, such as Azure SQL Database, Azure Blob Storage, and Azure Data Lake.
- **Online Services:** Provides connections to cloud applications like SharePoint, Microsoft Dynamics 365, Salesforce, and more.
- **Other:** Lists additional sources such as OData feeds, webpages, and APIs.

> ✅ **TIP** You must enable some connectors by selecting **File > Options and settings > Options > Preview features**. Connectors marked as Beta or Preview have limited support and should not be used in production environments.

Connecting to data

To connect to data in Power BI Desktop

1. Go to the **Home** ribbon.

2. Select the **Get data** dropdown arrow on the Home ribbon.

3. Choose the respective data source, such as Excel, SQL Server, or Web.

4. If the data source is not listed, select **More...** at the bottom of the list. This option opens a full gallery of available connectors grouped by category (File, Database, Power Platform, Azure, Online Services, Other, and so on).

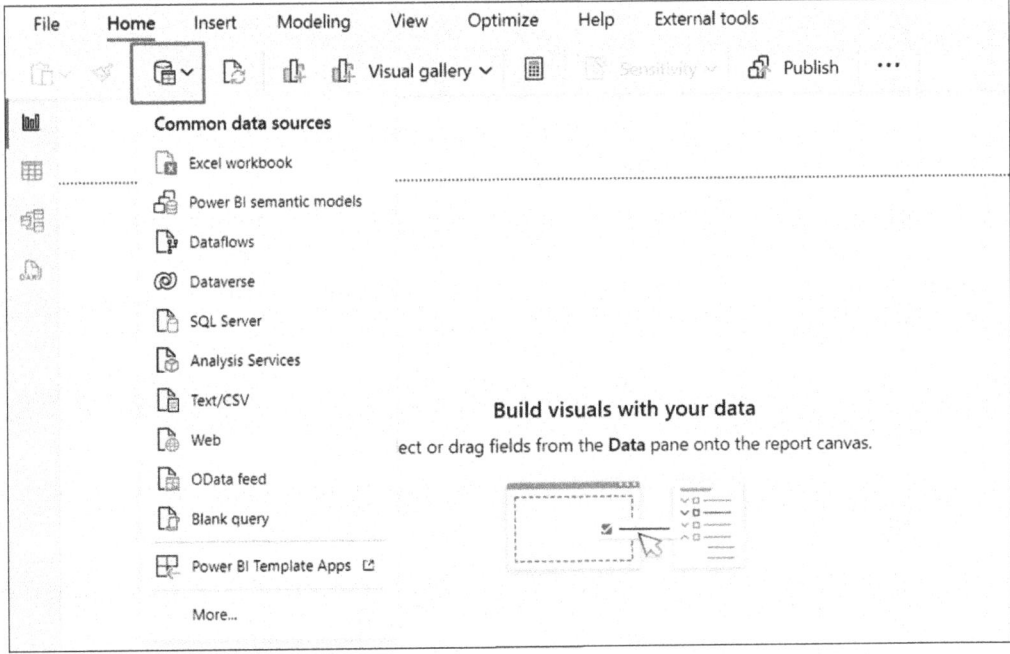

Get Data feature in Power BI Desktop.

5. Select the desired connector and follow the prompts to complete the connection.

Stages of connecting to data

When you connect to data in Power BI, the experience follows a series of common stages designed to guide you through the process. Although the exact experience may vary depending on the connector selected, the general flow includes

- **Connection Settings:** Define the information needed to connect, such as a file path or server name.

- **Authentication:** Provide credentials to securely access the data source. The method varies by connector (for example, Windows, Database, or API key).

- **Data Preview:** Review a sample of your data in the Navigator window or a preview dialog before loading or transforming it.

- **Query Destination:** Choose whether to load the data directly or transform data to open it in the Power Query Editor.

> ⚠️ **IMPORTANT** Some connectors might include all these stages, whereas others may skip some depending on their requirements. Always review the connector's documentation if you need specific details about its behavior.

Preview source data in Power Query

After you select a connector and provide the necessary connection details, Power BI opens the Navigator window. Here you can browse and preview the available tables, sheets, or objects from your data source. This preview helps you verify the structure and contents before loading the data into Power BI.

You can select one or multiple tables to import, depending on your reporting needs. After making your selection, you have two options:

- Select **Load** to load the data directly into your report to start building visuals right away.

- Select **Transform Data** to open the selected data in Power Query, where you can clean, shape, and prepare it before loading.

Power Query displays a live preview of your data that updates instantly as you apply each step. This feature helps you see how every change affects the data in real time, so you can spot mistakes and adjust quickly.

3

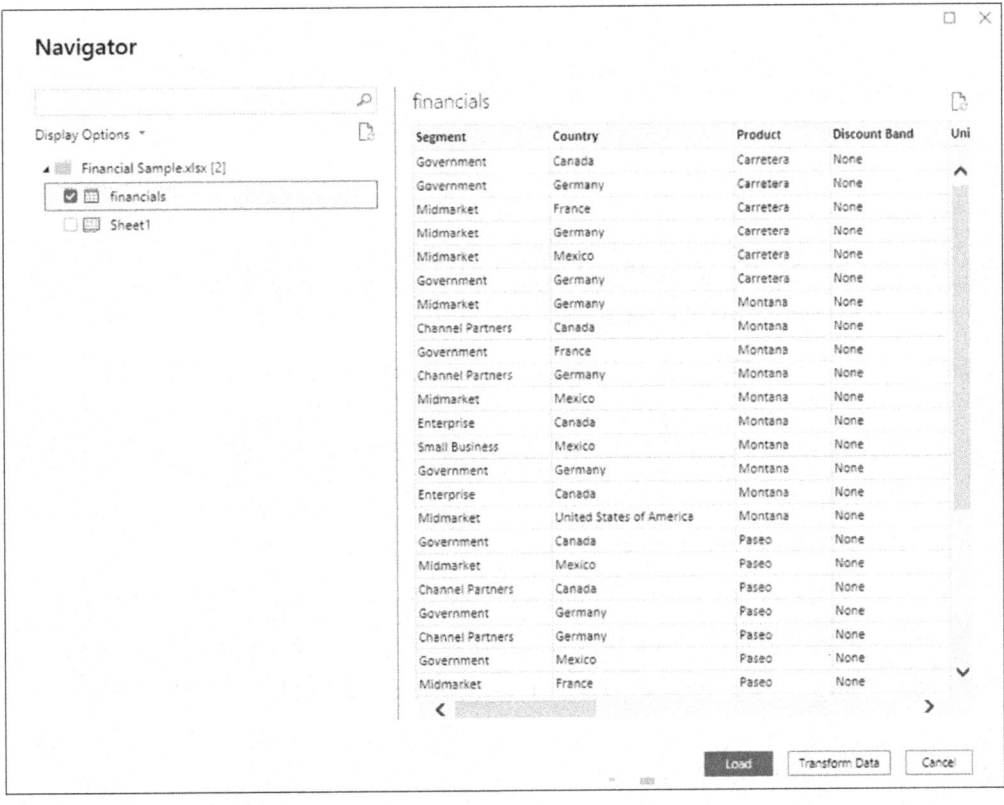

Power BI Navigator window.

 TIP If your data needs cleaning or adjustments, the recommendation is to select **Transform Data**. If your data is already prepared and ready to use, you can select **Load** to bring it directly into your model.

SEE ALSO You will learn how to apply data transformations in Chapter 4, "Transforming data with Power Query."

IMPORTANT Power Query shows a cached preview of only the first 1,000 rows to improve performance. This means you might not see the latest data or issues that appear outside the preview range. To refresh the preview of the query, select **Home > Refresh Preview** or select **Refresh All** to refresh all queries. Always validate the final data after applying transformations to ensure accuracy.

Connect to common data sources

Power BI Desktop makes it easy to connect to a wide range of data sources. In this section, you'll learn how to connect to the most common types, including files, databases, webpages, and online services.

 SEE ALSO You can find the full list of supported data sources here: https://docs.microsoft.com/en-us/power-bi/connect-data/power-bi-data-sources

Imagine you work for *Wide World Importers*, a company that specializes in sourcing and selling unique products from around the world. Senior leadership has asked you to build reports that combine information from different systems:

- Sales transactions stored in a SQL Server database, showing which products customers bought and which employees processed the sales

- Employee details, such as job titles and hire dates, stored in Excel workbooks managed by the Human Resources team

- Shipment records stored as JSON files in a cloud-based warehouse application

- Financial forecasts managed in Azure Analysis Services, used to predict future sales based on historical trends

These data sources are stored in different formats and systems, and they all provide critical information that you need to combine in your reports. To achieve this task, you must first connect to each source, extract the data, and then prepare and combine it using Power Query.

This process varies depending on the system, because working with a SQL Server database is different from connecting to an Excel workbook or importing JSON files.

After your data is connected and cleaned, you can build interactive reports in Power BI and publish them to the Power BI service, making them available for others in your organization to explore and use.

Get data from Excel and CSV files

Organizations often store data in different file formats. One common format is the flat file, which contains a single table of data with a simple structure, no relationships or hierarchies. Typical flat files include

- CSV files (.csv)

- Delimited text files (.txt)

- Excel workbooks (.xlsx, .xlsm), which can include multiple sheets, tables, and even data models.

Power BI enables you to connect to all these types of files using the Get Data experience.

To get data from an Excel file

1. In Power BI Desktop, go to the **Home** tab and select **Get Data**.

2. From the list, select **Excel workbook**.

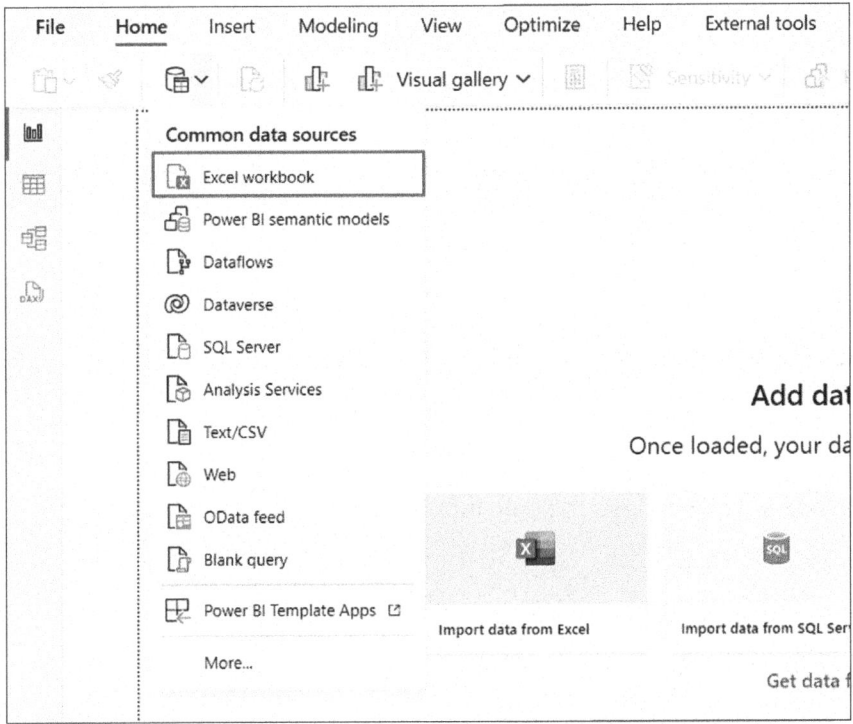

Get data from Excel.

3. Browse to the folder where the file is stored, select the file, and then select **Open**.

4. In the Navigator window, select the Excel sheet or table you want to import and review the data preview.

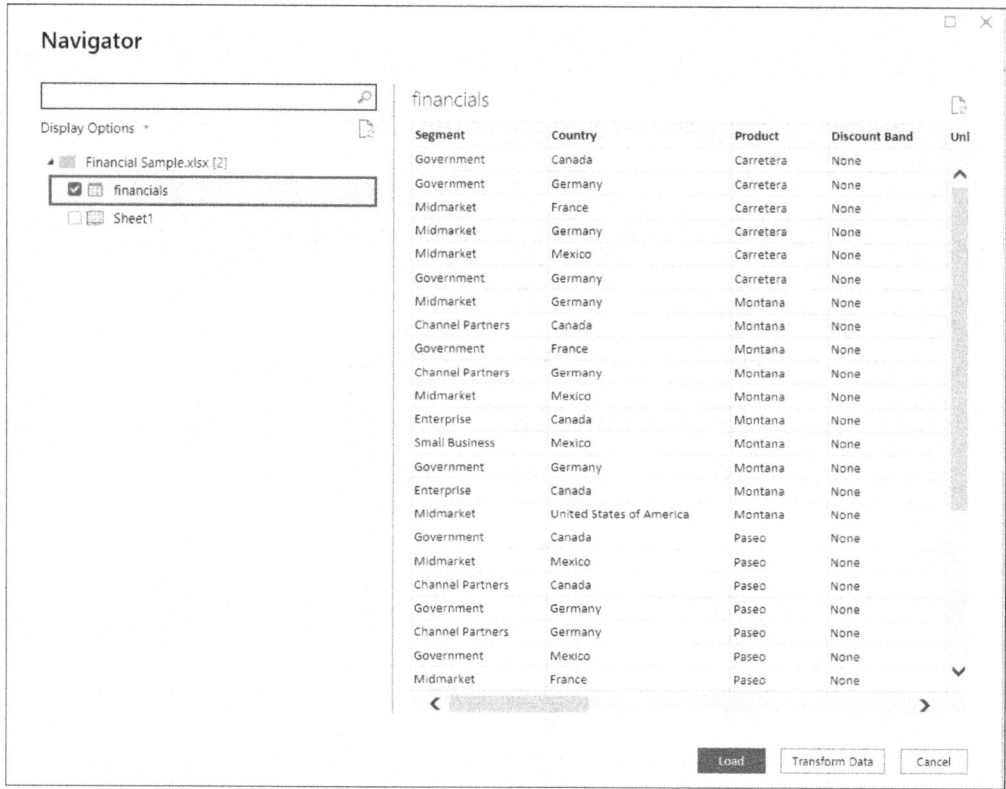

Navigator window in Power BI Desktop.

5. Choose **Load** to add it directly to your model or **Transform Data** to prepare it in Power Query.

6. Select **Close & Apply** to load the data into Power BI.

To get data from a CSV file

1. In Power BI Desktop, go to the **Home** tab and select **Get Data**.

2. From the list, select **Text/CSV**.

3. Browse to the folder where the file is stored, select the CSV file, and select **Open**.

4. In the preview window, review the data preview and verify that the file settings, such as delimiter or encoding, are correctly applied based on your file's structure.

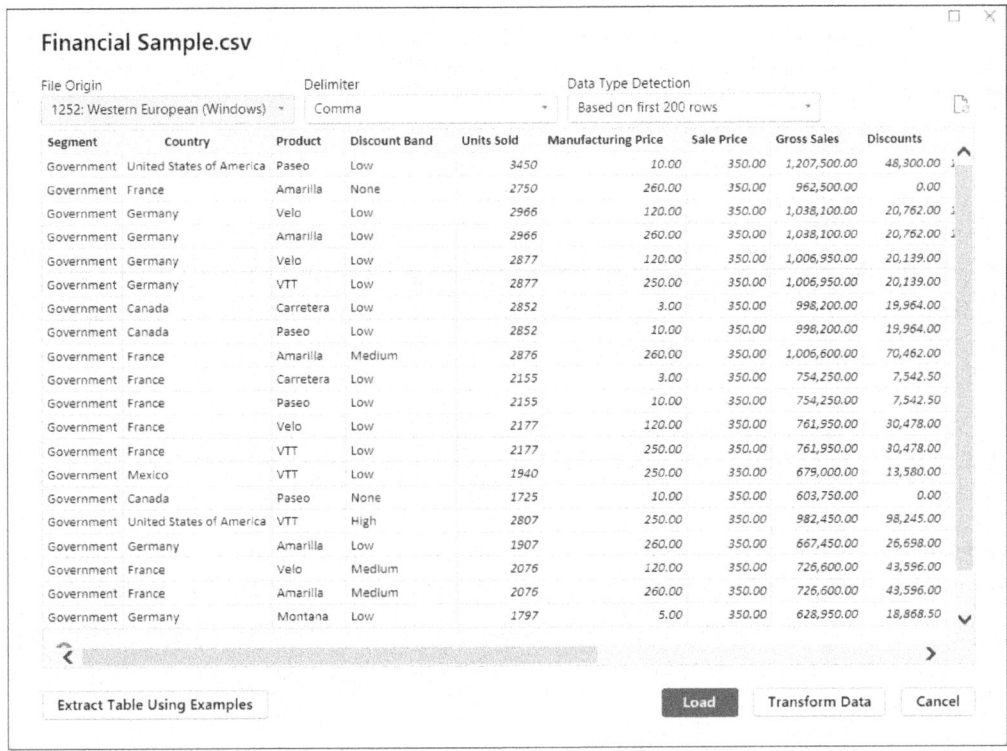

Data preview window for a CSV file.

5. Choose **Load** to add it directly to your model or **Transform Data** to prepare it in Power Query.

6. Select **Close & Apply** to load the data into Power BI.

 IMPORTANT When connecting to a CSV file, you can adjust several options in the preview window before loading the data:

File Origin: Select the character encoding used to read the file. If you see strange characters, try changing the encoding to Western European (Windows) or UTF-8.

Delimiter: Power BI typically detects the correct delimiter, such as Comma or Semicolon, but always verify and adjust if needed to correctly separate your columns.

Data Type Detection: Decide whether to detect data types based on the first 200 rows (faster) or the entire dataset (more accurate but slower).

TIP Select **Extract Table Using Examples** when your file doesn't have a clear table structure. You can define sample column names and sample data to guide Power BI in detecting the correct table layout automatically.

Get data from folders

If you work with multiple files that share the same structure and file type, such as monthly sales reports or daily log files, you don't need to import them one by one. Power BI lets you connect to a folder and combine all the files into a single table.

⚠ **IMPORTANT** This method works best when all files have the same structure. If your files have different columns or formats, you may need to clean them first.

Power BI automates this process by creating two elements: a sample query based on the first file and a function query that applies the same steps to all other files in the folder. This approach allows you to customize the process once and apply it to all files without extra effort.

 TIP You can modify the sample query at any time to add more transformations. Power BI will automatically apply your changes to all files.

To get data from a folder

1. In Power BI Desktop, go to the **Home** tab and select **Get Data**.

2. From the list, select **Folder**.

3. Browse to the folder where the files are stored, select the folder, and select **OK**.

Folder

Folder path

C:\   Browse...

          OK   Cancel

Folder connection window.

4. In the preview window, review the list of files and select **Transform Data** to perform any cleaning or filtering you may need.

5. Select the **Combine Files** icon next to the Content column and review the sample preview from the first file.

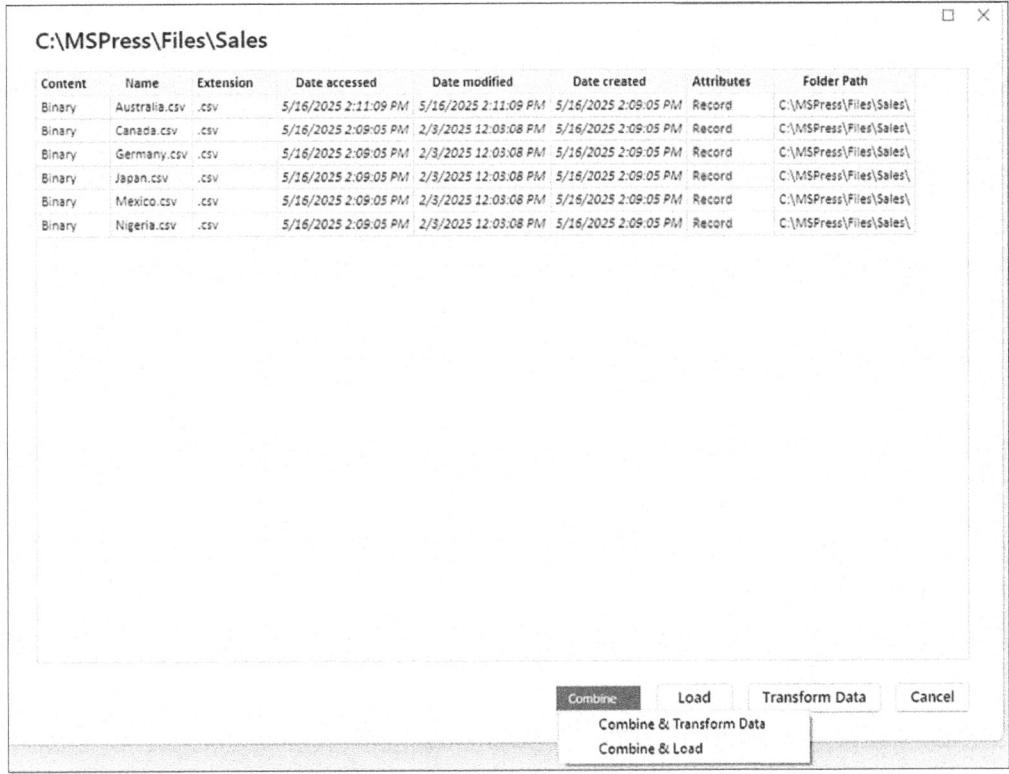

File preview and combination options in a folder.

6. Select **OK** to combine all files into a single table.

7. Review the combined data in Power Query and apply any additional transformations if needed.

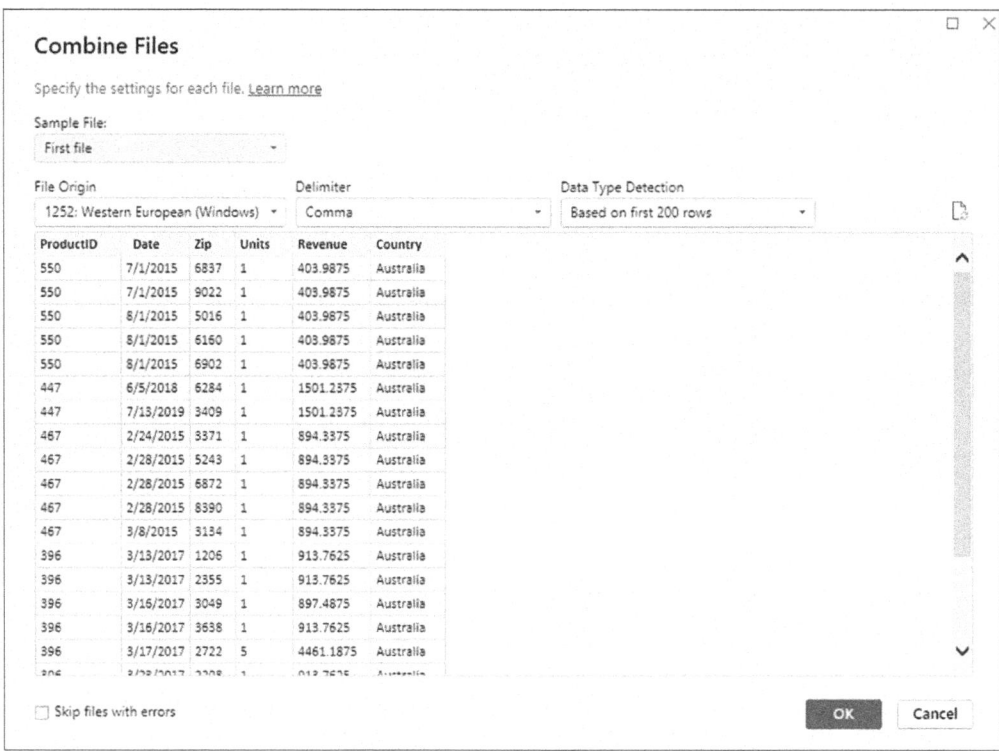

Data sample preview from the first file in the folder.

8. Select **Close & Apply** to load the combined data into Power BI.

Get data from relational data sources

Many organizations manage their business data in relational databases like SQL Server, Oracle, or MySQL. Power BI enables you to connect directly to these databases without needing to export data to flat files first. This approach makes it easier to keep your data updated and build reports based on live or regularly refreshed data.

To get data from SQL Server

1. In Power BI Desktop, go to the **Home** tab and select **Get Data**.

2. From the list, select **SQL Server**.

3. In the SQL Server database dialog, enter the server name and database name provided by your database administrator.

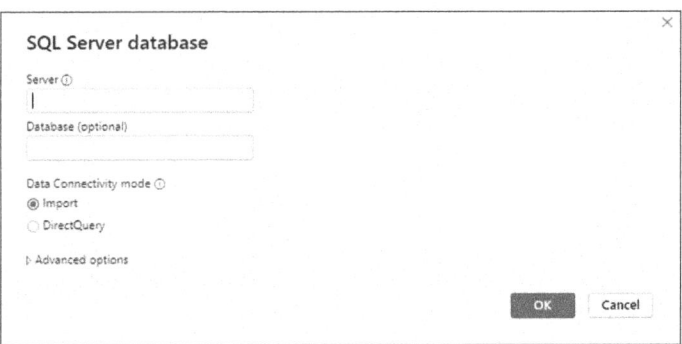

SQL Server connection settings.

4. Under Data Connectivity Mode, select **Import** (recommended) or **DirectQuery** and select **OK**.

> ⊘ **SEE ALSO** Learn more details about how Import and DirectQuery affect performance and data refresh in the "Select the appropriate storage mode" section later in this chapter.

5. In the authentication window, choose one of the following options:

   - **Windows:** Use your Windows or Azure Active Directory account.

   - **Database:** Enter the username and password provided for the database.

   - **Microsoft account:** Use your Microsoft credentials for Azure-based databases.

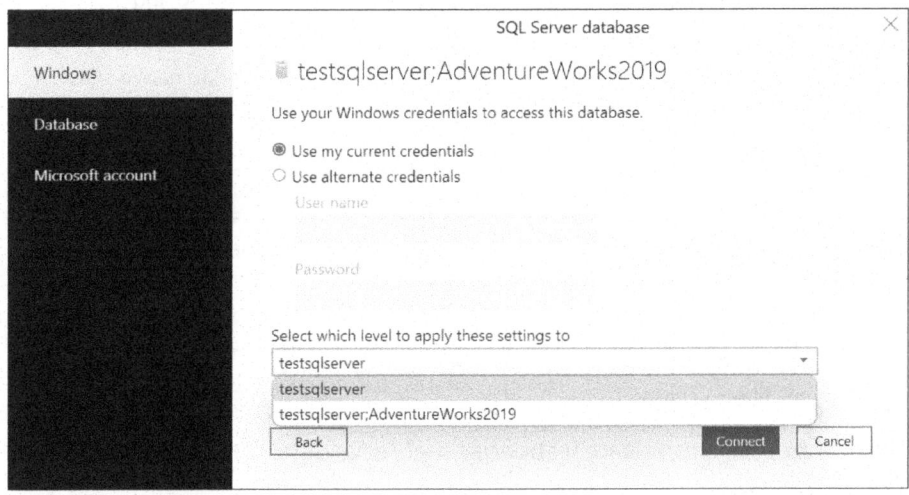

SQL Server authentication options.

6. Select a sign-in option, enter your username and password, and then select **Connect**.

7. In the Navigator window, browse the available tables or views.

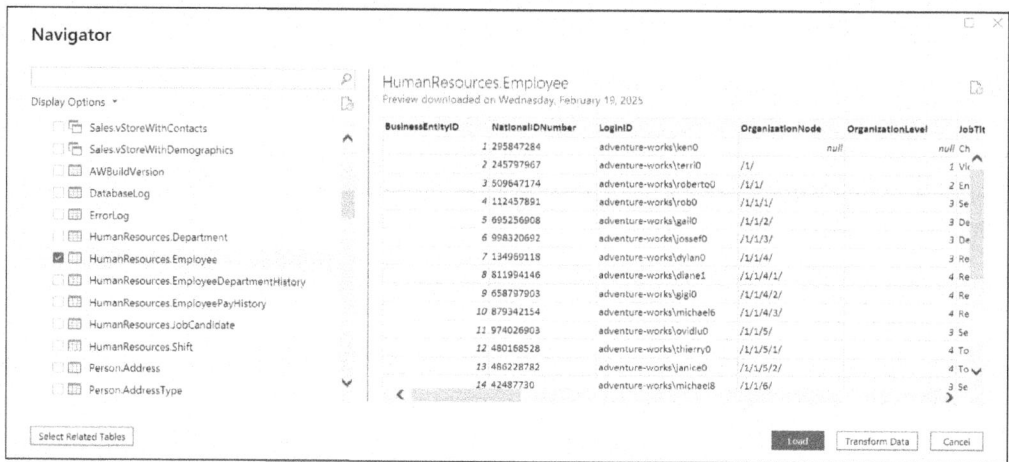

Navigator window for SQL Server.

8. Select one or more tables to load or select **Transform Data** to open them in Power Query.

9. Select **Close & Apply** to load the data into Power BI.

> ⚠️ **IMPORTANT** When connecting to SQL Server, Power BI can push transformations back to the source using a process called *query folding*. This means that filtering, grouping, and other operations can be executed directly by the database, improving performance and reducing memory usage in Power BI.
>
> Query folding happens automatically if the transformation can be translated to native SQL. However, some advanced steps may stop folding, causing the rest of the processing to happen in Power BI.

> **SEE ALSO** You'll explore how to check, preserve, and optimize query folding in Chapter 12, "Applying advanced topics and best practices."

Get data from the web

You can connect to public or private webpages that serve data, for example, HTML tables or APIs.

To get data from the web

1. In Power BI Desktop, go to the **Home** tab and select **Get Data > Web**.

2. In the From Web dialog, select **Basic**, enter the URL of the page you want to connect to, and select **OK**.

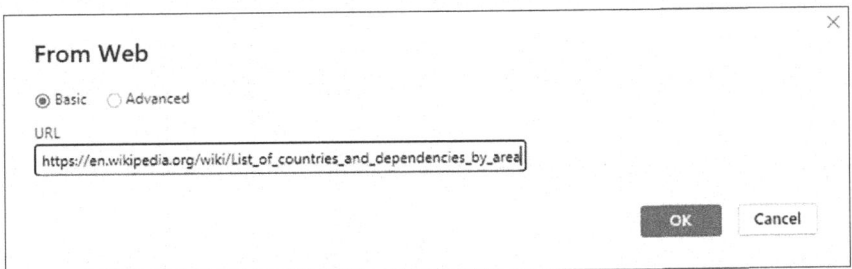

Web connection dialog.

3. Choose an authentication method:

   • **Anonymous** (for most public webpages)

   • **Windows**, **Basic**, **Web API**, or **Organizational account** (if credentials are required)

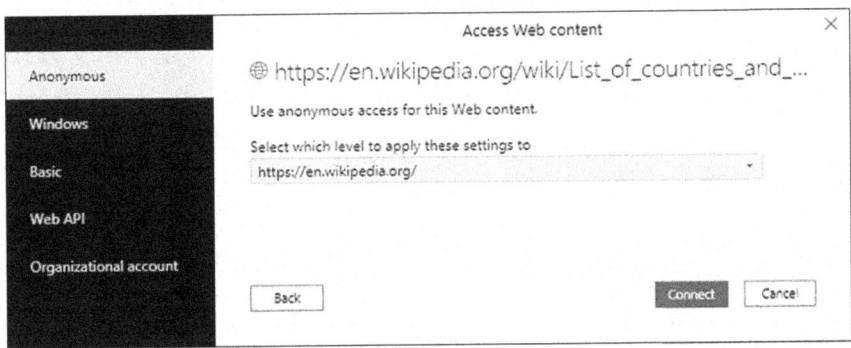

Authentication options for web connection.

4. Select the level of access you want to apply the authentication to and select **Connect**.

5. In the Navigator window, browse the list of detected tables or use the Web View tab to explore the page content.

6. Select the table you want to load or select **Add Table Using Examples** to define custom data extraction.

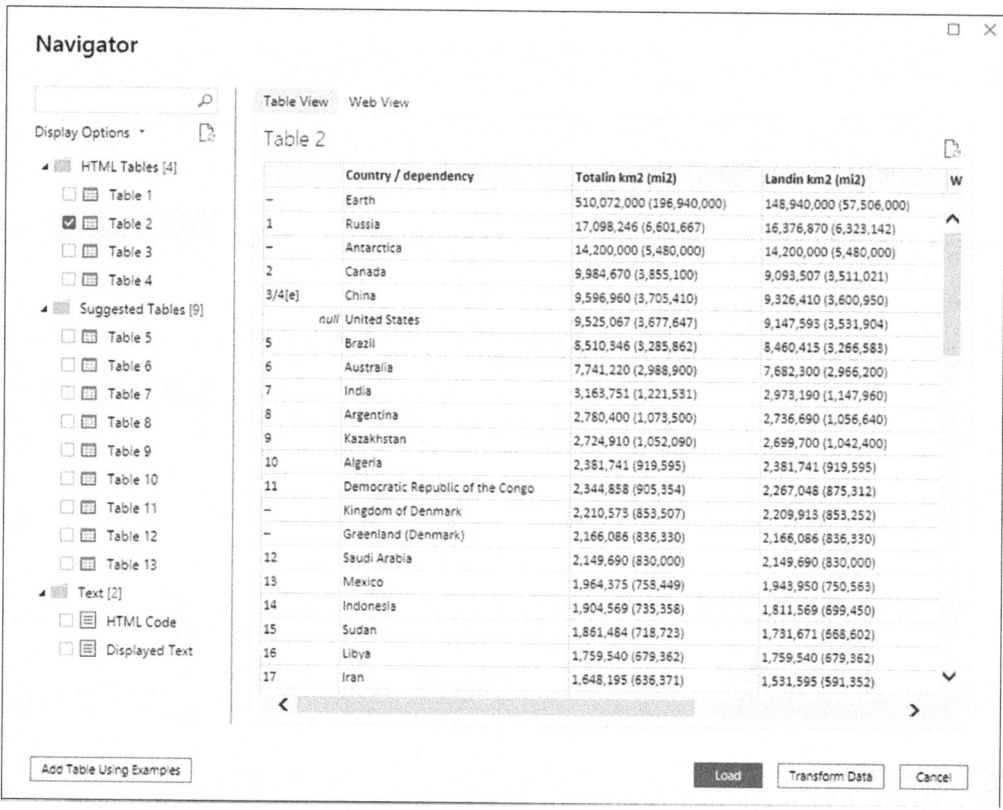

Web Navigator preview.

7. Select **Load** to import the data or **Transform Data** to open it in Power Query for further preparation.

8. Select **Close & Apply** to load the data into Power BI.

 TIP If Power BI detects multiple tables, use Web view to visually explore the page and pick the table you need.

 IMPORTANT Power BI remembers the authentication for the selected web address. You won't need to enter it again for the same site unless you change the settings.

Get data from online services

Many organizations use online applications like SharePoint, OneDrive, Dynamics 365, or Google Analytics to manage daily operations. Power BI allows you to connect to these services and combine their data with other sources to build richer reports and insights.

To get data from online services

1. In Power BI Desktop, go to the **Home** tab and select **Get Data**.

2. From the Online Services category, select **SharePoint Online List**.

3. In the SharePoint Online List dialog, enter your SharePoint site URL (not the full file path) and select **OK**.

4. In the authentication window, sign in with your Microsoft account and select **Connect**.

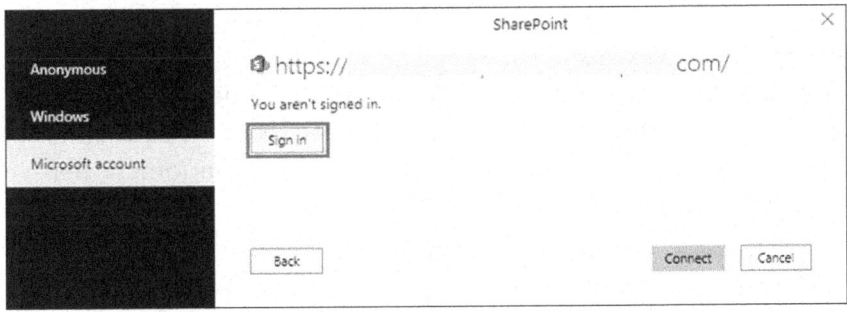

SharePoint authentication window.

5. In the Navigator window, browse the lists and tables available in your SharePoint site.

6. Select the list you want to import.

7. Choose **Load** to bring the data directly into Power BI or **Transform Data** to clean it in Power Query before loading.

8. Select **Close & Apply** to load the data into Power BI.

Select the appropriate storage mode

When you connect Power BI Desktop to a data source, you'll be asked to choose how Power BI should access the data. This choice has a big impact on performance, data refresh behavior, and report interactivity. Power BI offers three storage modes, each designed for different data scenarios:

- **Import:** This is the most common and default storage mode in Power BI. It creates a local copy of the data inside your Power BI file (.pbix), allowing you to work offline and benefit from faster performance because the data is pre-loaded in memory. This mode is ideal for small to medium datasets that don't require real-time updates.

> ✓ **TIP** You need to refresh the data to get updates.

> ⚠ **IMPORTANT** Changing the Storage mode of a table to Import is an irreversible operation. After this property is set up, you can't later change it to either DirectQuery or Dual.

- **DirectQuery:** This mode keeps the data in the source system, meaning no data is stored in Power BI. Instead, Power BI sends on-demand queries to the source. This mode is ideal for large datasets or when you need real-time data, ensuring you always see the most up-to-date results although it may perform slower depending on the data source's response time.

> ⚠ **IMPORTANT** Direct Query has limited DAX functionality, some visuals may be restricted, and performance depends on source speed.

- **Dual (Composite):** This mode combines both Import and DirectQuery. Power BI decides the best mode based on the context. It improves performance by using cached data when possible and switches to live queries when needed.

Comparison Table

Power BI offers three primary storage modes: Import, DirectQuery, and Dual. Each is suited for different performance and data access needs. Choosing the right mode depends on factors such as data source type, report refresh requirements, and how frequently the data changes.

The following table outlines the main characteristics, typical use cases, and key considerations of each mode to help you decide which is most appropriate for your reporting scenario.

Storage Mode	Best for	Key Considerations
Import	Fast reports, offline access	Requires scheduled or manual data refresh
DirectQuery	Real-time data, large datasets	May have slower report performance
Dual	Balanced performance and flexibility	Requires careful data modeling to avoid inconsistency

 TIP Not all connectors support all storage modes. For example, Excel works only with Import, whereas SQL Server supports both Import and DirectQuery.

Understand privacy levels

When combining data from multiple sources, such as an Excel file and an online service, Power BI evaluates the privacy level of each source to determine how much information it can safely share between them. This process helps protect sensitive data and prevent unintentional data leaks when merging or combining queries.

Power BI offers the following privacy levels:

- **Private:** This level contains sensitive or confidential data, such as personal files or internal company data. Power BI isolates this data and does not share it with other sources during query evaluation.

- **Organizational:** This level of privacy is safe to share within your organization, such as data from SharePoint sites or SQL databases, but not outside your organization.

- **Public:** This level includes data that is safe to share openly, such as public websites or open APIs. Power BI can freely combine this data with other sources.

To configure data source settings

1. Select **File > Options and settings > Data source settings**.

2. Select a data source from the list.

3. Select **Edit Permissions**.

4. Under Privacy Levels, select a privacy level. Be sure to choose the appropriate level.

5. Select **OK** and then select **Close**.

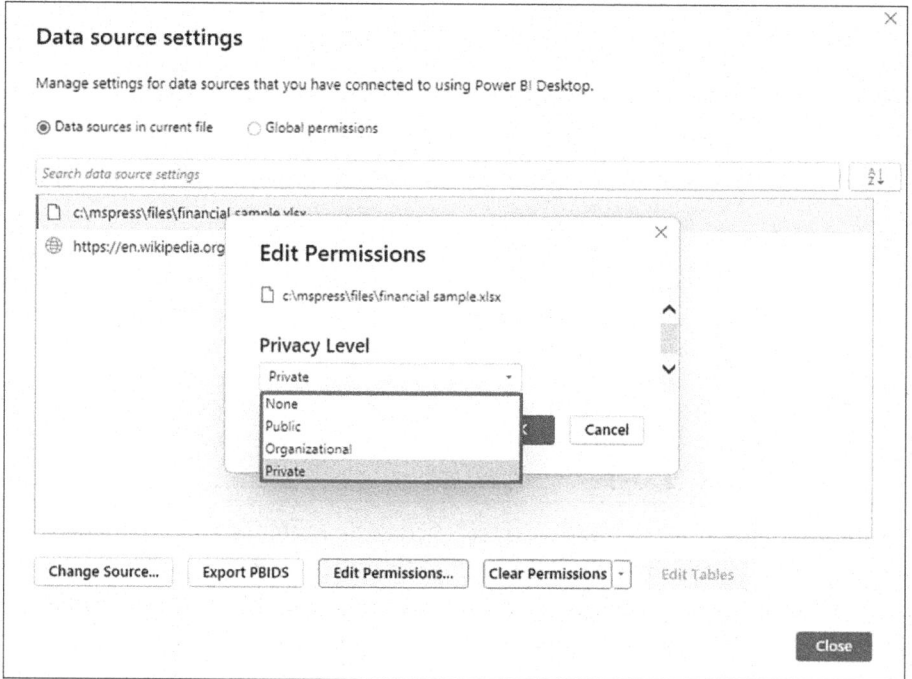

Data source settings privacy level selection.

 TIP If you're combining data only for personal use or testing, you can enable the **Ignore privacy levels** option in the Query Options. Be careful, though, because this option disables privacy checks globally.

IMPORTANT Always choose the most restrictive level needed for your scenario. If you're not sure, select **Private** to keep your data secure.

Skills review

In this chapter, you learned how to

- Navigate the Power Query Editor interface, including the ribbon, queries pane, data preview, and applied steps.

- Use the Get Data feature to connect to common data sources such as local files (Excel, CSV), folders, relational databases like SQL Server, online services, and webpages.

- Preview and validate source data before loading it into your Power BI report.

- Select the appropriate storage mode (Import, DirectQuery, or Dual) based on your performance and data freshness needs.

- Recognize the importance of properly configuring privacy levels to safely combine data without exposing sensitive information.

3

Practice tasks

Before you can complete these tasks, you must copy the book's practice files to your computer. The practice files for these tasks are in the Power-BISBS\C03 folder.

The introduction includes a complete list of practice files and download instructions.

Explore Power Query Editor

Before you connect to any data, take a moment to explore the Power Query Editor interface on your own. Open Power BI Desktop and enter the Power Query Editor by selecting **Home > Transform data**.

Explore the interface and reflect on the following questions:

1. What is the ribbon at the top used for? What kinds of options do you notice there?

2. What do you find in the Queries pane on the left side? Why do you think this area is important?

3. Can you spot the Query Settings pane on the right? What kind of information or steps does it show?

When you finish exploring, close Power Query without making changes.

Connect to common data sources

Get Data from Excel

Use the Financial Sample.xlsx file containing sales data. Follow these steps to connect to the data and review its structure:

1. Open Power BI Desktop.

2. Go to the **Home** tab and select **Get Data > Excel**.

3. Browse to the folder where Financial Sample.xlsx is saved and select **Open**.

4. In the Navigator window, review the list of available tables or sheets.

5. Select the **financials** table to preview the data and select **OK**.

6. Select **Close & Apply** to load the data into Power BI.

Get data from a folder

Use the Sales folder with several .csv files for different countries. To get data, follow these steps:

1. Select **Home** > **Get data** > **Folder**.

2. Browse to the Sales folder and connect.

3. Select **Combine & Transform Data** and review the data preview.

4. Select **OK**.

5. Select **Close & Apply** to load the data into Power BI.

Get data from the web

You need population data from Wikipedia. To get data, follow these steps:

1. Select **Home** > **Get data** > **Web**.

2. Enter this URL:https://en.wikipedia.org/wiki/ List_of_countries_and_dependencies_by_population

3. In the Navigator, review the detected tables.

4. Select the **List of countries and territories by total population** table and select **Transform Data**.

5. Select **Close & Apply** to load the data into Power BI.

Select the appropriate storage mode

Continue working from where you finished the previous task and then perform the following tasks:

1. On the left-side panel, switch to Model view.

2. Select any table in your model.

3. In the Properties pane, expand the Advanced section and locate the Storage mode setting.

Reflect on the following questions:

1. Why is Import the selected mode in your case?

2. Which storage mode would you choose if you needed real-time data?

Understand privacy levels

Continue working from where you finished the previous task and then perform the following tasks:

1. Select **File** > **Options and settings** > **Data source settings**.

2. Select **Edit Permissions**.

3. Review or update the Privacy Levels for your data sources:

   - Set Excel source to **Private**.

   - Set Web page to **Public**.

Reflect on why this step is important. What risks might you face if privacy levels are not set correctly?

Transforming data with Power Query

Practice files

You will need to use the practice files provided with this chapter to complete the practice tasks.

When you're working with data, in the best scenario, you will get that data in optimal conditions to be analyzed. However, usually the opposite happens, meaning that you will commonly have to make some change or transformation to make the data uniform, orderly, and meaningful. In other cases, you must enrich tables with new columns, correct errors, replace records, and so on based on the requirements of the analysis you're going to perform.

Power Query has at its disposal a series of features that, through the user interface and *without the need to know about languages*, allow you to transform the data, adjusting it with a series of clicks. This apparent simplicity hides a powerful advantage in Power BI because it enables you to adapt to the requirements of data quality and accuracy, without having to modify the data in the original source.

When we talk about data transformation, we refer to the operations or activities that will be carried out to ensure the quality of the data. Errors tend to cause problems because they affect the accuracy of the calculations, generate inconsistencies that will later have a negative impact on report design, and cause great damage—the loss of confidence in what is being presented.

In this chapter

- Understand Power Query
- Recognize the role of data quality and cleansing
- Define data types
- Apply columnar transformations
- Change table structures
- Combine and append tables

The main premise or prerequisite before loading data to the semantic model is to evaluate whether the data complies with what is necessary to start making calculations. If it does not, you will have to use a series of steps to adjust it. That is what you will learn in this chapter.

Understand Power Query

Power Query is the data preparation and transformation engine present in every connection you make in Power BI. This tool uses a powerful language called M that consists of more than 700 functions.

Power Query offers various predefined transformations to speed up the work, such as filtering records, selecting columns, sorting values, defining data types, adding new columns, merging, and appending queries. However, one of the most distinctive aspects is that you can achieve the desired result without knowing specifically what the right function is simply by using the user interface.

By using this tool, you can balance between knowing what is within reach with a couple of clicks and delving into specialized functions that will give you greater flexibility in approaching a scenario.

Recognize the role of data quality and cleansing

Working with clean data that has the required data quality is key because it will be reflected later when you're creating a report. Usually, inconsistencies come from the original data source or from intermediate processes that generate those inconsistencies. Although it is not impossible, you most likely will not encounter scenarios where the data is 100% optimal for immediate loading into the semantic model.

The consequences of loading messy data with errors can take many forms, from problems in the accuracy of calculations to inconsistencies that reflect repeated values or even the loss of records that distort the totality of the facts. That is why, being one of the first steps you take when working in Power BI, it allows you to make decisions about the status of the data to adjust and shape it to suit your needs.

Define data types

Assigning data types is an important step in ensuring quality. First, because it defines the nature of the data, classifying it, and second, because it establishes the transformation options available to you. Not all transformations work universally on the different data types; on the contrary, some will be enabled only for specific types.

4

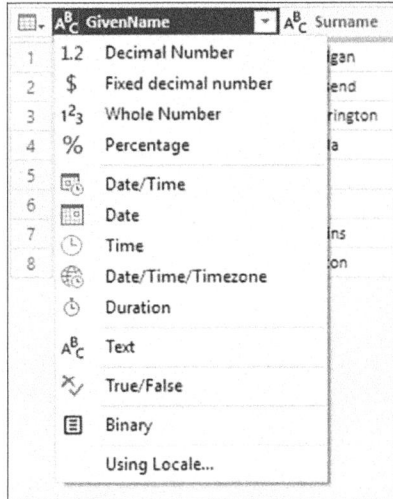

Available data types in columns.

You can define these data types by selecting the icon to the left of the column header where the different data types appear. By default, through its automatic detection, Power BI establishes the data types in each column; these types are reflected in the steps applied as "Change Type." Also, after having selected one or more columns (Ctrl + Left-click or Shift + Left-click to select a range of adjacent columns) from the Transform menu's Detect Data Type option, you can also assign them quickly.

> ✓ **TIP** In general, defining data types is one of the first steps you should evaluate when working in Power Query. You can see it as a requirement that will help you avoid conflicts by not assigning data types correctly or by omitting them.

Apply columnar transformations

Before you learn how to perform columnar transformations, you have to keep in mind the following: the transformations are performed on the columns coming from the table you have loaded in Power Query. However, you can also run transformations where the result will appear in new columns that will be part of the semantic model.

The Transform menu contains options that apply directly to one or more selected columns.

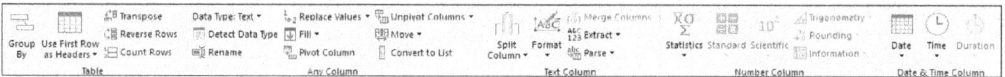

Transformation options on the Transform menu.

On the other side, in the Add Column menu, you can transform data by adding new columns. When you should choose between one option and the other depends mainly on the scenario, so there is no single way to go about this task.

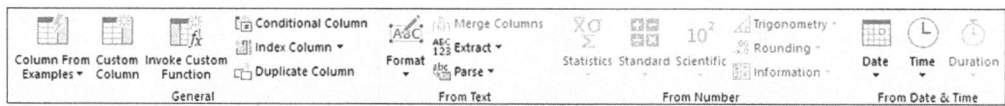

Transformation options on the Add Column menu.

Fill missing content

The records might have omissions. To fill them, you use a *fill up* or *fill down*. The differences between choosing one option or the other correspond to the orientation of the fill. Fill down takes into account the record immediately before consecutive null values, whereas fill up takes into account the record immediately following consecutive null values.

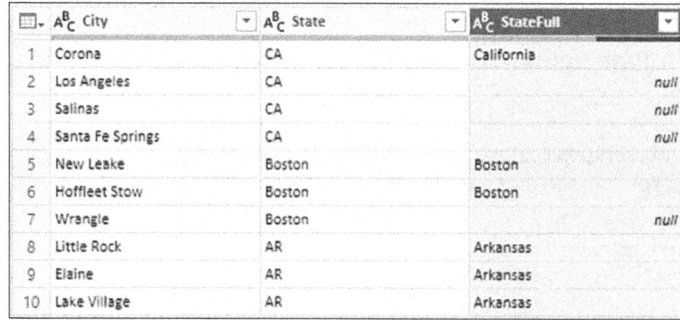

	ABC City	ABC State	ABC StateFull
1	Corona	CA	California
2	Los Angeles	CA	null
3	Salinas	CA	null
4	Santa Fe Springs	CA	null
5	New Leake	Boston	Boston
6	Hoffleet Stow	Boston	Boston
7	Wrangle	Boston	null
8	Little Rock	AR	Arkansas
9	Elaine	AR	Arkansas
10	Lake Village	AR	Arkansas

The StateFull column contains blank records to be filled in.

To perform a fill down

1. Select the **StateFull** column.

2. Select the **Transform** menu.

3. Select **Fill: Down**.

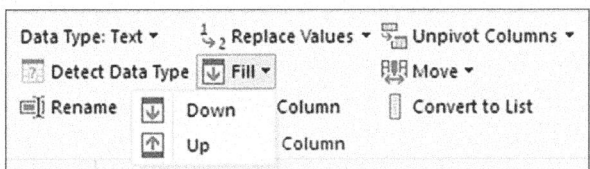

The direction of the arrows indicates the type of fill.

Applying a fill down fills the missing records, by copying the value from the previous row into the nulls, without altering rows that already contain data.

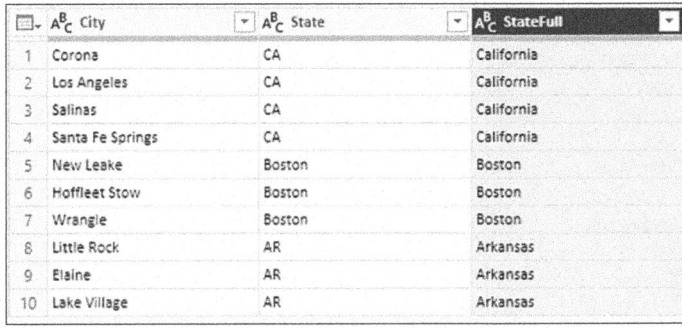

Now the StateFull column contains records in each of its rows.

Remove duplicates

Removing duplicate values is another recurring operation when you're transforming data. This time you will not access the operation from the Options menu but by right-clicking.

The columns contain duplicate values for Julian and Jamie.

To remove duplicates in the records

1. Select the **GivenName** column.

2. Right-click the column header.

3. Select **Remove Duplicates**.

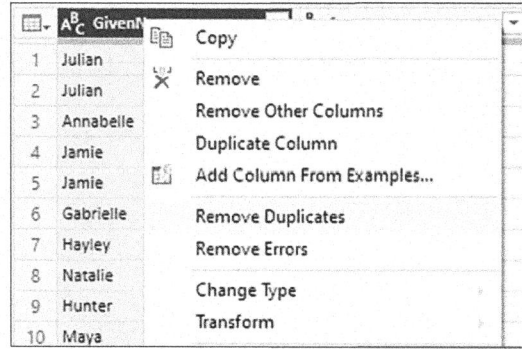

Select the Remove Duplicates option.

4. The duplicate records are removed.

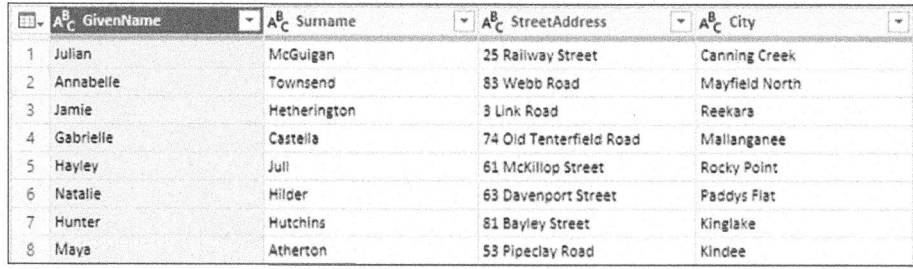

Now Julian and Jaime appear only once in the records.

Combine columns

Combining columns is a transformation operation that seeks to join two or more columns into one. The result is a unified column. Note that the first column selection is the one that will appear from left to right in the result.

To combine two columns into one by transformation

1. Select the **GivenName** column first and then the **Surname** column by holding down the Ctrl key.

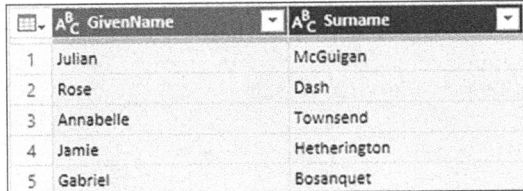

Select two columns.

2. From the Transform menu, select **Merge Columns**. In the Merge Columns dialog, select the **Space** separator type and type the name of the new column: **FullName**.

3. Press the **OK** button.

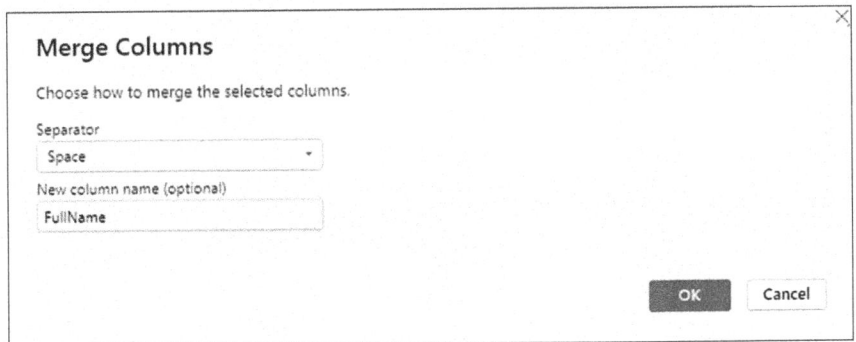

You can select different types of separators.

4.   The result is a single merged column.

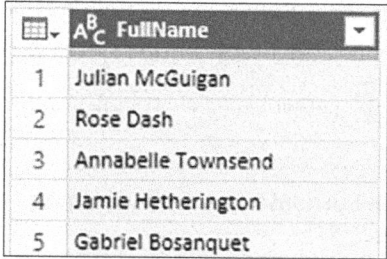

	A^B_C FullName
1	Julian McGuigan
2	Rose Dash
3	Annabelle Townsend
4	Jamie Hetherington
5	Gabriel Bosanquet

A single column with combined values.

 TIP You can use the Shift key to select multiple columns at the same time.

In the same way, you can create a new combined column while leaving the previous ones untouched.

To create a new column from the combination of two existing columns

1.   Select the **GivenName** and **Surname** columns.

2.   Select the **Add Column** menu.

3.   Select **Merge Columns**.

4.   Select the **Space** separator type and type the name of the new column: **FullName**.

5.   The result is a new column.

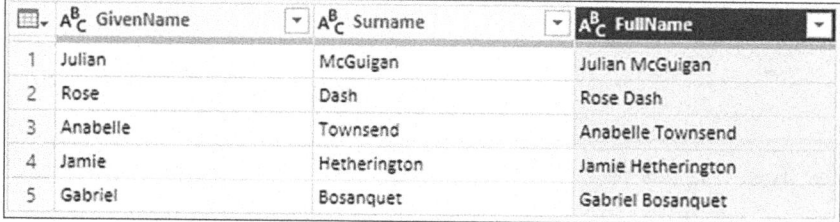

	A^B_C GivenName	A^B_C Surname	A^B_C FullName
1	Julian	McGuigan	Julian McGuigan
2	Rose	Dash	Rose Dash
3	Anabelle	Townsend	Anabelle Townsend
4	Jamie	Hetherington	Jamie Hetherington
5	Gabriel	Bosanquet	Gabriel Bosanquet

A new column named FullName presents the combined values.

Extract text

Among the available transformations, you also are able to extract text. In this case, you will extract the year that appears at the beginning of the Vehicle column.

	1²₃ CustomerKey	ABC GivenName	ABC Surname	ABC Vehicle
1	15	Julian	McGuigan	2000 Peugeot Kart Up
2	23	Rose	Dash	2005 Volvo XC90
3	36	Annabelle	Townsend	1999 Lancia Lybra
4	120	Jamie	Hetherington	2006 Dodge Durango
5	180	Gabriel	Bosanquet	1995 Morgan Plus 4

In the Vehicle column, the year will be deleted.

To extract text from a column

1. Select the **Vehicle** column.

2. Select the **Transform** menu.

3. From the Extract option, select **Text After Delimiter**.

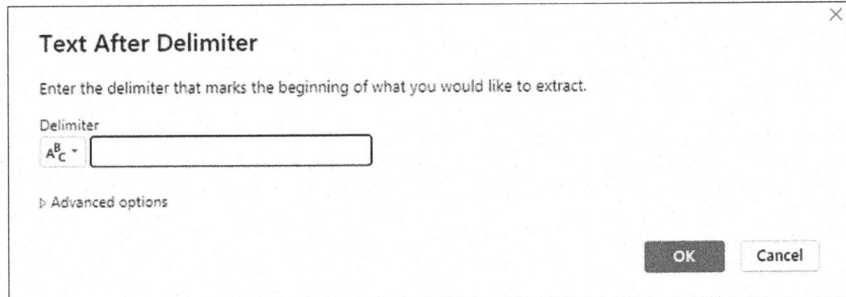

Text After Delimiter dialog.

4. Press space in the Delimiter box and then select **OK**.

5. The result is the vehicle model without the year.

	1²₃ CustomerKey	ABC GivenName	ABC Surname	ABC Vehicle
1	15	Julian	McGuigan	Peugeot Kart Up
2	23	Rose	Dash	Volvo XC90
3	36	Annabelle	Townsend	Lancia Lybra
4	120	Jamie	Hetherington	Dodge Durango
5	180	Gabriel	Bosanquet	Morgan Plus 4

Now the Vehicle column does not contain the year.

Replace values

Another recurring transformation step is replacing values. In this case, you will select the current value and then type the desired value.

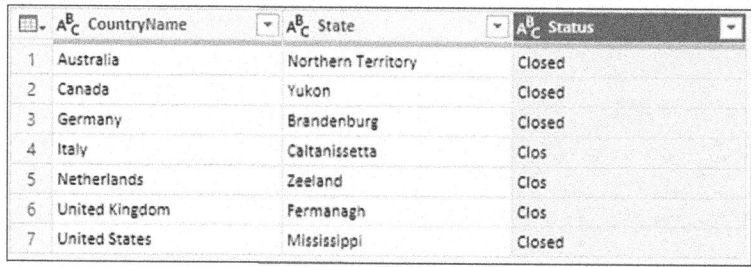

	ABC CountryName	ABC State	ABC Status
1	Australia	Northern Territory	Closed
2	Canada	Yukon	Closed
3	Germany	Brandenburg	Closed
4	Italy	Caltanissetta	Clos
5	Netherlands	Zeeland	Clos
6	United Kingdom	Fermanagh	Clos
7	United States	Mississippi	Closed

The Status column contains records to be replaced.

To replace values in a column

1. Select the **Status** column.

2. Select the **Transform** menu.

3. Select **Replace Values**.

4. Type in the value to find: **Clos**.

5. Type in the value to be replace with: **Closed**.

6. Under the Advanced options, check the **Match entire cell contents** box.

7. Press the **OK** button.

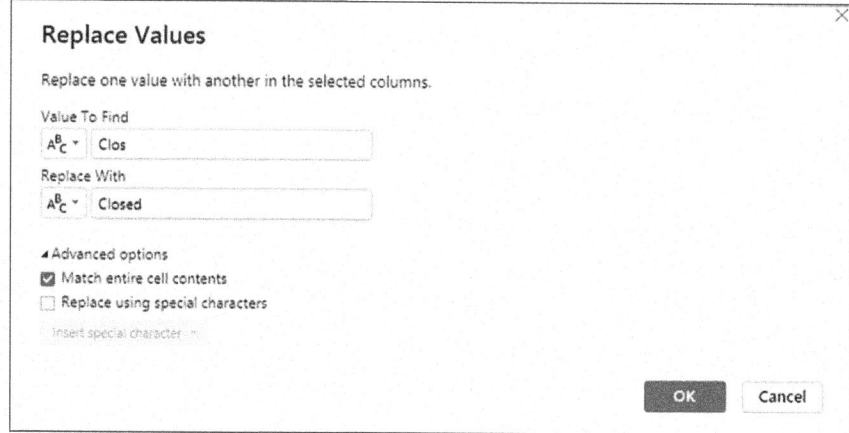

A search and replace values box appears.

The resulting column shows the replaced values.

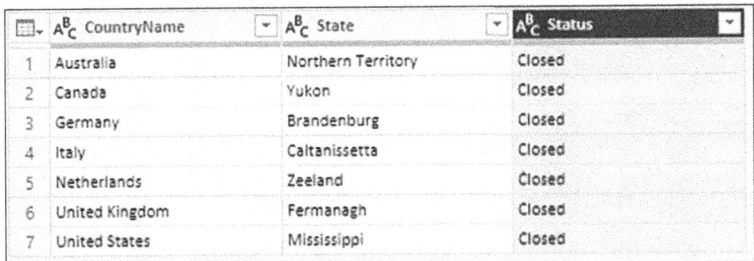

	AᴮC CountryName	AᴮC State	AᴮC Status
1	Australia	Northern Territory	Closed
2	Canada	Yukon	Closed
3	Germany	Brandenburg	Closed
4	Italy	Caltanissetta	Closed
5	Netherlands	Zeeland	Closed
6	United Kingdom	Fermanagh	Closed
7	United States	Mississippi	Closed

Now all records contain the word Closed.

Column from examples

So far you have learned one way to extract texts, but that is not the only way. One convenient method enables you to perform various transformations, starting from examples. Here you will create a column that extracts the color of the product description by typing directly in the cell of the new column.

	1²₃ ProductCode	AᴮC ProductName	1.2 Cost	1.2 Price
1	101001	Contoso 512MB MP3 Player E51 Silver	6,62	12,99
2	101002	Contoso 512MB MP3 Player E51 Blue	6,62	12,99
3	101003	Contoso 1G MP3 Player E100 White	7,4	14,52
4	101004	Contoso 2G MP3 Player E200 Silver	11	21,57
5	101005	Contoso 2G MP3 Player E200 Red	11	21,57

The ProductName column contains the color to be extracted.

To create a new column from examples

1. Select the **Add Column** menu.

2. From the tab, select **Column From Examples > From Selection**.

3. Select the **ProductName** column.

4. In the new column that appears on the right, double-click the header and change the name to **Color**.

5. In the first row, type **Silver** and press Enter.

6. To confirm the creation of the column, select **OK**.

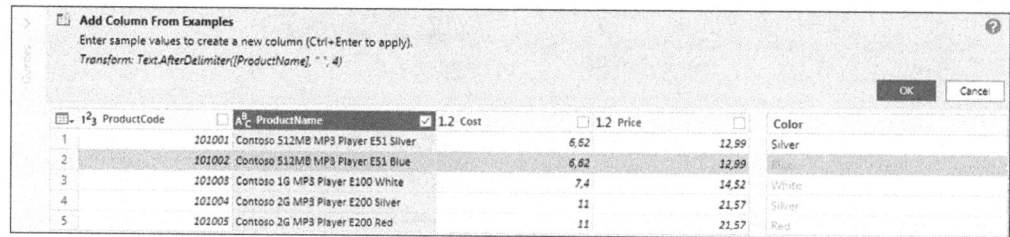

The result is a new column, except that the color comes from the product description.

 TIP In some cases you might need to type examples in other cells so that the Power Query Engine understands what you are trying to achieve.

Grouping data

Grouping data allows you to reduce the number of visible records in the table, transforming them into a summarized version where the values will not be repeated. This operation can be useful when you want to avoid presenting all the values in detail. In this case, you will sum the values in the Quantity column, making the repeated values in the ProductName column disappear.

The ProductName column contains repeated products.

To group data

1. Select the **Transform** menu.

2. Choose **Group By**.

3. In the New column name field, enter **Total Quantity**.

4. In the Operation field, select **Sum**.

5. In the Column field, choose **Quantity**.

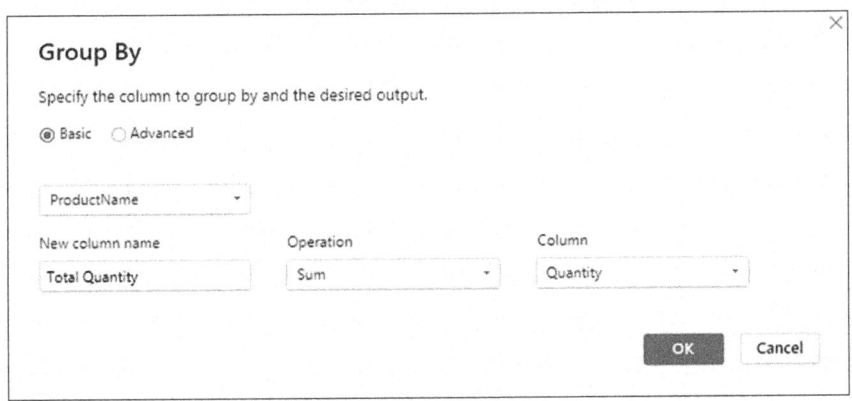

Dialog with the data grouping options according to the available columns.

When you select **OK**, the table that originally had 10 rows will be reduced to 4 rows. Also, the previous Quantity values will disappear and become the summation presented in the new Total Quantity column.

A^B_C ProductName	1.2 Total Quantity
1 WWI 1GB Pulse Smart pen E50 Silver	2
2 WWI Desktop PC1.80 E1802 White	9
3 MGS Dungeon Siege: Legends of Aranna M330	3
4 Contoso 1G MP3 Player E100 White	1

Table grouped from the sum of the Quantity column.

Change table structures

You can apply transformations not only to columns, but you also can modify the structure of a table so that you can adapt it to analyze data in semantic models. Unlike what you have seen in the previous transformations that focus on changing the records, the following transformations seek to modify the tables at a general level.

Unpivot

Unpivoting is an operation that allows you to move one or more columns to reduce them, thus simplifying the table to perform operations. You select only the column that will remain static or unchanged, right-click it, and choose **Unpivot Other Columns**.

	1²3 Year	1²3 Australia	1²3 Canada	1²3 France
1	2015	880	2022	524
2	2016	1158	2403	509
3	2017	1383	2799	665
4	2018	2947	5652	1324
5	2019	3603	6850	1716
6	2020	1415	2586	593
7	2021	2343	3830	1100
8	2022	4118	6585	2396
9	2023	3303	5421	1726
10	2024	1003	1547	357

The values are separated by the countries in each column.

When you execute the transformation, the table structure changes. You will see only three columns: Year, Attribute (which replaces the country name), and Value, which is the value of each country.

	1²3 Year	A⁸c Attribute	1²3 Value
1	2015	Australia	880
2	2015	Canada	2022
3	2015	France	524
4	2016	Australia	1158
5	2016	Canada	2403
6	2016	France	509
7	2017	Australia	1383

Now the table contains three columns.

In the formula bar at the top of the result, the following syntax appears in the M language:

```
= Table.UnpivotOtherColumns(#"Changed Type", {"Year"}, "Attribute", "Value").
```

This expression has been executed in the language automatically. However, you also can change the names of the columns directly from the formula bar, replacing the words "Attribute" with "Country" and "Value" with "Quantity".

The most important point about this transformation is that you can take advantage of how Power BI performs calculations, because when all the values are in the same column, you simplify subsequent arithmetic operations.

Pivot Column

If different events are recorded in a column, you still can perform calculations or other operations; however, it is advisable to transfer those events to a tabular (columnar) scheme where each column contains its specific attribute or observation.

To perform this operation, you must select the **Type** column, and then from the Transform menu, select **Pivot Column**. Then a dialog will appear where you have to choose the column that contains the values.

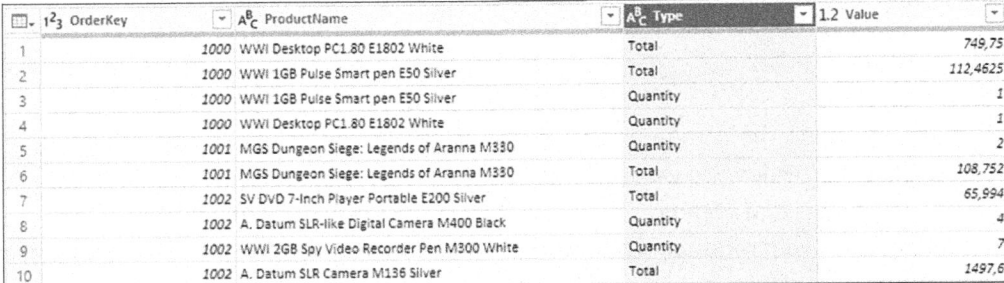

1²₃ OrderKey	AᵇC ProductName	AᵇC Type	1.2 Value
1	1000 WWI Desktop PC1.80 E1802 White	Total	749,75
2	1000 WWI 1GB Pulse Smart pen E50 Silver	Total	112,4625
3	1000 WWI 1GB Pulse Smart pen E50 Silver	Quantity	1
4	1000 WWI Desktop PC1.80 E1802 White	Quantity	1
5	1001 MGS Dungeon Siege: Legends of Aranna M330	Quantity	2
6	1001 MGS Dungeon Siege: Legends of Aranna M330	Total	108,752
7	1002 SV DVD 7-Inch Player Portable E200 Silver	Total	65,994
8	1002 A. Datum SLR-like Digital Camera M400 Black	Quantity	4
9	1002 WWI 2GB Spy Video Recorder Pen M300 White	Quantity	7
10	1002 A. Datum SLR Camera M136 Silver	Total	1497,6

The Type column contains both Quantity and Total records.

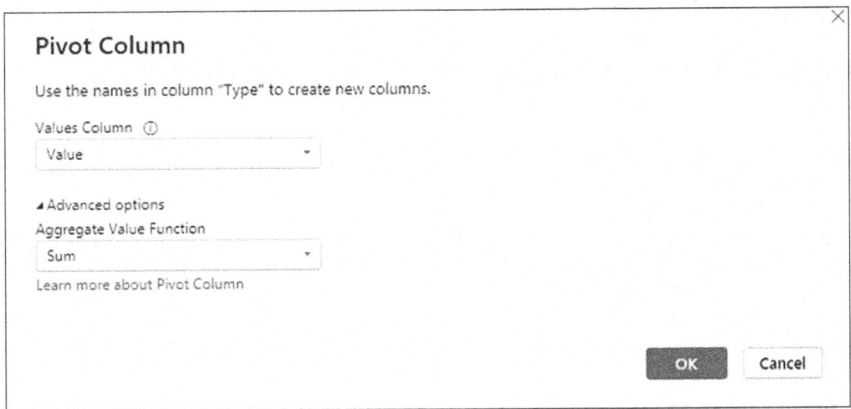

Dialog where you choose the column containing the values.

The result is presented in a table that separates the Quantity and Total records into their own columns.

	1²₃ OrderKey	Aᴮ_C ProductName	1.2 Quantity	1.2 Total
1	1000	WWI 1GB Pulse Smart pen E50 Silver	1	112,4625
2	1000	WWI Desktop PC1.80 E1802 White	1	749,75
3	1001	MGS Dungeon Siege: Legends of Aranna M330	2	108,752
4	1002	A. Datum SLR Camera M136 Silver	3	1497,6
5	1002	A. Datum SLR-like Digital Camera M400 Black	4	1260,16
6	1002	SV DVD 7-Inch Player Portable E200 Silver	1	65,994
7	1002	WWI 2GB Spy Video Recorder Pen M300 White	7	950,25
8	1003	NT Wireless Bluetooth Stereo Headphones M402 Green	3	224,9775
9	1004	Adventure Works 19" Color Digital TV E35 Brown	2	229,44
10	1004	Contoso DVD 58 DVD Storage Binder M55 Silver	1	8,334

Table with quantities and total shown separately.

Combine and append tables

In many scenarios, the data needed for analysis is distributed across multiple tables. Power Query provides two essential operations to consolidate this information: combining tables and appending tables. These transformations allow you to unify attributes and avoid redundancy in the semantic model, ensuring a cleaner and more efficient data structure.

Combining tables

When performing a merge, you add new columns from other tables into the current table. This operation requires fields in common and is beneficial when you need to unify some attributes from other tables into one.

Here is the first table, named sales:

	OrderDate	1²₃ ProductKey	1²₃ Quantity	1.2 UnitPrice
1	1/1/2015	48	1	112,4625
2	1/1/2015	460	1	749,75
3	1/1/2015	1730	2	54,376
4	1/1/2015	955	4	315,04
5	1/1/2015	62	7	135,75
6	1/1/2015	1050	3	499,2
7	1/1/2015	1608	1	65,994
8	1/1/2015	85	3	74,9925
9	1/1/2015	128	2	114,72
10	1/1/2015	2079	1	499,455

The ProductKey column is a common field in another table called product.

Here is the second table, named product:

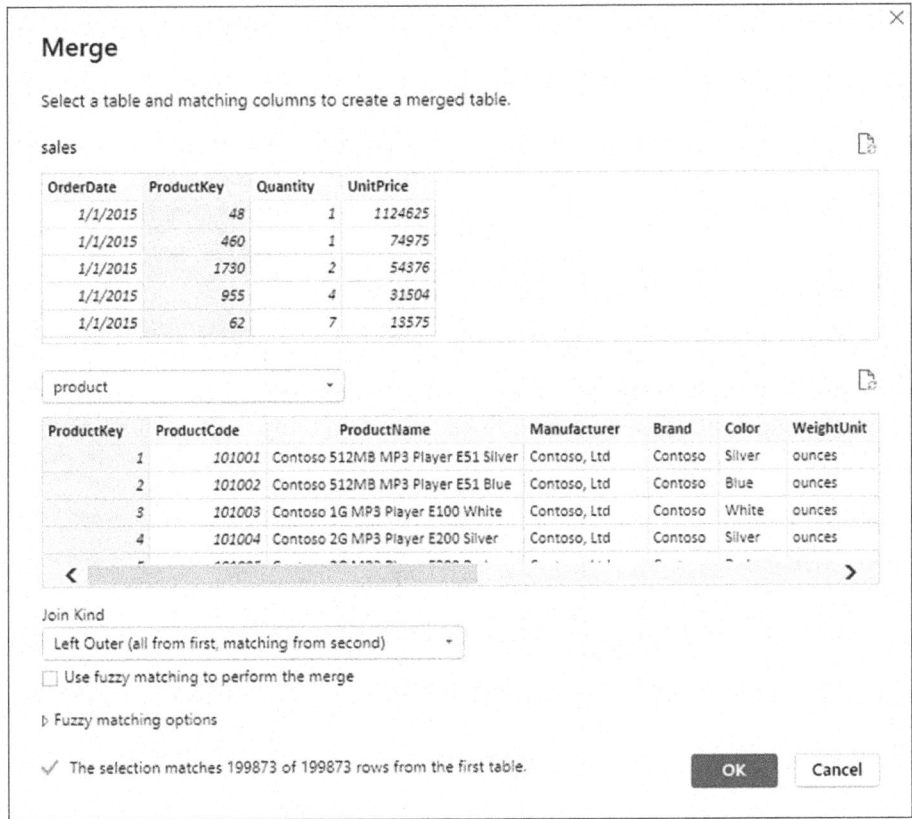

1²₃ ProductKey	1²₃ ProductCode	AᵇC ProductName
1	1	101001 Contoso 512MB MP3 Player E51 Silver
2	2	101002 Contoso 512MB MP3 Player E51 Blue
3	3	101003 Contoso 1G MP3 Player E100 White
4	4	101004 Contoso 2G MP3 Player E200 Silver
5	5	101005 Contoso 2G MP3 Player E200 Red
6	6	101006 Contoso 2G MP3 Player E200 Black
7	7	101007 Contoso 2G MP3 Player E200 Blue
8	8	101008 Contoso 4G MP3 Player E400 Silver
9	9	101009 Contoso 4G MP3 Player E400 Black
10	10	101010 Contoso 4G MP3 Player E400 Green

The product table contains the same ProductKey column from the sales table that will allow you to merge the tables.

To perform the merge, you must select the table in the query panel. Then from the Home menu, select **Merge Queries**. Then you will see a dialog where you must select both tables and the common column (in this case, **ProductKey**) and select **OK**.

Merge

Select a table and matching columns to create a merged table.

sales

OrderDate	ProductKey	Quantity	UnitPrice
1/1/2015	48	1	1124625
1/1/2015	460	1	74975
1/1/2015	1730	2	54376
1/1/2015	955	4	31504
1/1/2015	62	7	13575

product

ProductKey	ProductCode	ProductName	Manufacturer	Brand	Color	WeightUnit
1	101001	Contoso 512MB MP3 Player E51 Silver	Contoso, Ltd	Contoso	Silver	ounces
2	101002	Contoso 512MB MP3 Player E51 Blue	Contoso, Ltd	Contoso	Blue	ounces
3	101003	Contoso 1G MP3 Player E100 White	Contoso, Ltd	Contoso	White	ounces
4	101004	Contoso 2G MP3 Player E200 Silver	Contoso, Ltd	Contoso	Silver	ounces

Join Kind

Left Outer (all from first, matching from second)

☐ Use fuzzy matching to perform the merge

▷ Fuzzy matching options

✓ The selection matches 199873 of 199873 rows from the first table.

OK   Cancel

The default merge type is Left Outer.

The type of combination refers to the conditions that will be set. A *Left Outer* merge implies that the initial table (sales) will keep all its records. On the other hand, from the other table (product), only those values that match the previous table will be extracted. The result is presented as a new column called product.

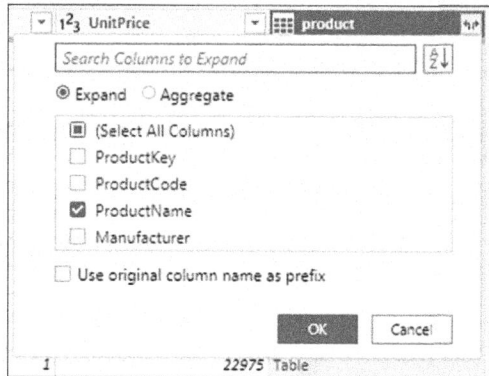

In the header you can expand the available columns.

	OrderDate	ProductKey	Quantity	UnitPrice	ProductName
1	1/1/2015	48	1	112,4625	WWI 1GB Pulse Smart pen E50 Silver
2	7/2/2015	48	1	112,4625	WWI 1GB Pulse Smart pen E50 Silver
3	1/1/2015	460	1	749,75	WWI Desktop PC1.80 E1802 White
4	2/1/2015	460	1	749,75	WWI Desktop PC1.80 E1802 White
5	13/1/2015	460	2	749,75	WWI Desktop PC1.80 E1802 White
6	19/5/2015	460	4	749,75	WWI Desktop PC1.80 E1802 White
7	16/6/2015	460	1	749,75	WWI Desktop PC1.80 E1802 White
8	1/1/2015	1730	2	54,376	MGS Dungeon Siege: Legends of Aranna M330
9	21/5/2015	1730	1	54,376	MGS Dungeon Siege: Legends of Aranna M330
10	1/6/2015	3	1	10,89	Contoso 1G MP3 Player E100 White

The result is the addition of the ProductName column in the sales table.

Although the default combination type is a Left Outer, you can take advantage of other types, depending on the type of requirement. The important point is that all of them perform operations in one way or another so that two tables, when combined, can include or exclude records.

Appending tables

Appending tables corresponds to placing a table under another one, maintaining the structure and correlation in its records so that there will be no omissions. This way, you will avoid loading the semantic model with more than one table that contains the same structure.

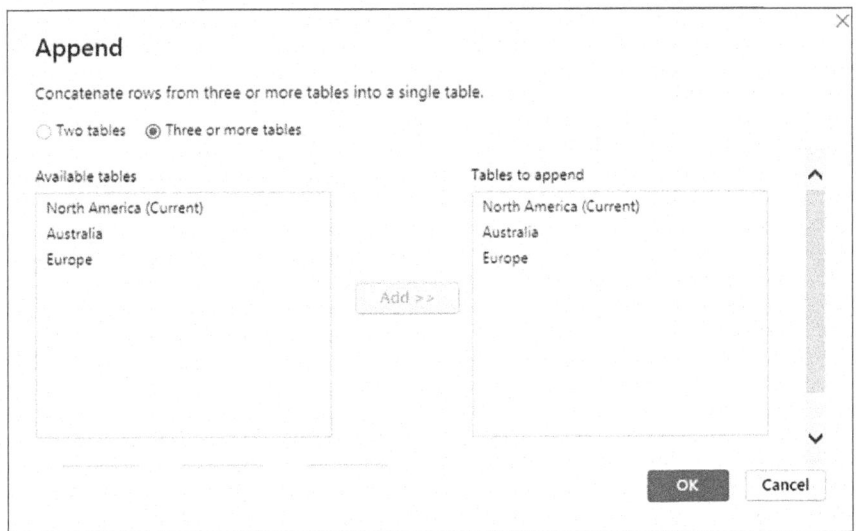

	¹²₃ CustomerKey	Aᴮ_C Continent	Aᴮ_C GivenName	Aᴮ_C Surname	Aᴮ_C City
1	200009	North America	Wilbert	Salisbury	St Gregoire De Nicolet
2	200016	North America	Amy	Willis	Oshawa
3	200040	North America	Johnny	Paulsen	London
4	200043	North America	Lucas	Weisner	Toronto
5	200046	North America	Rick	Wallace	Toronto
6	200055	North America	James	Ford	Sherwood Park
7	200066	North America	Gregg	Rush	Montreal
8	200084	North America	Mary	Ouellette	Toronto
9	200085	North America	Reina	Diaz	Earlton
10	200105	North America	Lilly	Anderson	Barrie

The customer table contains records from North America only.

In the Home menu, under the Combine section, you will see the button to append queries. There, you will see options to append two or more tables.

You must select the tables to be appended.

To avoid loading all the tables to the semantic model after they have been unified, right-click on the Australia and Europe tables and select the **Enable load** option. This selection disables their individual load, keeping only the unified table active. Finally, the unified table for North America changes its name to Regions.

 IMPORTANT To ensure uniformity of the records, the names of each of the columns must be the same. Otherwise, new columns will be added to the query append result.

Skills review

In this chapter, you learned how to

- Use Power Query in data transformation.

- Recognize the importance of data quality and cleanliness.

- Assign data types and their relationship to transformations.

- Apply various transformations (fill values, remove duplicates, merge columns, extract text, replace values, add columns from examples, group data).

- Apply advanced table transformations using unpivot and pivot columns.

- Simplify the semantic model from combinations and table appends.

Practice tasks

Before you can complete these tasks, you must copy the book's practice files to your computer. The practice files for these tasks are in the PowerBISBS\C04 folder.

The introduction includes a complete list of practice files and download instructions.

Understand Power Query

Considering the role that Power Query plays in the data transformation and cleansing process:

1. Why is data preparation and the transformation engine such as Power Query important in information analysis?

2. What advantages does process automation in Power Query offer compared to a manual approach in Excel?

3. Do you think the use of tools such as Power Query reduces the need for advanced programming skills or increases their importance?

Recognize the role of data quality and cleansing

Considering the impact of data quality and data cleansing:

1. Why is it crucial to work with clean data before creating a report in Power BI?

2. Do you think data quality is more important than the amount of information available?

Define data types

Data type assignment is one of the initial steps before starting to perform transformations:

1. Why is it essential to correctly assign the data type in Power Query?

2. What are the advantages of automatic data type detection in Power BI?

Apply columnar transformations

Using the file "Chapter 4 - Applying columnar transformations," perform the following tasks:

1. Make a connection to the Replace_values table.

2. Select the **Country** column.

3. From the Transform menu, select **Fill Up**.

Change table structures

Using the file "Chapter 4 - Changing table structures," perform the following tasks:

1. Make a connection to the Pivot_Column table.

2. Select the **Type** column.

3. From the Transform menu, select **Pivot Column**.

4. In the dialog, select the **Value** column containing the values.

Combine and append tables

Using the file "Chapter 4 - Combining and appending tables," perform the following tasks:

1. Make a connection to the product and sales tables.

2. Select the sales table and select **Merge Queries** from the Home menu.

3. Select the product table as the second table.

4. Select the **ProductKey** column in both tables and select **OK**.

5. Expand the following records in the new product column: ProductName and Manufacturer (uncheck the **Use original column name as prefix** box).

Creating a simple semantic model

5

Practice files

No practice files are necessary to complete the practice tasks in this chapter.

A semantic model represents the backbone of a report in Power BI by defining how data will be transferred between tables, columns, relationships, and calculations that you will create later. Its behavior assumes a series of techniques and concepts developed by the business intelligence industry to store and process data.

The semantic model defines and manages various properties, including how relationships between tables are established, the data types assigned to columns, field aggregations and hierarchies, security settings, and other advanced features. However, the advantage is that most are configured through the user interface, and others are automatically predefined.

The importance of creating a semantic model efficiently will be reflected in your ability to perform different operations easily. Sometimes, achieving the expected result is complicated because, in general terms, it is not aligned with the requirements of calculations and report design.

In this chapter

- Understand the fundamentals of the semantic model
- Define relationships between tables
- Differentiate types of relationships
- Control cross-filter direction
- Manage active and inactive relationships
- Customize the semantic model and manage its properties

In this chapter, you will learn how to create a simple semantic model using the main features that are important to consider when creating a report in Power BI.

Understand the fundamentals of the semantic model

This section covers the key features that define how the semantic model is used. Creating relationships and configuring properties are essential steps that, often imperceptibly, shape the outcome of your reports. This is the starting point; everything that comes after is based on this foundation.

Single table

The first thing you need to understand is this: The level of abstraction you find in Power BI can be summarized in tables; they are simply tables that communicate with each other. However, you can apply techniques to them to get the most out of them according to their structure.

In its simplest form, a semantic model can consist of a single table. That table contains all the available records, organized through a series of columns that classify their observations.

OrderDate	Quantity	UnitPrice	ProductName	GivenName	CountryFull
5/9/2018	1	163,9918	Litware Microwave 2.2CuFt M125 Silver	John	United States
25/4/2015	1	87,2	SV 16xDVD M330 Silver	John	United States
25/4/2015	1	381	Contoso Water Heater 2.6GPM E0900 Blue	John	United States
12/3/2015	1	28,4625	NT Bluetooth Active Headphones E202 Black	John	United States
27/2/2015	1	300,8	A. Datum All in One Digital Camera M200 Green	John	United States
27/2/2015	1	30,1	MGS Rise of Nations: Thrones and Patriots2009 E145	John	United States
19/1/2018	1	233,991	Contoso DVD 14-Inch Player Portable L100 Silver	John	United States
21/2/2015	1	4,823	MGS Hand Games men M300 Yellow	John	United States
14/5/2015	1	86,25	WWI Wireless Bluetooth Stereo Headphones M270 Silver	John	United States
23/2/2015	1	34,794	SV DVD Player M110 Silver	John	United States

The sales table contains six columns.

The most obvious aspect is that some of its attributes, such as columns, may have repeated records when all the data is stored in a single table. For example, in the CountryFull column, you can see the country United States repeated.

Using a single table is more common than it seems, but it has its limitations. As you learn about creating semantic models, you will realize that using a single table is not the first option if you want to build something that can continue to grow and adapt to new requirements over time.

Two or more tables

Unlike using a single table, the approach known as *dimensional modeling* aims to separate observations into different entities or tables. This is where relationships come into play, acting as highways for transferring data, and the classification of table types, whether they are *facts* or *dimensions*.

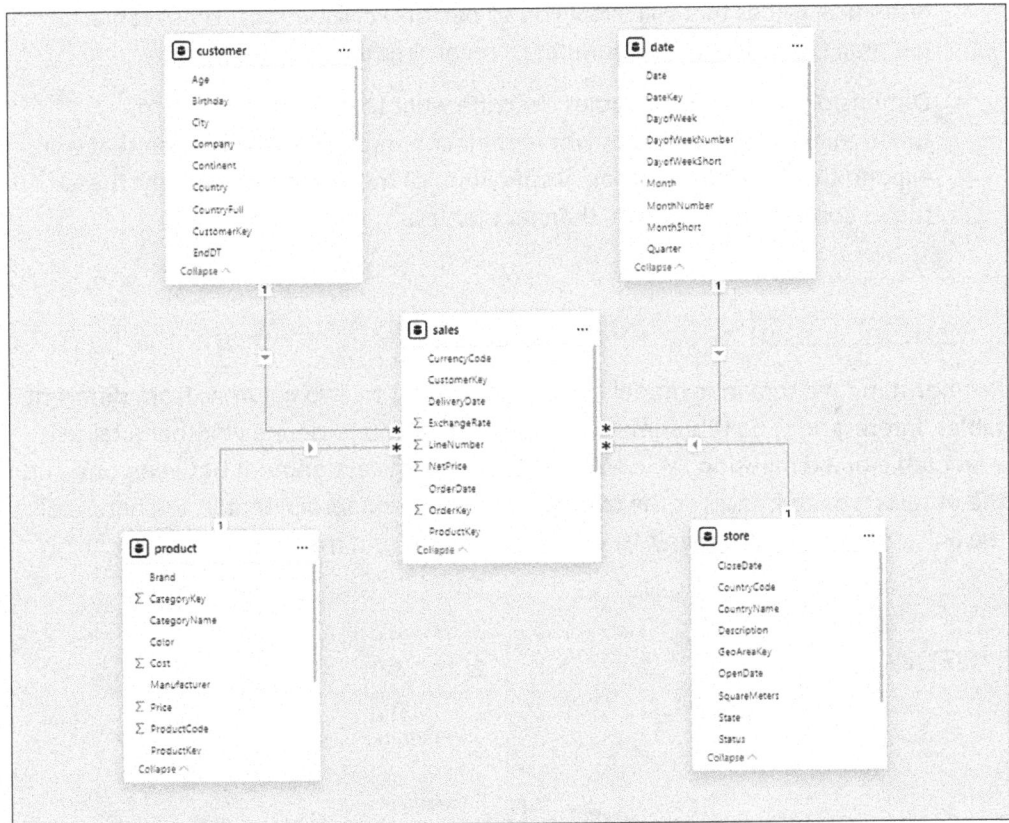

Star schema: The facts table named sales is in the center, surrounded by the dimension tables named customer, date, product, and store.

Applying dimensional modeling techniques (separating tables) creates what is known as a *star schema*. This approach is recommended to take advantage of the full range of features offered by Power BI. Likewise, adopting this type of schema helps reduce complexity when creating calculations in the Data Analysis Expressions (DAX) language, having a significant impact on the ability to continue growing, indexing more data, and bringing reports to new requirements without detracting from their capabilities.

Types of tables

You should be familiar with two types of tables when working under a star schema.

- **Fact tables:** These tables contain columns that define an event that has occurred. When you inspect fact tables, you will notice that they have correlatives in their records, sequences, or dates that may be repeated or numerical values that will allow you to perform calculations. These tables generally contain a larger number of records in the semantic model.

- **Dimension tables:** These tables describe what the fact tables record, functioning as lookup tables where their columns store information that will expand the understanding or classification of those events. Similarly, these tables contain fewer records than fact tables.

Define relationships between tables

Relationships in a semantic model are defined based on two columns from different tables. Interestingly, no table-level property allows you to define whether a table is a fact table or a dimension table. What establishes the assignment between one and the other is what is known as the *cardinality in the relationship*, that is, the nature of the link: one-to-many or many-to-one, one-to-one, and many-to-many.

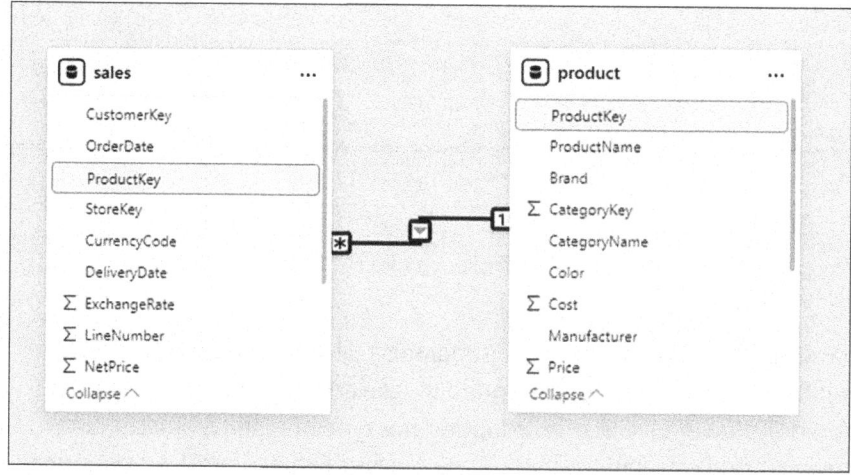

Between this sales fact table and product dimension table, the relationship type is one-to-many.

From the Model view in Power BI, you can identify that the product table is a dimension table because the relationship shows the number one (1), which is the side where the column being used as the key to connect to the fact table contains unique values; they are not repeated. On the other hand, the sales fact table is on the many side with the asterisk symbol (*), which can be interpreted to mean that the product codes that appear in that table are repeated.

To create a new relationship

1. Go to the Model view.

2. From the Home menu, select **Manage relationships**.

3. Select **New relationship** using the product and sales tables.

4. Select the **ProductKey** column in both tables.

5. Select **Save**.

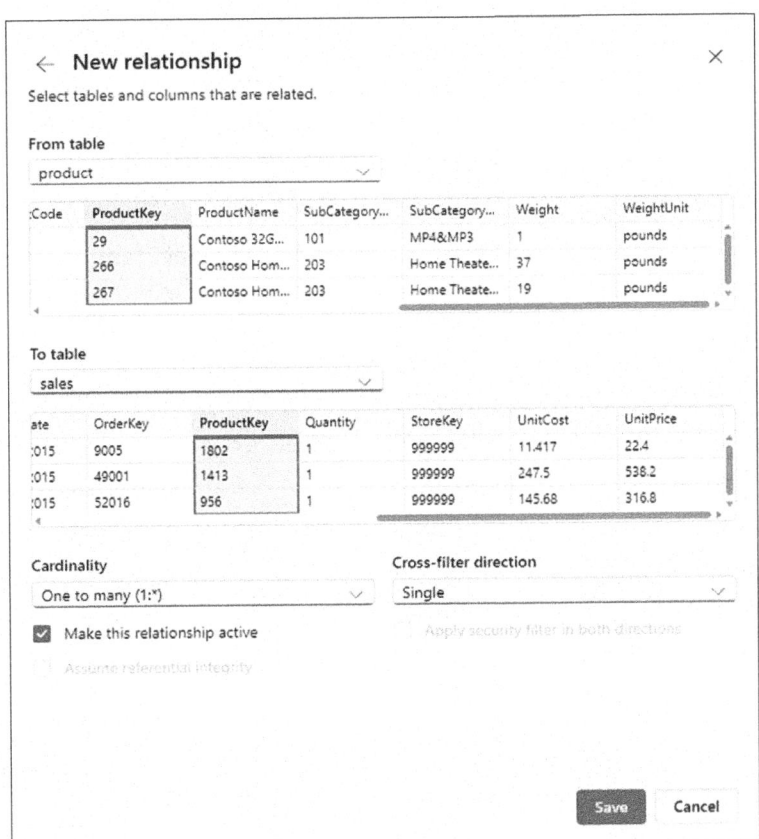

In this dialog for creating new relationships, you must select the tables and columns that will serve as keys.

The engine will automatically select the correct columns to create a new relationship if both have the same data type and name assigned to them. If not, you must locate them in the table and select them one by one.

 TIP From the Model view, you can also create new relationships by selecting a column with a mouse click and dragging it to another column in a corresponding table.

Differentiate types of relationships

Although at first glance all relationships seem the same, their differences can completely alter the results you obtain. Here you will learn to identify them and understand how each one behaves.

One-to-many (1:*) or many-to-one (*:1)

- This is the most common type of relationship and is the one that Power BI will create by default. You can identify it visually because the fact table contains an asterisk (*), whereas the dimension table contains the number one (1). However, if both columns contain unique values, it may instead create a one-to-one (1:1) relationship automatically.

- It represents a type of relationship where the column from the fact table records repeated values. In contrast, the corresponding column in the dimension table contains unique values.

One-to-one (1:1)

- This is a type of relationship where both columns contain unique records in each of the tables.

- Having the same type of cardinality is redundant and unnecessarily increases the number of tables in the model. In these cases, it is recommended to combine the tables as you saw in the preceding chapter to unify them into a single table.

Many-to-many (*:*)

- In this type of relationship, the values in the columns are repeated in both tables. They do not require unique values as in one-to-many relationships.

■ This is considered the most complex type of relationship and is "situational" because the consequences of not understanding what governs its behavior range from the appearance of a concept called ambiguity in the semantic model to the possibility of generating erroneous results at the calculation level.

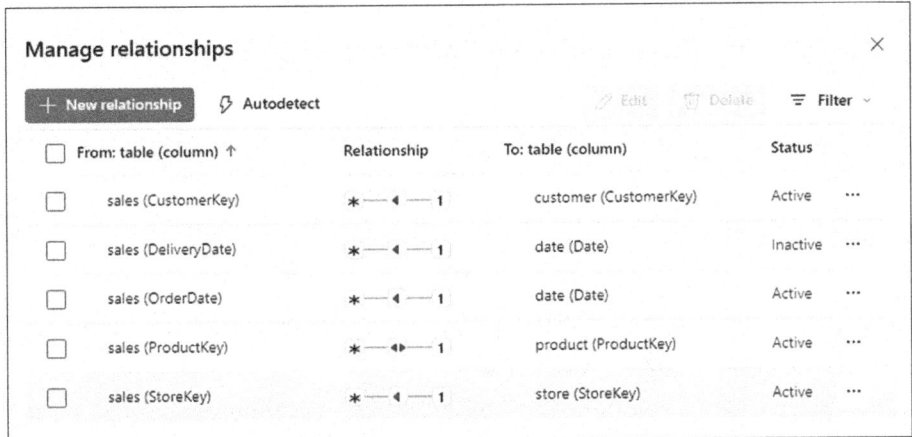

In the Manage relationships box, you can simultaneously view all relationships in the semantic model, the relationship type, the columns involved, and the status.

In the Manage Relationships, you can find a button called Autodetect. Selecting it will perform a complete check of the tables in the semantic model to detect whether valid relationships exist. Although this feature is very useful, it is recommended that you take special care and validate whether these are indeed the correct relationships.

> **TIP** In the Manage Relationships, you can select the **Filter** button to filter the types of relationships that exist in the semantic model and the cross-filter direction in each of the tables.

Control cross-filter direction

You can think of cross-filter direction as the way in which data will be able to travel in one direction or another between the different tables that make up the semantic model—something like the lanes on a highway that define its direction. This behavior is known as *filtering data* and is essential for you to be able to interact between the different values contained in the tables.

When cross-filter direction is set in one direction only:

- Only one table can filter the values of the other.
- This is the default type of relationship in one-to-many or many-to-one relationships.
- The table on the one (1) side can filter the data in the table on the many (*) side, but not vice versa.

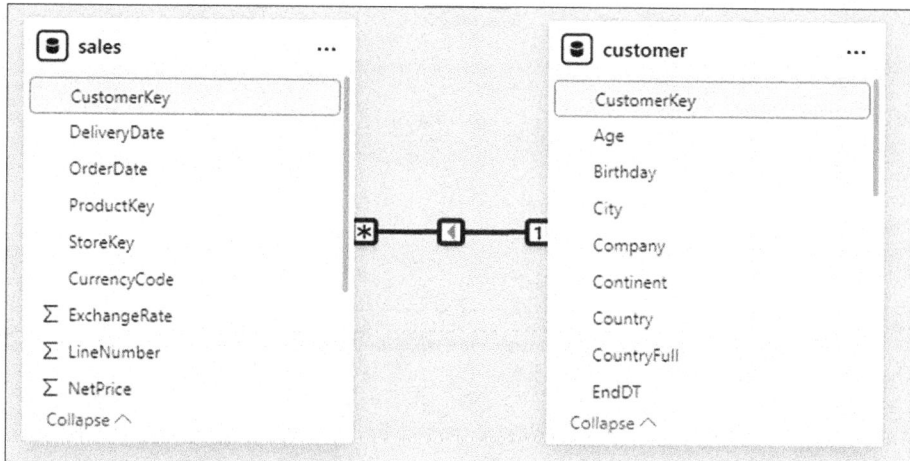

Between the sales fact table and the customer dimension table, the cross-filter direction is defined in a single direction.

One way to identify which table filters the other is to look at the direction of the arrow on the line that physically represents the relationship. In the preceding image, you can see how the filter travels from the customer dimension table on the one (1) side to the sales table on the many (*) side. In the middle, you can see the arrow pointing to the left.

If the cross-filter direction is set in both directions:

- Both tables will be able to filter each other's data, whether it is dimension or fact data.
- If the semantic model contains more than one fact table, modifying the cross-filter direction in both directions can cause ambiguity.
- It can potentially decrease performance.
- This is the default filter type for many-to-many relationships (although you can change its configuration later).

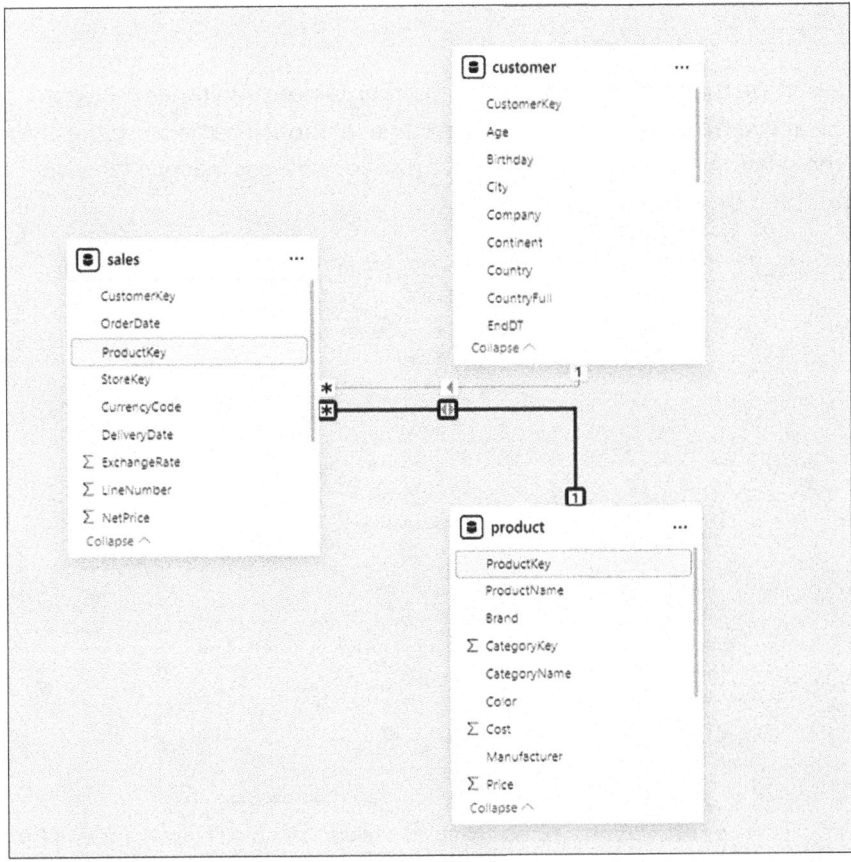

Between the sales fact table and two dimension tables, customer and product, the cross-filter direction between the sales and product tables is defined in both directions.

You can identify whether the filter direction is set in both directions by looking at the arrows; in the preceding image, both point to the sales and product tables. You can also modify the filter direction without having to do so from the physical or visible relationships; to do so, you can use the CROSSFILTER function in the DAX language. This function allows you to manipulate the filter direction virtually and situationally, but only in scenarios that warrant it, and not generally when modifying from the relationships between tables.

As with many-to-many relationships, changing the filter direction in both directions without understanding the consequences can cause conflicts. On the one hand, ambiguity could reappear in the semantic model because data highways (relationships) will be able to travel in both directions. And, on the other hand, changing the filter direction between each of the tables could have a negative effect on performance.

Manage active and inactive relationships

A table can have more than one relationship with other tables simultaneously, but only one can be active. You can visually identify active relationships because the line representing the relationship between the tables is solid, whereas inactive relationships are represented by a dashed line.

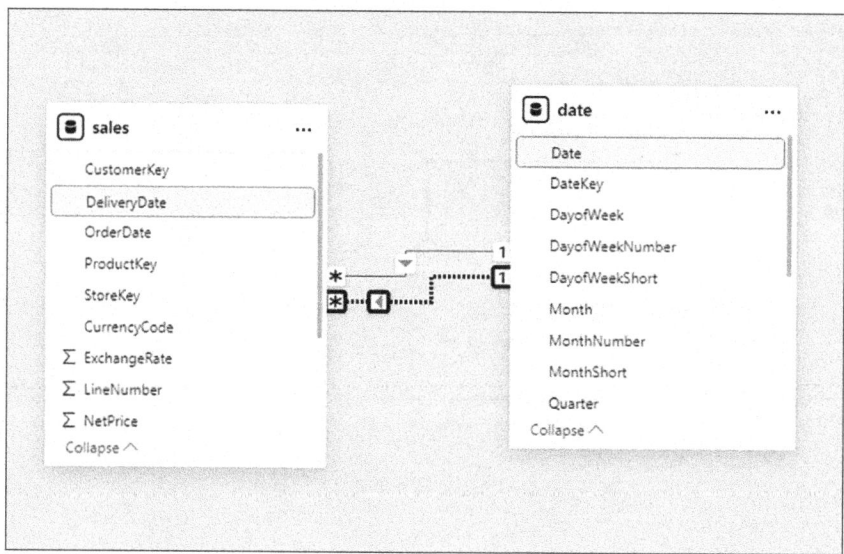

Between the sales fact table and date dimension table, the inactive relationship is reflected in a dashed line.

In general terms, you can create the necessary relationships between the tables that make up a semantic model. However, for a filter to travel through inactive relationships, you will need to use a specific function in the DAX language, namely USERELATIONSHIP. This function activates the existing inactive relationships in the semantic model.

The use of inactive relationships in a semantic model will be determined by the type of filtering and calculation you want to achieve. For example, when sales are presented based on the billing date compared to the shipping date, different results may be reflected depending on the time horizon being viewed.

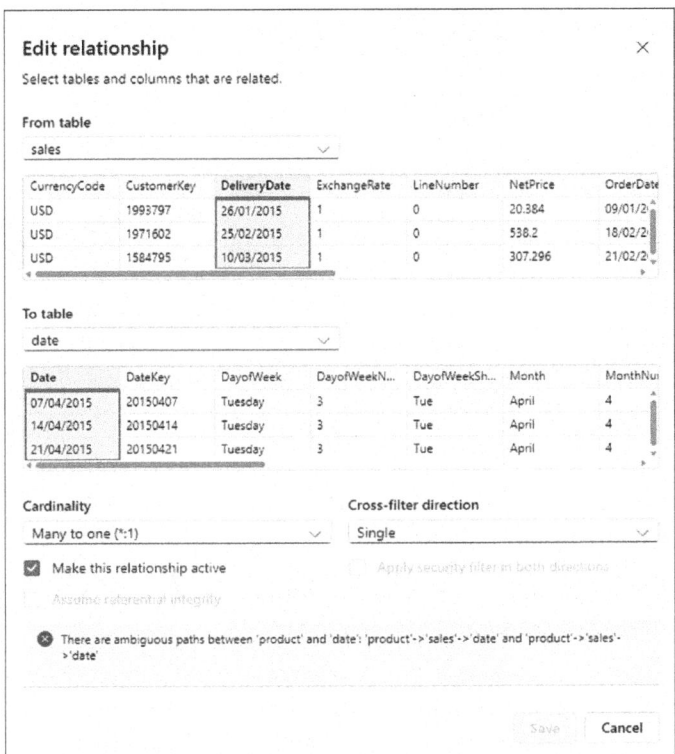

Edit relationship ✕

Select tables and columns that are related.

From table

sales ∨

CurrencyCode	CustomerKey	DeliveryDate	ExchangeRate	LineNumber	NetPrice	OrderDate
USD	1993797	26/01/2015	1	0	20.384	09/01/2:
USD	1971602	25/02/2015	1	0	538.2	18/02/2:
USD	1584795	10/03/2015	1	0	307.296	21/02/2:

To table

date ∨

Date	DateKey	DayofWeek	DayofWeekN...	DayofWeekSh...	Month	MonthNu:
07/04/2015	20150407	Tuesday	3	Tue	April	4
14/04/2015	20150414	Tuesday	3	Tue	April	4
21/04/2015	20150421	Tuesday	3	Tue	April	4

Cardinality   **Cross-filter direction**

Many to one (*:1) ∨   Single ∨

☑ Make this relationship active   ☐ Apply security filter in both directions

☐ Assume referential integrity

❌ There are ambiguous paths between 'product' and 'date': 'product'->'sales'->'date' and 'product'->'sales'->'date'

Save   **Cancel**

When using this dialog for creating new relationships, if you try to activate a new relationship in a table with an existing relationship, a restriction warning will appear.

As you can see from the preceding image, only one relationship can be active in each table. When you want to activate them, you must choose whether to swap who should be active or inactive or use the DAX language to activate it through functions.

Customize the semantic model and manage its properties

In addition to being functional, a semantic model must also be clear and efficient. In this section, you will learn how to refine and adjust it using different features that improve its comprehension and organization.

Column tools

From the Table view, you have access to a series of additional settings for both columns and tables. Here you can adjust and create structures, formats, properties, order, groupings, relationships, and calculations.

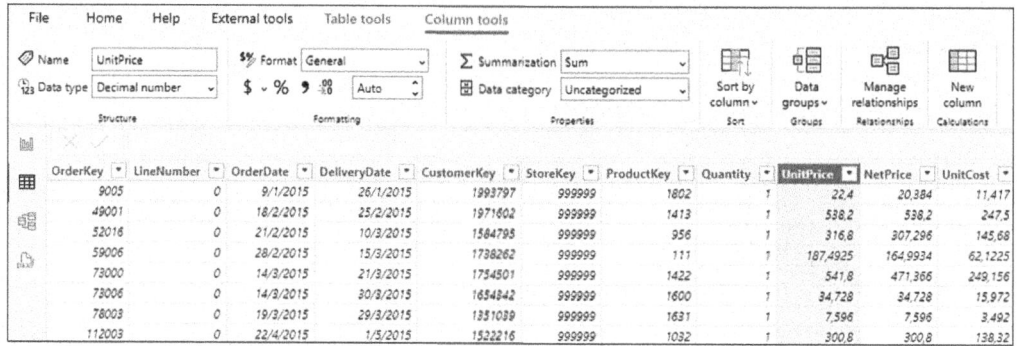

On the Column tools tab, if a column is selected, you can change certain settings.

Let's look at some of them:

- **Name:** This setting allows you to change the name of the column (you can also do this by right-clicking or pressing the F2 key).

- **Data type:** Although the data type is defined initially from Power Query, you can modify it again here from the semantic model.

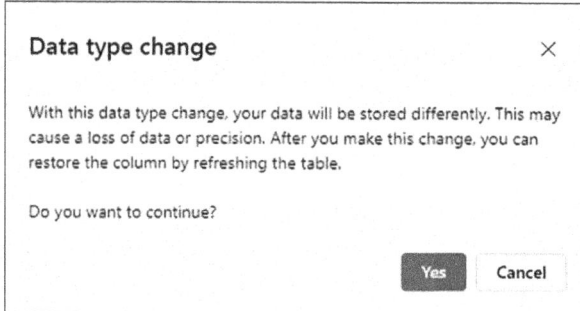

When you change the data type, a Data type change warning about the possible consequences will appear.

- **Format:** This setting defines how data will be represented at the report level.

- **Summarization:** In most numeric columns, the default aggregation (Sum) is expected, but you can change it to average, minimum, maximum, count, and distinct count.

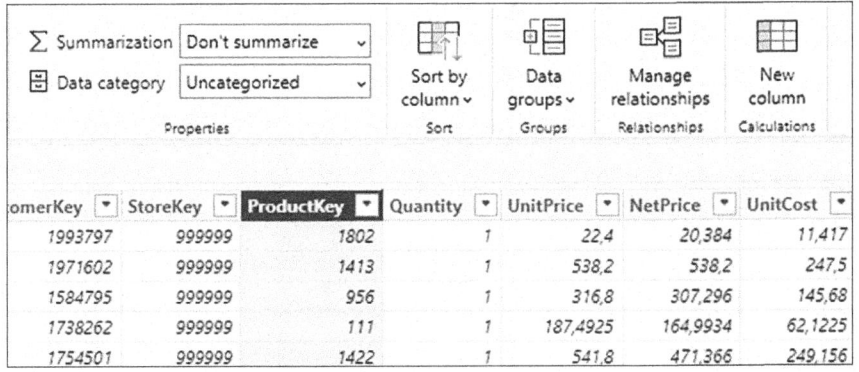

omerKey ▼	StoreKey ▼	**ProductKey** ▼	Quantity ▼	UnitPrice ▼	NetPrice ▼	UnitCost ▼
1993797	999999	1802	1	22,4	20,384	11,417
1971602	999999	1413	1	538,2	538,2	247,5
1584795	999999	956	1	316,8	307,296	145,68
1738262	999999	111	1	187,4925	164,9934	62,1225
1754501	999999	1422	1	541,8	471,366	249,156

On the Column tools tab, the summary type for a ProductKey column that serves as a relationship between tables is set to Don't summarize.

Sometimes, even though some columns are numeric data types, defining them as a sum aggregation type is not functional because they will not be used for subsequent mathematical calculations.

- **Data category:** Beyond data types, categorization allows you to establish new behaviors. For example, if the data type is decimal, you can additionally set it as latitude or longitude, which is necessary when you're using maps with that level of precision.

- **Sort by column:** Using this setting, you can sort a column based on the fields of another column, allowing for a different order.

- **Data groups:** This setting generates a new column that groups the categorical or continuous values in the table.

To create a new group

1. With the CategoryName column selected, select **New data groups**.

2. Enter the name of the new group column: **NewCategory**.

3. Select the values **Audio, Cell phones**, and **Computers**, and then select **Group**.

4. Change the name by double-clicking the header and entering **Personal technology**.

5. In the lower-right corner, check the **Include Other Group** box.

6. Select **OK**.

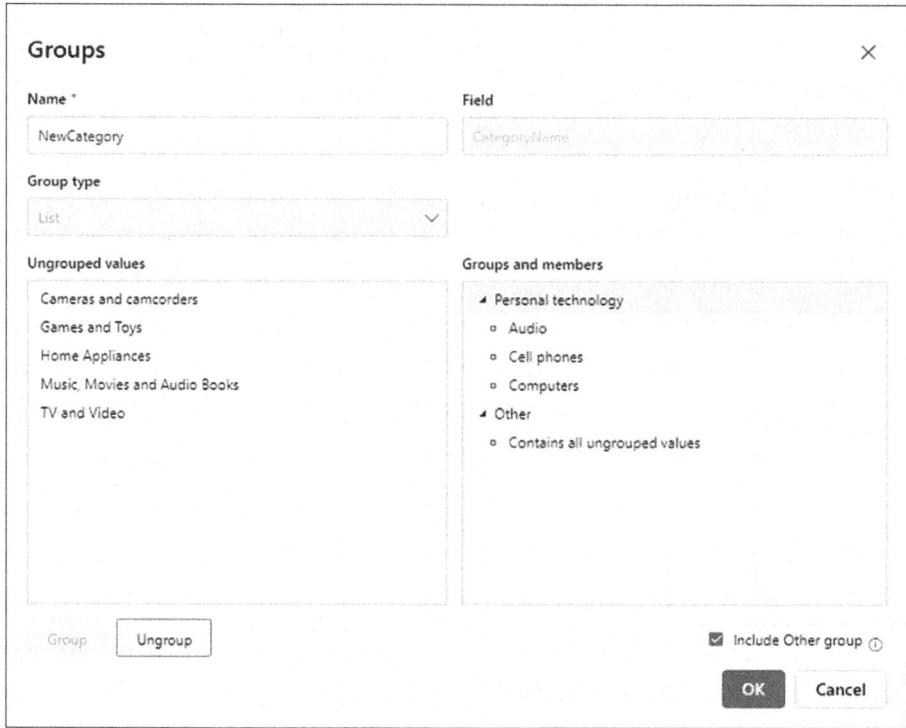

In the Groups dialog, you can group categorical and continuous (numerical) values.

The result is a new column that is now part of the semantic model containing the defined groupings. If you need to edit its structure, right-click it and select the **edit groups** option to return to the creation dialog.

Other properties

Tables have other settings that allow you to adjust behaviors considered *subtle* but useful as you use Power BI. In the Model view, when you select a table, you can see the Properties and Data tabs on the right, which are divided into the representation of each table and the model section where other items are set.

In the Properties tab, you can change the name of the table, assign a description that will be displayed when you hover the mouse cursor over it, hide it, set synonyms for natural language searches, and perform other settings related to Excel integrations.

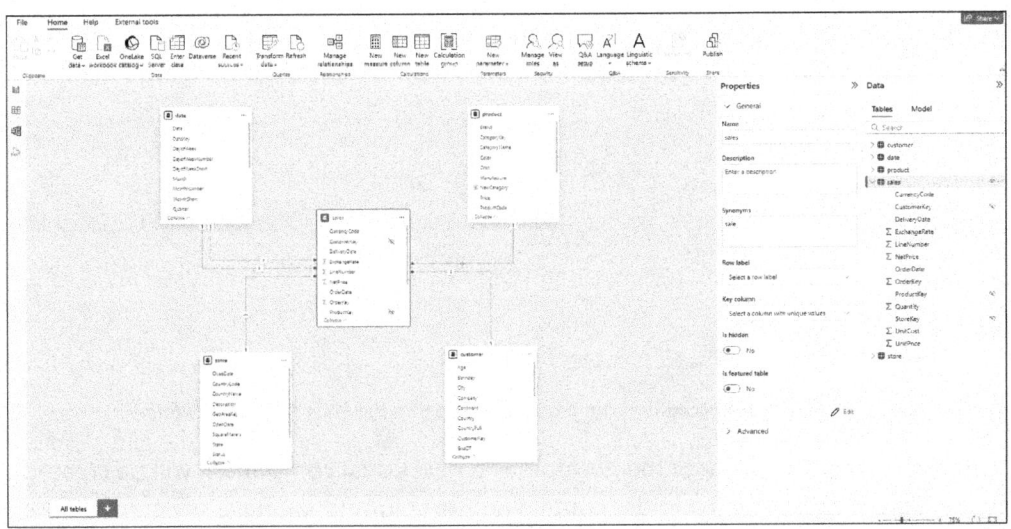

In the Model view, related tables and the Properties and Data tabs are displayed.

When you select a column, you will see options like those found in Column tools, but with some differences.

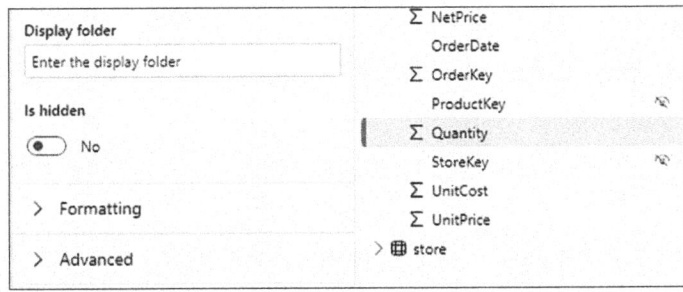

In the column properties, several options are available when you're selecting a column.

One difference is the ability to group the columns or calculations you will create later into folders. In this case, you just need to select one or more columns and assign a name to the folder.

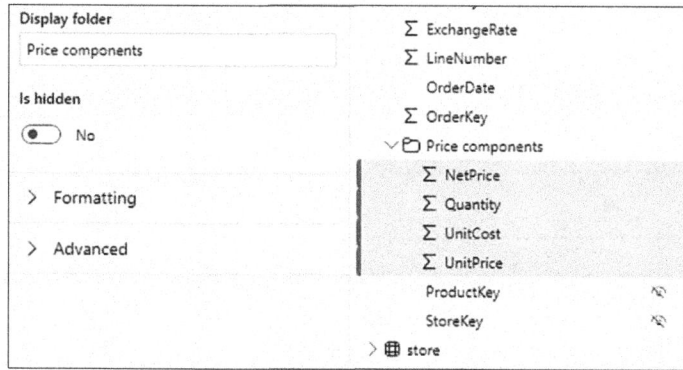

In the column properties, several columns are grouped together in the Price components folder.

When you enter the name of the new folder, a new visual component will be created in the table in the form of a folder containing the columns you have selected.

Layouts

You can use layouts to create new tabs from the Model view with a selection of tables that need to be organized individually. This is a good option when you need to separate tables with common attributes or objectives.

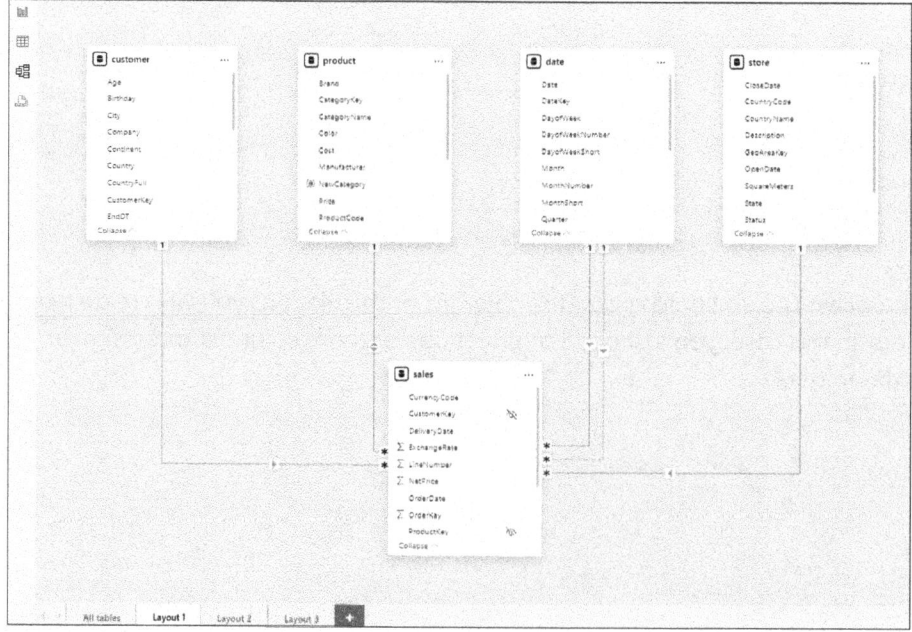

The Model view shows the dimension tables displayed at the top, with the single fact table below.

To create a layout, all you have to do is select the green tab with the plus sign at the bottom. A new tab will open where you can drag and drop the tables you need. In the preceding image, you can see a visual layout where the dimension tables are at the top while the fact table is below.

 IMPORTANT This layout doesn't affect the semantic model at all; you're simply organizing the tables and their relationships differently.

Skills review

In this chapter, you learned how to

- Identify a semantic model and its role within Power BI.

- Differentiate between a single table and a dimensional model using a star schema.

- Establish relationships between tables.

- Identify the types of relationships available and their behavior in the model.

- Configure the direction of cross-filtering between tables.

- Customize the model by adjusting properties such as formats, data types, categories, and folders.

5

Practice tasks

No practice files are necessary to complete the practice tasks in this chapter, but there are files to build the semantic model. Copy the book's practice files to your computer. The practice files for these tasks are in the PowerBISBS\C05 folder.

Understand the fundamentals of the semantic model

Considering the fundamental role of the semantic model in Power BI:

1. Why is the semantic model considered the backbone of a report in Power BI?

2. Why is using the star schema recommended for building scalable and maintainable models?

Define relationships between tables

Reflect on how tables connect and interact with each other:

1. What determines whether a table should be considered a fact table or a dimension table in Power BI?

2. What visual cues distinguish fact and dimension tables in the Model view?

Differentiate types of relationships

Understanding how different relationship types affect model behavior:

1. What are the key differences between one-to-many, one-to-one, and many-to-many relationships?

2. Why is the many-to-many (*:*) relationship considered a special situation that can cause errors?

Control cross-filter direction

Taking control over how filters travel between related tables:

1. Why should filters in both directions be used with caution?

2. What is the CROSSFILTER function in DAX, and in what scenario might it be useful?

Manage active and inactive relationships

When there are multiple relationships between two tables:

1. What distinguishes an active relationship from an inactive one in the Model view?

2. How can the USERELATIONSHIP function be used in DAX?

3. Why might it be necessary to maintain more than one relationship between the same tables?

Customize the semantic model and manage its properties

Improving the clarity and structure of the model:

1. What is the purpose of visualization folders in Power BI?

2. How can sorting one column by another influence the presentation of a report?

3. Why is it important to define data categories and aggregation behaviors for numeric fields?

Performing basic calculations with DAX

6

Practice files

No practice files are necessary to complete the practice tasks in this chapter.

The analytical language of DAX expressions is responsible for querying the semantic model. When you are unable to obtain a result through the various automatic operations offered by Power BI, such as dragging and dropping elements into the canvas, adopting a calculation suggested by Copilot, or performing other predefined calculations, doing it step by step using specific functions allows you to access not only specific results but also new behaviors that will be reflected in the report design.

Remember that, although the automation and simplification of calculation processes continues to increase, knowing the fundamentals that govern a language is helpful because, as you study, you will be able to question what already exists, understand it, modify it, and adapt it to your needs.

In this chapter

■ Explore the DAX Execution framework

■ Write basic syntax and apply common functions

■ Perform conditional calculations

■ Understand CALCULATE and its impact on filter context

■ Integrate visual calculations

In this chapter, you will learn how to perform basic calculations in the language responsible for building the calculations that together will bring to life each of the visual objects used in Power BI.

Explore the DAX execution framework

DAX can be used to request information from the semantic model through queries about its structure and metadata, and similarly to define security controls; however, this chapter will focus on its application for *creating calculations*. There are also various elements, or "artifacts," within Power BI where this language can be executed.

Calculated columns

Calculated columns are new columns added to a table to enrich it. At first, it may be more intuitive to create a calculation where the result is generated in a new artifact (calculated column) that can be seen immediately.

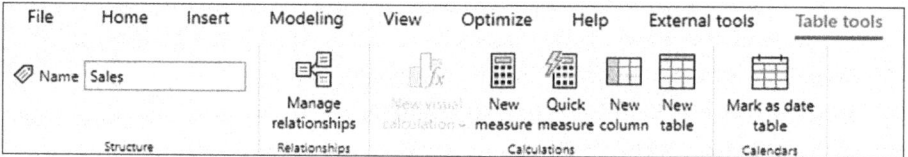

On the Table tools tab, when you select a table, various options for creating calculations will appear.

You can create a calculated column by right-clicking a table, selecting the **New Column** option, or using the Table tools or Column tools tabs.

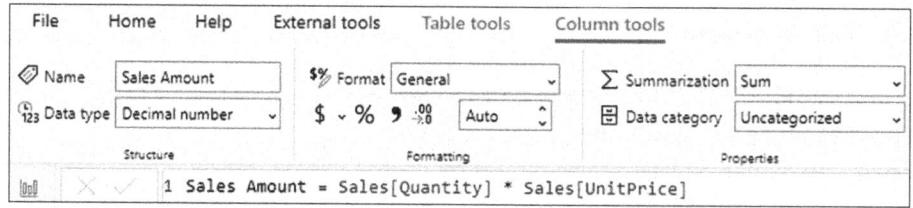

In the Table view, selecting New column activates the formula bar in DAX.

The new calculated column called Sales Amount multiplies the Quantity and UnitPrice columns. One of the distinctive features of referencing a column in a syntax is that it will always be prefixed with the table name; see the word *Sales* before the square brackets in each column.

Quantity ▼	UnitPrice ▼	NetPrice ▼	UnitCost ▼	CurrencyCode ▼	ExchangeRate ▼	Sales Amount ▼
1	22.4	20.384	11.417	USD	1	22.4
1	538.2	538.2	247.5	USD	1	538.2
1	316.8	307.296	145.68	USD	1	316.8
1	187.4925	164.9934	62.1225	USD	1	187.4925
1	541.8	471.366	249.156	USD	1	541.8
1	34.728	34.728	15.972	USD	1	34.728

New calculated column: Sales Amount.

Another noticeable difference when creating calculated columns is their nature: *They are created from expressions in DAX,* maintaining the same functionalities as any other column within the semantic model.

Measures

At first, measures may seem more abstract than calculated columns because their results cannot be seen unless you use them within a visual object. To create a measure, right-click a table and select **New Measure** or go to the Table tools tab.

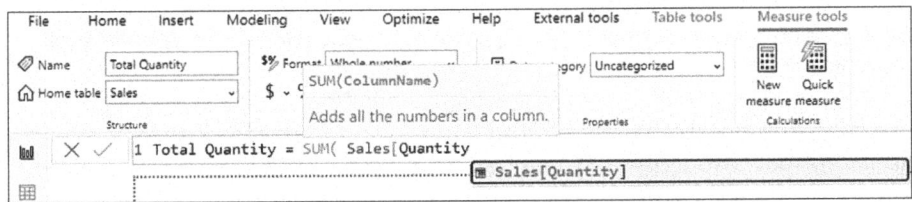

New measure: Total Quantity.

 TIP You can use the Tab key to help you type references within a syntax. *Intellisense* is responsible for suggesting functions and fields based on what you're typing.

Unlike a calculated column, a measure is more flexible because it does not take up space in the semantic model; it only stores expressions and can be reused constantly. However, when a result or behavior can be achieved through a measure, the use of calculated columns tends to be avoided.

One way to explain this is as follows: Measures are the norm when you think about creating a calculation in DAX; *calculated columns, on the other hand, are considered the exception.*

6

Calculated tables

Over the years, Power BI has introduced new features that have rendered calculated tables obsolete. However, they are useful in specific scenarios, so it is important to be familiar with them.

Basically, a calculated table behaves and has the same functionalities as any other table in the semantic model, but it is created from expressions in DAX. The example below shows a table containing records from the sales table where the quantity is greater than seven.

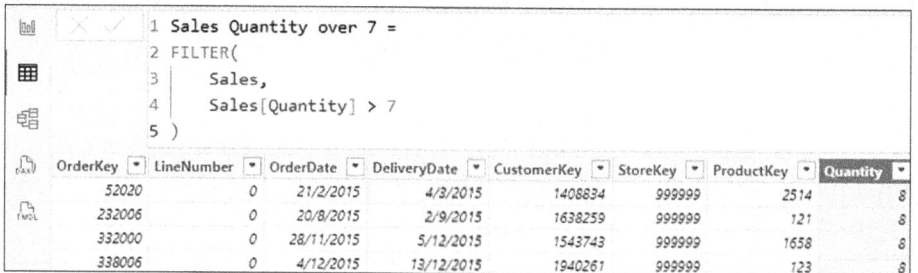

In this new calculated table, Sales Quantity over 7 displays only the records from the sales table where the quantity is greater than seven.

In the past, it was common to create a temporary calculated table to "visualize" a result in tabular format. This approach changed when the DAX Query view appeared, which allows you, among other things, to do the same thing without having to generate a new table in the semantic model.

Visual calculations

Visual calculations offer a different approach when creating calculations in DAX. They are designed to reduce the complexity of recurring operations, and their main distinction is seen in their execution, *which is unique to the visual object you have used.* This method departs from the classic way of the language, where calculations are always subject to the layout of tables and relationships between them.

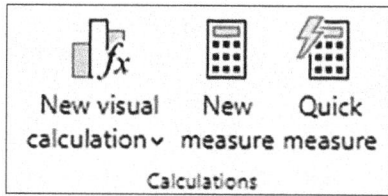

When a visual object is selected, the option to recalculate the visual will be enabled.

A visual calculation is created, executed, and its limits are found in the visual object. Unlike measures, it cannot be reused (unless you copy and paste the visual object) and does not propagate through relationships in the semantic model. Nor does it replace what you can usually achieve, but it is an addition that provides flexibility and simplicity.

	Total Quantity	Accumulated Quantity
Color		
Azure	1,408	1,408
Black	173,216	174,624
Blue	30,782	205,406
Brown	20,333	225,739
Gold	22,330	248,069
Green	11,098	259,167
Grey	51,641	310,808
Orange	5,657	316,465
Pink	18,047	334,512
Purple	1,788	336,300
Red	36,477	372,777
Silver	118,442	491,219
Silver Grey	1,718	492,937
Transparent	681	493,618
White	119,214	612,832
Yellow	15,538	628,370

The formula bar reads: `1 Accumulated Quantity = RUNNINGSUM( [Total Quantity])`

On the Visual calculation formula bar, when you select Fx, templates with recurring calculations will appear. The RUNNINGSUM function performs a cumulative calculation based on the Total Quantity measure.

In visual calculations, a single line can simplify an operation that, compared to classic DAX, requires combining functions and understanding contexts in the language.

Write basic syntax and apply common functions

No matter what calculation you're going to create, you always start with the name and then refer to the functions after the equal sign. You can write everything on a single line or indent using the Shift+Enter key combination. Likewise, DAX is not case sensitive and does not cause conflicts in the result if you write the syntax in upper- or lowercase.

It is also common to use comments in some parts of the code to document and remember what you have done in the past. Comments can be a single line starting with -- or //, with the rest considered part of the comment.

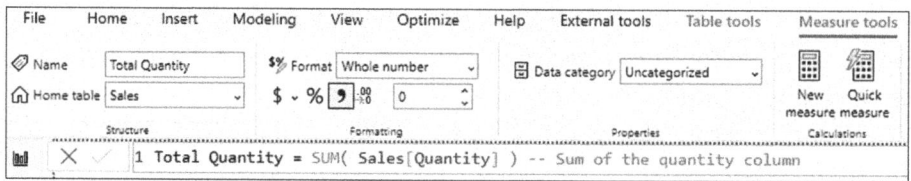

Measure: Total Quantity. On the right side, a comment about the operation performed is displayed using a double dash --.

You can also write multiline comments starting with /* and ending with */.

Another useful feature that can help you change the way you think when creating a calculation is *variables* because they allow you to encapsulate calculations in stages with the possibility of executing them sequentially.

```
 1 Quantity Pct =
 2 /*
 3 Description: percentage of quantity with respect to the total colors selected
 4 */
 5 VAR _Numerator = [Total Quantity] -- Numerator
 6 VAR _Denominator =
 7     CALCULATE ( [Total Quantity], ALLSELECTED ( 'Product'[Color] ) ) -- Denominator
 8 VAR _Result =
 9     DIVIDE ( _Numerator, _Denominator ) -- Division
10 RETURN
11     _Result
```

Measure: Quantity Pct. In a syntax, you can combine the use of multiline comments and variables.

To use variables

1. Start with the word VAR.

2. Define the name of the variable (for example: **_Numerator on line 5**).

3. After the equal sign, write the expression.

4. Create as many variables as you need.

5. Call up the result with the word RETURN.

In the image, first the variable _Numerator is created and then _Denominator.
It is in the variable _Result where the previous variables are reused within the DIVIDE function in line 9, ending the operation with the word RETURN.

Thinking sequentially has a learning curve. At this point, you may find it a little complicated, but using variables has other benefits, such as more efficient evaluation, more readable code, and the ability to debug parts of the code. Plus, you avoid the creation of intermediate measures that can be evaluated in the same syntax.

IMPORTANT Variables are not mandatory in DAX, but they offer substantial advantages and benefits.

Similarly, you can reuse existing calculations to create other variations. In the following image, the Quantity Pct measure, which represents the percentage of quantities, uses another existing measure, [Total Quantity].

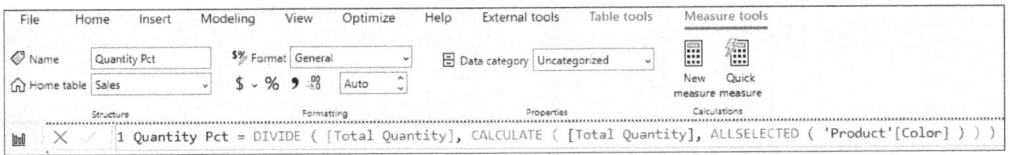

Measure: Quantity Pct. The previous measure is shown but written without indentation or variables.

On the other hand, when you create calculations in DAX, you will see two types of results:

- **Scalar value:** This single piece of data occupies a cell in the result, represented by a number, text, date, or logical (Boolean) value.

- **Table:** This structured set of rows and columns contains multiple organized values.

 IMPORTANT Measures always return scalar values. Although functions generate tables, measures cannot return table values, and those functions cannot be used directly on measures.

Aggregation functions

Aggregation functions allow you to create aggregates on columns of the semantic model, obtaining a scalar value. Functions such as SUM, AVERAGE, MIN, MAX, and COUNT perform summations, averages, minimums, maximums, and record counts.

Most require a single parameter, for example, using the SUM function:

```
Total Quantity = SUM( Sales[Quantity] )
```

Likewise, the native columns of the table generate automatic aggregations that can be changed in the visual object options.

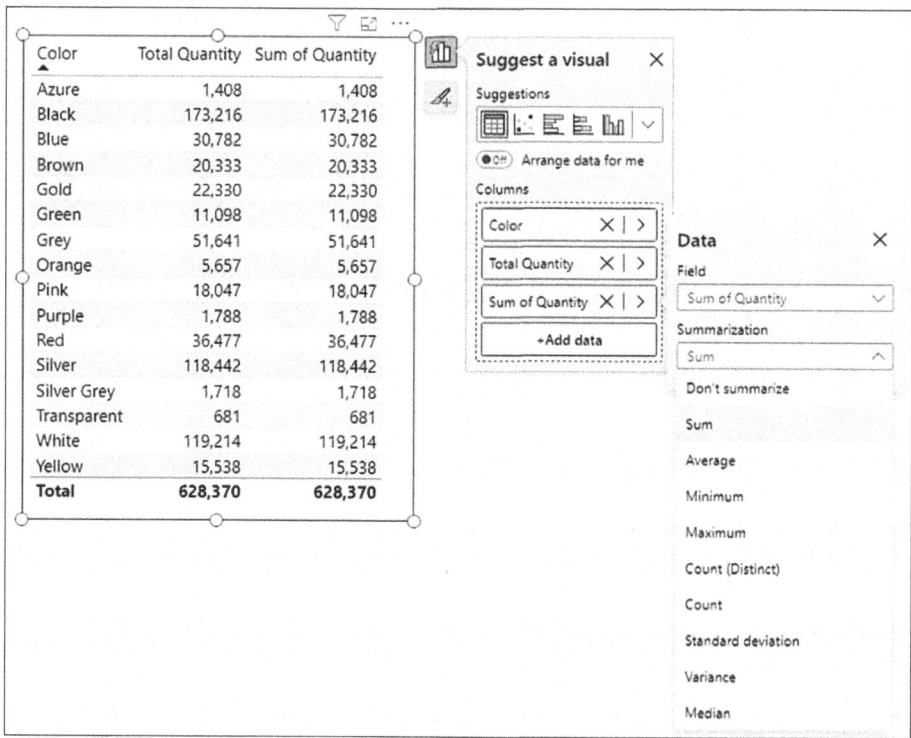

In this table with the Total Quantity measure and automatic aggregation of the Quantity column, the result is the same, but the column allows you to change the summary type.

This behavior can be confusing at first because the result is the same when compared to a measure. However, native columns are avoided in these cases. Instead, new measures are created, and they have the advantage of being reused later in other calculations, automatically reflecting any changes.

One of the most common operations is counting rows. Some functions adapt to the requirement:

- **COUNT:** Counts the number of rows in a column of values such as numbers, dates, and text strings, excluding blank values. Here we count the number of products sold:

```
Number of Products Sold = COUNT( Sales[ProductKey] )
```

- **DISTINCTCOUNT:** Counts the number of distinct values in a column, including blank values. In this case, we count the number of unique sales orders:

```
Number of Unique Orders = DISTINCTCOUNT( Sales[OrderKey] )
```

- **COUNTROWS:** Counts the number of rows in a table. Here we count the number of products available in the catalog:

```
Number of Products in Catalog = COUNTROWS( 'Product' )
```

Color	Number of Product Sold	Number of Unique Orders	Number of Products in Catalog
Azure	431	430	14
Black	55,028	41,001	602
Blue	9,795	9,285	200
Brown	6,497	6,286	77
Gold	7,203	6,923	50
Green	3,542	3,463	74
Grey	16,484	14,930	283
Orange	1,840	1,817	55
Pink	5,750	5,572	84
Purple	580	576	6
Red	11,718	10,944	99
Silver	37,603	30,628	417
Silver Grey	526	525	14
Transparent	227	227	1
White	37,756	30,740	505
Yellow	4,893	4,753	36
Total	**199,873**	**83,130**	**2,517**

This table shows various measures using the COUNT, DISTINCTCOUNT, and COUNTROWS functions.

In the preceding image, you can see how the color of the products can offer different results based on the count performed, whether you're looking for a column count, a single count, or a count that considers all the columns in a table.

Aggregations with more than one column

When an operation requires more than one column reference, you use iterator functions. You can identify them because most end with an *X*. SUMX, AVERAGEX, MINX, and MAXX are some of the available functions.

Previously, you learned how to calculate gross sales from a calculated column by referencing the Sales[Quantity] and Sales[UnitPrice] columns without using any functions. If you wanted to achieve the same result, but in a measure, you might be tempted to do the following:

```
Incorrect Sales Amount = SUM ( Sales[Quantity] ) * SUM ( Sales[UnitPrice] )
```

In reality, however, you need to use the SUMX iterator:

```
Correct Sales Amount = SUMX ( Sales, Sales[Quantity] * Sales[UnitPrice] )
```

Brand	Incorrect Sales Amount	Correct Sales Amount
A. Datum	21,554,001,148	4,708,419
Adventure Works	1,005,083,907,561	48,944,440
Contoso	1,949,207,250,724	36,764,434
Fabrikam	193,588,656,564	20,793,846
Litware	33,986,858,531	6,995,101
Northwind Traders	12,170,824,063	2,421,865
Proseware	207,409,160,923	17,664,634
Southridge Video	279,002,607,646	9,932,170
Tailspin Toys	24,068,509,507	1,626,949
The Phone Company	776,214,376,092	30,074,180
Wide World Importers	806,568,323,999	36,749,276
Total	**43,306,225,902,972**	**216,675,316**

This table uses two versions of the Sales Amount measure. Note the substantial difference in the results.

At this point, DAX language theory comes into play and influences the result. Although both versions use the arithmetic multiplication operator (*), the SUMX version is the correct one. Iterators are the only type of function that allows access to what is known as *row context* from a measure. In comparison, calculated columns, by their nature, already run in that context; therefore, simply referencing the columns is sufficient.

The iterators in their first parameter request the table by which they will traverse the expression row by row. Then, in the second parameter, the columns involved in the calculation are incorporated. Similarly, it is possible to perform calculations with several columns but from different tables:

```
Total Product Cost = SUMX ( Sales, Sales[Quantity] * RELATED (
'Product'[Cost] ) )
```

By using the RELATED function, you can access columns from related tables in the semantic model. In this case, the quantities are in the sales table while the cost is in the product table.

Perform conditional calculations

In simple terms, logic is a question that can give you two possible results: *one true* and *one false*. In DAX, an IF function allows you to establish logic. Let's see how to use it in a calculated column to classify product colors based on color temperature.

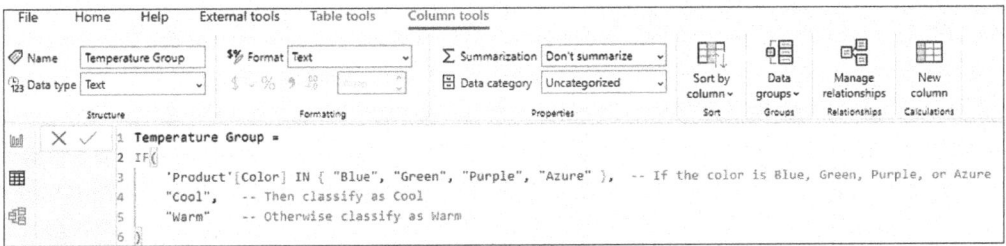

In this Table view, a new column is calculated using the IF function.

In this case, the true result will be classified as cold if the color is registered as blue, green, purple, or azure. Otherwise, it will be classified as warm, with the result being false. Note the use of the IN operator on line 3, which evaluates whether 'Product'[Color] matches any value in a single-column table defined using curly brackets {}.

You can also apply logic by combining the SWITCH and TRUE functions with clean, readable syntax for multiple conditions when evaluating ranges of values.

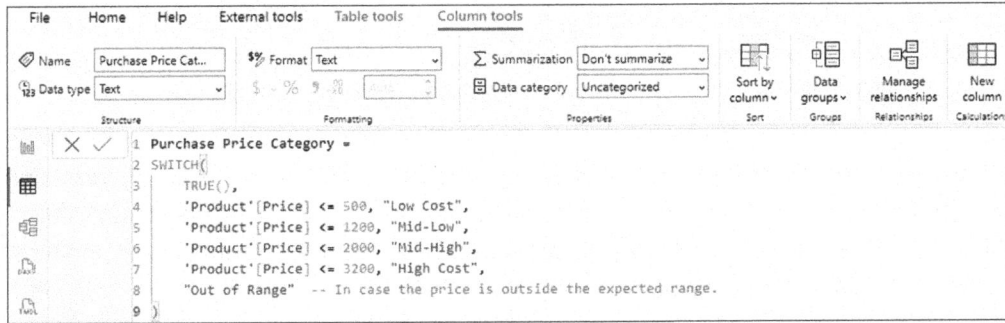

In this Table view, a new column is calculated using the SWITCH and TRUE functions.

Keep in mind that the order of the conditions influences the result because the evaluation is performed from top to bottom. By having the correct order, you allow each range to be mutually exclusive and the price to be classified correctly, without one condition overlapping another.

6

Understand CALCULATE and its impact on filter context

If there is one function that is different from any other in the DAX language, it is CALCULATE. It is the only one that can modify the *filter context*. However, this context *can be changed without using any function* through various visual objects that simultaneously form part of a report.

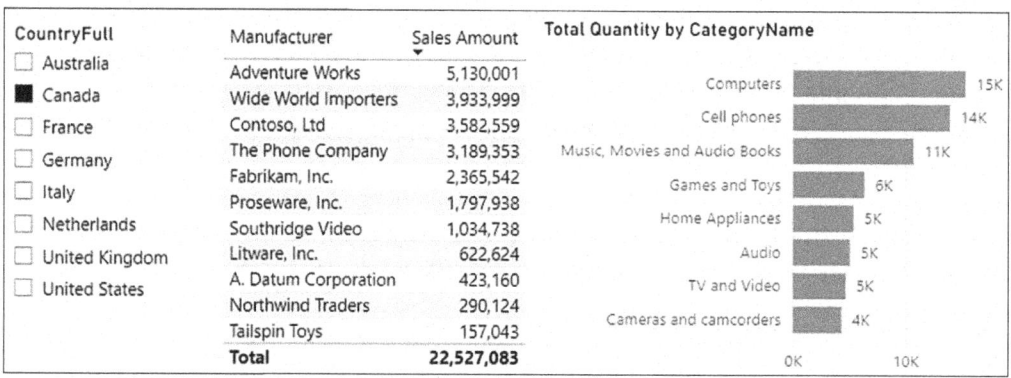

This Report view shows a segmenter, a table, and a bar chart. The filter context is modified by selecting Canada in the slicer.

In this case, the filter context is modified by selecting Canada as the country, reducing the visible records in the table and bar chart that use the [Sales Amount] and [Total Quantity] measures. Likewise, each visual object is affected by Manufacturer and CategoryName when presenting the results in detail.

You can replicate the same behavior of the slicer selecting the country Canada by using CALCULATE as follows:

```
Sales Amount (Canada) = CALCULATE( [Sales Amount],
Customer[CountryFull] = "Canada" )
```

The first parameter is the expression that CALCULATE will evaluate, the measure [Sales Amount], and then the filter argument on the CountryFull column that will be equal to Canada.

Manufacturer	Sales Amount	Sales Amount (Canada)
Adventure Works	48,944,440	5,130,001
Contoso, Ltd	36,764,434	3,582,559
Wide World Importers	36,749,276	3,933,999
The Phone Company	30,074,180	3,189,353
Fabrikam, Inc.	20,793,846	2,365,542
Proseware, Inc.	17,664,634	1,797,938
Southridge Video	9,932,170	1,034,738
Litware, Inc.	6,995,101	622,624
A. Datum Corporation	4,708,419	423,160
Northwind Traders	2,421,865	290,124
Tailspin Toys	1,626,949	157,043
Total	**216,675,316**	**22,527,083**

In this Report view table, CALCULATE modifies the filter context by displaying only sales from Canada.

6

You can also apply more than one filter simultaneously from the same table.

```
1 Sales Amount US-male =
2 CALCULATE(
3     [Sales Amount], -- Calculates the total sales amount
4     Customer[CountryFull] = "United States", -- Filter #1: Only include customers from the US
5     Customer[Gender] = "male" -- Filter #2: And only if their gender is male
6 )
```

Manufacturer	Sales Amount	Sales Amount (Canada)	Sales Amount US-male
Adventure Works	48,944,440	5,130,001	13,214,485
Contoso, Ltd	36,764,434	3,582,559	9,981,358
Wide World Importers	36,749,276	3,933,999	9,853,836
The Phone Company	30,074,180	3,189,353	7,889,206
Fabrikam, Inc.	20,793,846	2,365,542	5,342,992
Proseware, Inc.	17,664,634	1,797,938	4,381,484
Southridge Video	9,932,170	1,034,738	2,691,686
Litware, Inc.	6,995,101	622,624	1,850,710
A. Datum Corporation	4,708,419	423,160	1,227,283
Northwind Traders	2,421,865	290,124	636,302
Tailspin Toys	1,626,949	157,043	436,372
Total	**216,675,316**	**22,527,083**	**57,505,714**

In this Report view, applying both filters changes the filter context of the measure to focus only on a specific customer segment.

> **IMPORTANT** When you add more than one filter in CALCULATE, all the conditions must be met at the same time for the result to be considered valid.

Here another example applies filters from different tables.

```
1  Sales Amount US-male-Azure =
2  CALCULATE(
3      [Sales Amount], -- Calculates the total sales amount
4      Customer[CountryFull] = "United States", -- Filter #1: Only include customers from the US
5      Customer[Gender] = "male", -- Filter #2: And only if their gender is male
6      'Product'[Color] = "Azure" -- Filter #3: The product must also have the color Azure
7  )
```

Manufacturer	Sales Amount	Sales Amount (Canada)	Sales Amount US-male	Sales Amount US-male-Azure
Adventure Works	48,944,440	5,130,001	13,214,485	
Contoso, Ltd	36,764,434	3,582,559	9,981,358	
Wide World Importers	36,749,276	3,933,999	9,853,836	
The Phone Company	30,074,180	3,189,353	7,889,206	
Fabrikam, Inc.	20,793,846	2,365,542	5,342,992	
Proseware, Inc.	17,664,634	1,797,938	4,381,484	
Southridge Video	9,932,170	1,034,738	2,691,686	
Litware, Inc.	6,995,101	622,624	1,850,710	
A. Datum Corporation	4,708,419	423,160	1,227,283	107,624
Northwind Traders	2,421,865	290,124	636,302	
Tailspin Toys	1,626,949	157,043	436,372	
Total	**216,675,316**	**22,527,083**	**57,505,714**	**107,624**

In this Report view, the CALCULATE function allows you to add multiple filters, either from the same table or from related tables.

Similarly, you can apply filters with operators other than equality—in this case, greater than.

```
1  Sales Amount Contoso > 100 =
2  CALCULATE(
3      [Sales Amount], -- Calculates the total sales amount
4      Sales[UnitPrice] > 100, -- Filter #1: Only include items with UnitPrice greater than 100
5      Product[Brand] = "Contoso" -- Filter #2: And only if the brand is Contoso
6  )
```

Manufacturer	Sales Amount	Sales Amount (Canada)	Sales Amount US-male	Sales Amount US-male-Azure	Sales Amount Contoso > 100
Adventure Works	48,944,440	5,130,001	13,214,485		
Contoso, Ltd	36,764,434	3,582,559	9,981,358		33,611,666
Wide World Importers	36,749,276	3,933,999	9,853,836		
The Phone Company	30,074,180	3,189,353	7,889,206		
Fabrikam, Inc.	20,793,846	2,365,542	5,342,992		
Proseware, Inc.	17,664,634	1,797,938	4,381,484		
Southridge Video	9,932,170	1,034,738	2,691,686		
Litware, Inc.	6,995,101	622,624	1,850,710		
A. Datum Corporation	4,708,419	423,160	1,227,283	107,624	
Northwind Traders	2,421,865	290,124	636,302		
Tailspin Toys	1,626,949	157,043	436,372		
Total	**216,675,316**	**22,527,083**	**57,505,714**	**107,624**	**33,611,666**

In this Report view, the CALCULATE function allows you to apply multiple filters by combining different operators.

A common calculation in report creation is the presentation of percentages or ratios. Using the DIVIDE function, you can ensure that divisions by zero do not generate an error. And, to get the denominator, you can use CALCULATE with REMOVEFILTERS or ALLSELECTED to modify the percentage representation according to the external filters being applied.

The two measures used:

```
REMOVEFILTERS Quantity =
DIVIDE (
    [Total Quantity], -- Numerator
    CALCULATE ( [Total Quantity], REMOVEFILTERS ( ( 'Product'[Manufacturer]
) ) -- Denominator
)
ALLSELECTED Quantity =
DIVIDE (
    [Total Quantity], -- Numerator
    CALCULATE ( [Total Quantity], ALLSELECTED ( 'Product'[Manufacturer] ) )
-- Denominator
)
```

Manufacturer	Total Quantity	REMOVEFILTERS Quantity	ALLSELECTED Quantity
Contoso, Ltd	166,594	26.51%	34.64%
Southridge Video	88,653	14.11%	18.43%
The Phone Company	81,162	12.92%	16.88%
Adventure Works	64,397	10.25%	13.39%
Proseware, Inc.	36,396	5.79%	7.57%
Fabrikam, Inc.	29,337	4.67%	6.10%
A. Datum Corporation	14,357	2.28%	2.99%
Total	**480,896**	**76.53%**	**100.00%**

Manufacturer
- ☑ A. Datum Corporation
- ☑ Adventure Works
- ☑ Contoso, Ltd
- ☑ Fabrikam, Inc.
- ☐ Litware, Inc.
- ☐ Northwind Traders
- ☑ Proseware, Inc.
- ☑ Southridge Video
- ☐ Tailspin Toys
- ☑ The Phone Company
- ☐ Wide World Importers

In this Report view, the CALCULATE function allows you to combine other functions that ignore the filter context.

A striking behavior becomes evident when using the same column from the CALCU-LATE filter argument in a visual object. This behavior is known as *overwriting filters*, which is one of the various operations performed by this function.

```
1 Computer Sales = CALCULATE( [Sales Amount], 'Product'[CategoryName] = "Computers" )
```

CategoryName	Sales Amount	Computer Sales
Computers	95,455,485	95,455,485
Cell phones	34,072,137	95,455,485
Home Appliances	27,894,562	95,455,485
TV and Video	21,371,304	95,455,485
Cameras and camcorders	19,511,997	95,455,485
Music, Movies and Audio Books	11,047,059	95,455,485
Audio	5,572,789	95,455,485
Games and Toys	1,749,984	95,455,485
Total	**216,675,316**	**95,455,485**

In this Report view, by design, the CALCULATE function overwrites the filters applied to the visual object when the same field is used in the filter argument.

If you want to keep only the value for Computer Sales in the corresponding cell, leaving the other categories blank, you can use the KEEPFILTERS function.

```
1 Computer Sales Keepfilters =
2 CALCULATE (
3     [Sales Amount],
4     KEEPFILTERS ( 'Product'[CategoryName] = "Computers" )
5 )
```

CategoryName	Sales Amount	Computer Sales	Computer Sales Keepfilters
Computers	95,455,485	95,455,485	95,455,485
Cell phones	34,072,137	95,455,485	
Home Appliances	27,894,562	95,455,485	
TV and Video	21,371,304	95,455,485	
Cameras and camcorders	19,511,997	95,455,485	
Music, Movies and Audio Books	11,047,059	95,455,485	
Audio	5,572,789	95,455,485	
Games and Toys	1,749,984	95,455,485	
Total	**216,675,316**	**95,455,485**	**95,455,485**

In this Report view, the KEEPFILTERS function preserves the filter context applied to the visual object, preventing it from being overwritten by CALCULATE.

CALCULATE has a series of functions known as *behavior modifiers*. One of these is USERELATIONSHIP, which is used exclusively to activate an inactive relationship between two tables.

```
1 Sales Amount USERELATIONSHIP =
2 CALCULATE (
3     [Sales Amount],
4     USERELATIONSHIP ( Sales[DeliveryDate], 'Date'[Date] )
5 )
```

Year	Sales Amount	Sales Amount USERELATIONSHIP
⊟ **2023**	**33,902,636**	**34,063,594**
February	4,566,763	4,434,706
January	3,756,961	3,969,356
May	3,011,561	3,016,881
June	2,983,523	2,962,393
December	2,963,667	2,947,633
November	2,716,481	2,713,089
September	2,694,009	2,685,978
August	2,684,536	2,579,167
October	2,586,159	2,599,103
July	2,433,545	2,554,571
March	2,282,743	2,499,133
April	1,222,689	1,101,584
Total	**33,902,636**	**34,063,594**

In this Report view, the USERELATIONSHIP function activates an inactive relationship with the delivery date to calculate sales according to that context.

Whether filtering data, ignoring, overwriting the filter context, or activating semantic model behaviors, CALCULATE is the most versatile function and one of the most complex to understand as calculations increase in complexity.

Integrate visual calculations

As you learned at the beginning of the chapter, visual calculations are the most important change that has been introduced in the language because they eliminate the influence of the semantic model on calculations. Instead, visual objects set the limits and rules.

Let's look at other examples where visual calculations simplify recurring operations.

To refer to previous rows, you can use the PREVIOUS function.

Year	Month	Sales Amount	Sales Growth MoM
2023	January	3,756,961	
	February	4,566,763	21.55%
	March	2,282,743	-50.01%
	April	1,222,689	-46.44%
	May	3,011,561	146.31%
	June	2,983,523	-0.93%
	July	2,433,545	-18.43%
	August	2,684,536	10.31%
	September	2,694,009	0.35%
	October	2,586,159	-4.00%
	November	2,716,481	5.04%
	December	2,963,667	9.10%
	Total	33,902,636	

In the Visual calculation formula bar, the PREVIOUS function allows you to refer to the previous row.

In this case, you use the DIVIDE and PREVIOUS functions to calculate the percentage change in Sales Amount compared to the previous month. If you look closely, you will see downward arrows, or parameter pickers, next to the measures.

```
X ✓ fx   1  Sales Growth MoM =
         2  DIVIDE(
         3       ⓥ[Sales Amount] - PREVIOUS( ⓥ[Sales Amount]), -- Numerator
         4       PREVIOUS( ⓥ[Sales Amount] ) --   ▦ [Month]
         5  )                                      ▦ [Sales Amount]
Year   Month     ¡Sales Amount¡ Sales Growth MoM  ▦ [Year]
```

The Visual calculation formula bar shows parameter pickers, which help you obtain the available values.

These parameter pickers serve as shortcuts to obtain values available in the visual object. Note that only [Month], [Sales Amount], and [Year] appear; that is, nothing that has not been added to the visual object will appear.

Another advantage of visual calculations is their ability to adapt dynamically to the fields used without the need to reference those fields in the syntax.

```
X ✓ fx   1  Rank =
         2  RANK (
         3      DENSE,
         4      ⓥ ROWS,
         5      ORDERBY ( ⓥ[Sales Amount], DESC )
         6  )
```

CountryFull	Rank	Sales Amount
Australia	5	12,505,756
Canada	4	22,527,083
France	7	6,746,637
Germany	3	22,994,080
Italy	8	6,391,250
Netherlands	6	8,710,902
United Kingdom	2	22,998,757
United States	1	113,800,852
Total	**1**	**216,675,316**

This Visual calculation formula bar shows how to create a ranking of countries based on Sales Amount.

The preceding image shows a ranking using the RANK function, which, in the event of a tie, uses its first argument DENSE to establish a sequential order (1-2-3...). Then ROWS determines the direction of the ranking in the table, and ORDERBY sorts according to the [Sales Amount] measure in descending order with DESC.

However, the most important point is that *there is no reference to the CountryFull column*. This approach allows the ranking to dynamically adapt to any categorical value you add to the visual object—unlike classic DAX, where you have to specify the column to which a ranking will be created, making it more restrictive.

Skills review

In this chapter, you learned how to

- Explore the DAX execution framework and recognize how and where calculations are created, processed, and evaluated within the semantic model.

- Write DAX expressions using basic syntax and apply common functions such as SUM, COUNT, DISTINCTCOUNT, and COUNTROWS to perform aggregations.

- Create conditional logic using the IF function and structured expressions with SWITCH and TRUE to classify or segment values.

- Use the CALCULATE function to modify the filter context, enabling dynamic calculations based on one or more filter conditions.

- Combine filters from the same or related tables using operators like =, >, and IN to fine-tune the scope of your measures.

- Create visual calculations in the Report view to display month-over-month comparisons, dynamic rankings, and other context-sensitive insights without altering the semantic model.

6

Practice tasks

No practice files are necessary to complete the practice tasks in this chapter, but see the files in the PowerBISBS\C06 folder for a basis for the next chapter.

Explore the DAX Execution framework

Understanding how and where DAX expressions are evaluated:

1. In which views can DAX calculations be created in Power BI, and what distinguishes each type of calculation (column, measure, table)?

2. Why is it important to understand where a calculation runs when building a data model?

Write basic syntax and apply common functions

Applying core aggregation functions in your measures:

1. What's the difference between COUNT, DISTINCTCOUNT, and COUNTROWS?

2. How does SUMX differ from SUM, and when is it necessary to iterate row by row?

Perform conditional calculations

Building logic to classify or segment data:

1. Why is SWITCH TRUE often preferred over nested IF statements when evaluating multiple conditions in DAX?

2. Why does the order of evaluation matter when writing multiple conditions using SWITCH TRUE?

Understand CALCULATE and its impact on filter context

Modifying filters to create dynamic expressions:

1. How would you use CALCULATE to filter sales data by country and gender without modifying the visual directly?

2. How does applying multiple filters in CALCULATE affect the result compared to applying only one?

Integrate visual calculations

Creating calculations directly from visuals without editing the model:

1. How would you build a month-over-month comparison or a product ranking directly in the Report view?

2. What are the advantages of visual calculations over semantic model measures in specific reporting scenarios?

Building your first report

7

Practice files

You will need to use the practice files provided with this chapter to complete the practice tasks.

A report represents how visual objects together give meaning to data. It is analytical visual communication put into practice, where everything you have learned comes together. It is possibly one of the most attractive and fun parts because by dragging and dropping elements onto the canvas, you will immediately create visualizations.

Here you'll explore a variety of visual objects that adapt and leverage data from the semantic model tables. Each of these graphics will allow you to express what you want to communicate in an intuitive, dynamic, and functional way.

In this chapter, you will learn how to create your first report in Power BI Desktop using a variety of visual objects, slicers, and complementary features.

Explore the Report view

The Report view is the place where you add each of the visual objects to the canvas. By default, the canvas has a size of 1280 x 720 pixels, corresponding to the 16:9 widescreen format. You can change this format in the Format pane using other sizes such as 4:3, letter, tooltip, and custom.

In this chapter

- Explore the Report view
- Understand types of visual objects
- Insert and customize visual objects
- Organize layout and apply slicers and filters

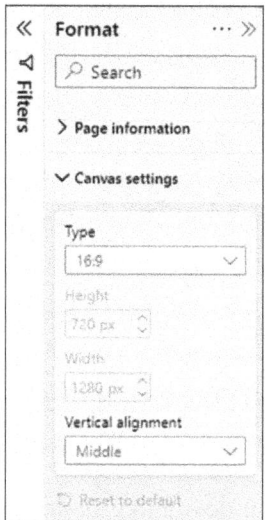

Using the Canvas settings, you can modify the size of the sheet and its vertical alignment.

You can add visual objects in several ways. In the Insert menu at the top of the ribbon, you will find several options, as well as other elements such as text boxes, buttons, shapes, and images.

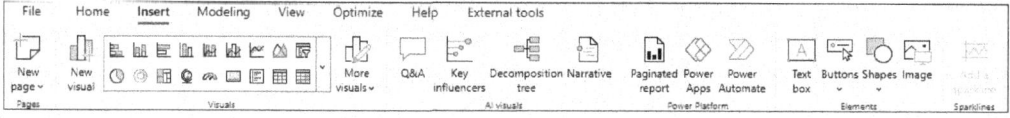

From the Insert menu, you can add visual objects and other elements.

Another option is to add objects from the canvas by right-clicking and selecting **Add visual**.

Right-click anywhere on the canvas to add visual objects.

However, the most familiar and immediate way to add an object is through the Visualizations pane (also referred to as the Build pane) in the upper-right corner.

The Visualizations pane offers suggestions for adding visual objects.

The Visualizations pane allows you to view a larger number of visual objects simultaneously. In addition, by selecting the ellipsis menu (…), you can add other visual objects from AppSource or from a file.

> **TIP** If you find a visual object that is not generally available, you can activate its preview version by selecting **Options and settings > Options > Preview features**.

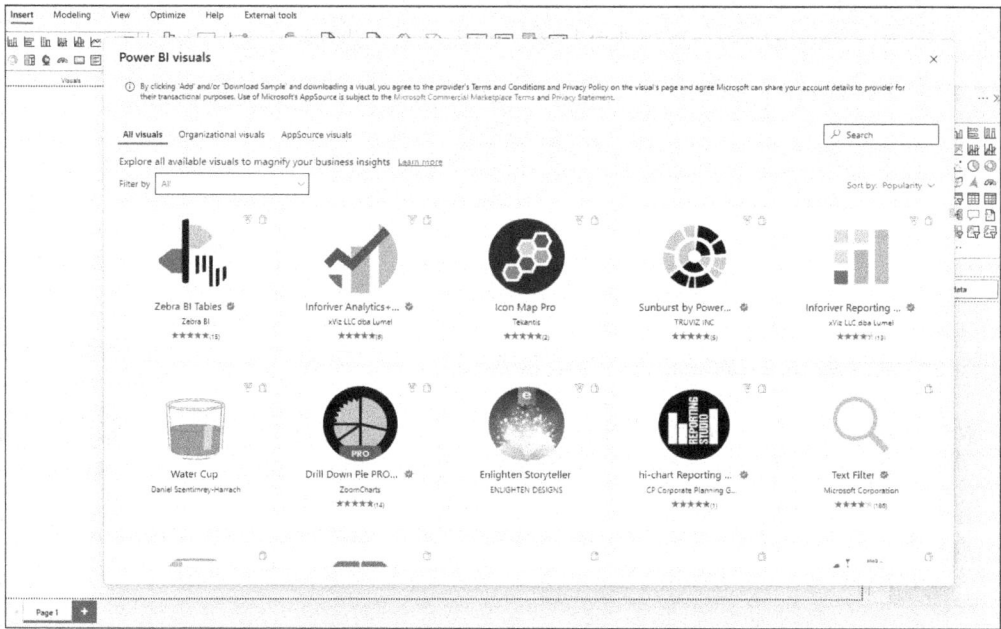

From this list of visual objects in AppSource, you can filter and sort according to your requirements.

Custom visual objects are developed by the community and specialized providers. They provide an alternative when you're looking for something with specific characteristics and behaviors.

Filters pane

Different types of filters are applied in the Filters pane. In simple terms, a filter reduces a query or number of visible records so that they meet a certain criterion—for example, a specific color selection being azure or blue, a logic where the price must be greater than, or a date that must be between two periods.

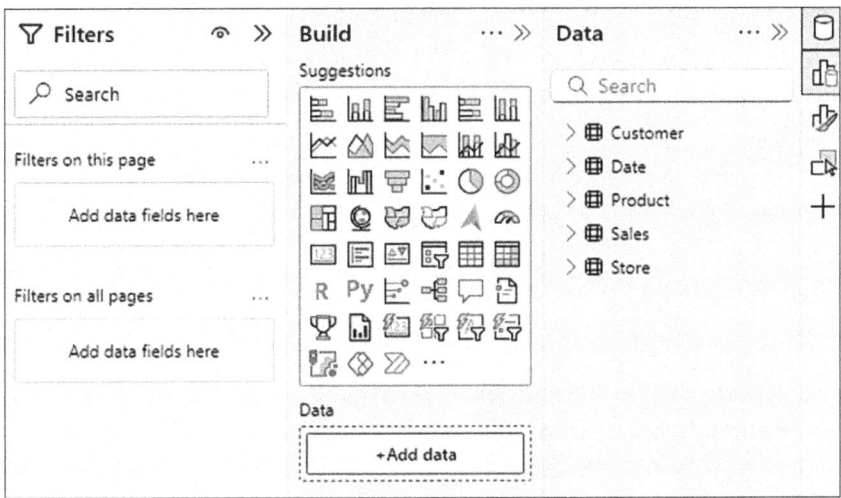

Different types of filters can be added to the Filters pane, coming from columns and measures in the semantic model.

Filters are configured and affect the report in different ways

- **Filters in this visual object:** Only to a specific visual object

- **Filters on this page:** To all visual objects within a page

- **Filters on all pages:** To all visual objects on all pages

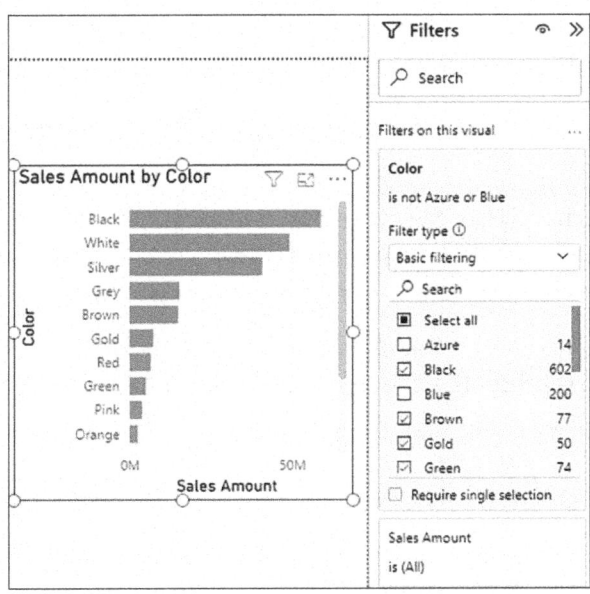

This stacked bar chart is filtered by color that is not azure or blue.

These types of filters applied from the Filters pane are used simultaneously with visual objects called slicers. They give you flexibility and the ability to decide which data in the report should be filtered and how.

 IMPORTANT The type of data coming from a column or measure determines the type of filter you can apply in the Filters pane.

Understand types of visual objects

In Power BI, visual objects such as columns, bars, lines, circles, matrices, cards, and others not only present data but also contextualize it, organize it hierarchically, and guide analytical reading. Choosing between them involves your understanding of the communicative purpose of the report and the type of data that best suits each one.

Deciding when and how to use these visual objects is affected by technical and human factors. However, beyond design, accuracy, aesthetics, and interactivity, the goal is for them to be functional and useful for the purpose of the report.

Let's look at some key visual objects.

Column charts

Column charts display comparisons between categories. Their variants highlight absolute quantities, groupings, or relative proportions.

- **Stacked column chart:** In this chart, the bars are divided into segments to show parts of the total by category.

- **Clustered column chart:** This chart is like the preceding one except that it shows values using vertical bars grouped by category. This type of chart is useful for comparing different elements on the same time or category axis.

- **100% Stacked column chart:** This chart is the same as the stacked column chart except that each column represents 100% of the total, showing the relative proportion between categories.

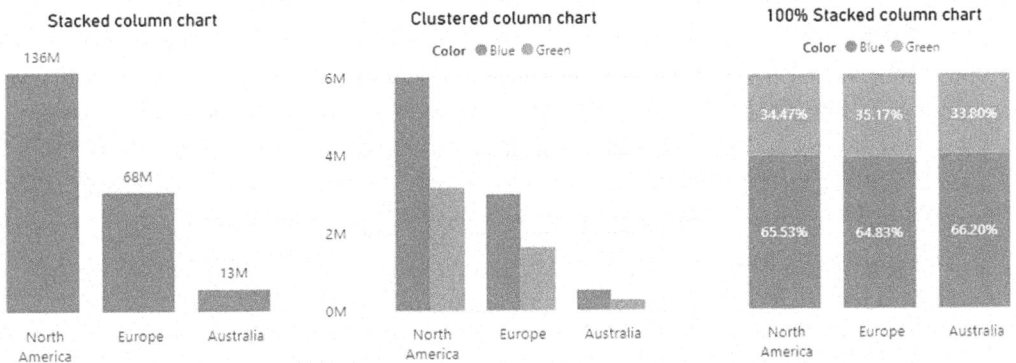

A comparison of stacked, clustered, and 100% stacked column charts for different continents.

 IMPORTANT Bar charts offer the same functionality as column charts but are oriented horizontally.

7

Line and area charts

Line and area charts represent sequences or time series. Lines highlight trends; areas add volume and accumulation to the analysis.

- **Line chart:** This chart connects data points with lines to show trends over time or ordered sequences.

- **Area chart:** This chart is similar to a line chart, but the area under the line is shaded to show volume.

- **Stacked area chart:** This chart accumulates multiple data lines to show how they contribute to the total.

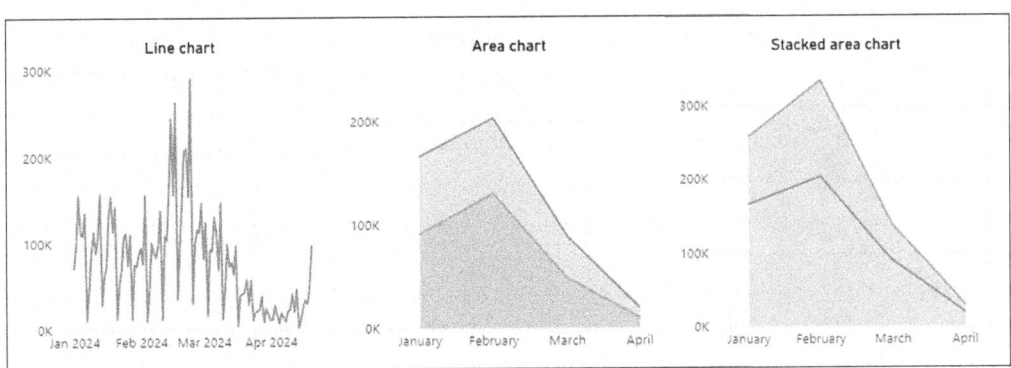

Line, area, and stacked area charts show data trends over time.

Trend analysis and contribution charts

Trend analysis and contribution charts reveal patterns, accumulations, and sequential changes in ordered data. They are ideal for temporal and progressive analysis.

- **Line and stacked column chart:** This chart allows you to view two different measures, one as a line and the other as columns, in the same chart.

- **Ribbon chart:** This chart shows changes in ranking over time between different categories.

- **Waterfall chart:** This chart shows how positive and negative values affect a cumulative total value.

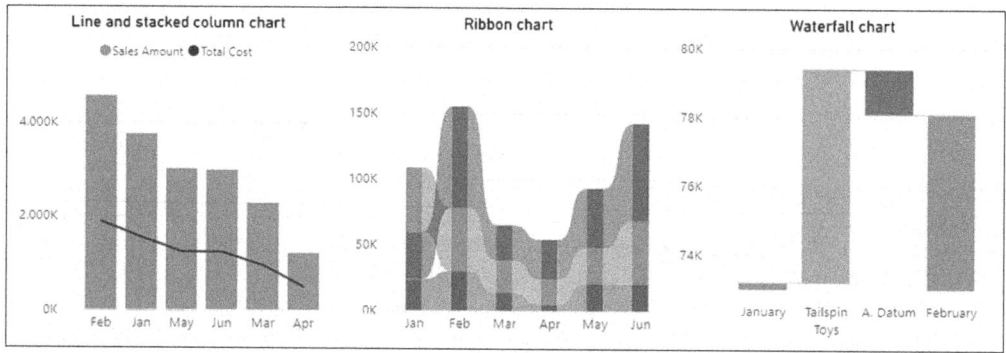

Line and stacked column, ribbon, and waterfall charts provide trend and contribution analysis.

Relationship and proportion charts

Relationship and proportion charts represent nonlinear comparisons between elements and values.

- **Scatter chart:** This chart shows relationships between two numerical variables.

- **Pie chart:** This chart represents proportions in a circle divided into sections.

- **Treemap:** This chart shows hierarchical proportions as rectangular blocks within an area.

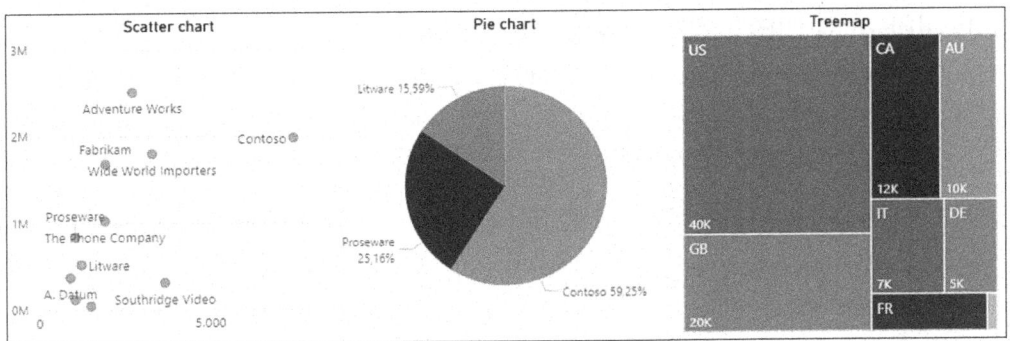

Scatter, pie, and treemap charts provide relationship and proportion analysis.

Key indicators and metrics

Key indicators and metrics summarize relevant values for performance monitoring.

- **Card (new):** This visual object displays one or more values, ideal for highlighting totals or performance figures.

- **Multi-row card:** This visual object shows several list values, one per row.

- **Key Performance Indicator (KPI):** This visual object shows the current value, the target, and a trend, ideal for performance indicators.

- **Gauge:** This visual object represents a value against a target, in the form of a speedometer.

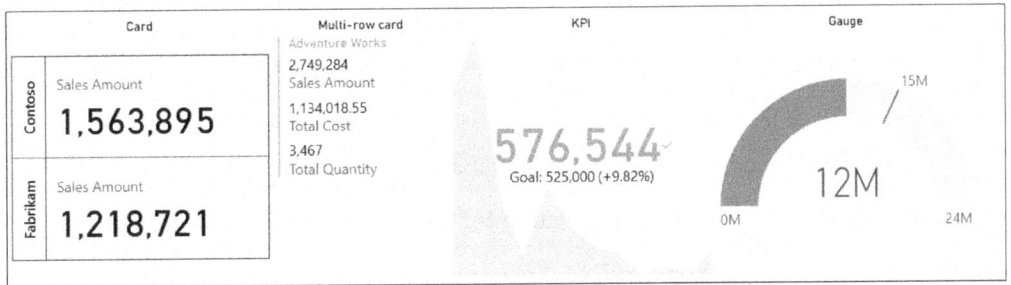

The visual objects shown include a card displaying sales across two brands, a multi-row card presenting various calculations from Adventure Works, a KPI showing monthly performance against a target, and a gauge representing a value in relation to its target and maximum value.

Tabular and hierarchical visualizations

Tabular and hierarchical visualizations allow you to explore data in detail or within grouped structures. They are ideal for comparing figures, breaking down information by category, and presenting measures in financial and organizational contexts.

- **Table:** This visual object displays tabular data without hierarchies.

- **Matrix:** This advanced table allows hierarchical groupings and measures in rows or columns.

Month	Table Sales Amount	Total Cost		Brand	Matrix Canada	Italy	United States	Total
January	2,254,770	933,210		⊞ **A. Datum**	**19,561**	**9,803**	**204,982**	**234,346**
February	2,840,034	1,173,890		⊟ **Adventure Works**	**280,560**	**92,744**	**1,508,092**	**1,881,397**
March	1,177,115	485,979		Coffee Machines	3,204	10,395	10,880	**24,479**
April	537,132	225,757		Desktops	124,790	24,593	809,513	**958,896**
May	1,240,087	502,568		Lamps			1,989	**1,989**
June	863,686	350,758		Laptops	15,145	15,692	212,833	**243,669**
July	630,784	259,643		Monitors	11,852	13,382	119,970	**145,203**
August	557,965	230,582		Televisions	125,569	28,683	352,908	**507,160**
September	339,739	144,995		⊞ **Contoso**	**118,766**	**33,882**	**843,976**	**996,623**
October	411,387	172,093		⊞ **Fabrikam**	**166,249**	**38,197**	**615,924**	**820,370**
November	361,764	153,229		⊞ **Litware**	**17,961**	**6,642**	**79,690**	**104,294**
December	576,544	242,860		⊞ **Northwind Traders**	**7,486**	**3,881**	**59,104**	**70,470**
Total	**11,791,005**	**4,875,564**		**Total**	**610,583**	**185,149**	**3,311,769**	**4,107,500**

Table and matrix visualizations for detailed and hierarchical data analysis.

Slicers

Slicers are visual filters that allow you to select or enter values to adjust the results displayed in the report.

- **Slicer:** This filter allows you to select values and filter data immediately.

- **Text slicer:** This filter allows you to enter values directly to apply filters.

Date and text slicers for dynamic filtering and targeted data selection.

7

Insert and customize visual objects

With everything you have learned, it's time to start creating your first report. It will be a *business analysis* using some of the calculations previously created in DAX.

This analysis will be read from left to right, starting at the top with a card containing KPIs on sales revenue, customers served, and quantities sold. Then, in a time series (line chart), you can view sales over a period. You will also present sales broken down by continent in a stacked bar chart.

At the bottom, you can view different types of category analysis, from the behavior of customers served (ribbon chart) to the distribution of margin and sales by price category.

Card

The card will allow you to compare growth with the previous year. These will be the first measures you will use:

```
Sales Amount = SUMX( Sales, Sales[Quantity] * Sales[UnitPrice] )
Total Quantity = SUM( Sales[Quantity] )
Clients served = DISTINCTCOUNT( Sales[CustomerKey] )
```

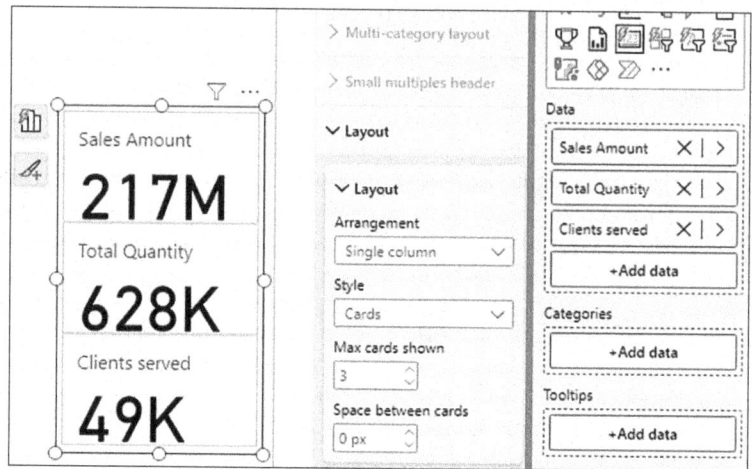

The Sales Amount, Total Quantity, and Clients served measures are displayed in these visual objects.

By default, the card orientation is horizontal (single row), so you will change it to vertical (single column) and the spacing between cards to zero. You will set the font size of the values for each measurement to **20**.

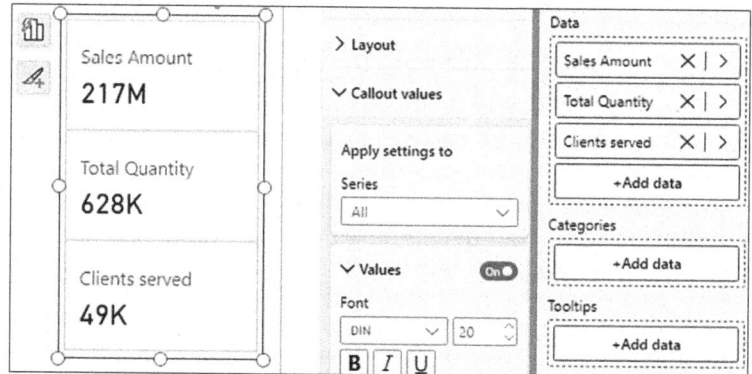

When values are modified by selecting All, the change applies to all measurements.

You can make individual adjustments to each measurement so that the quantities and customers served are displayed with thousand separators.

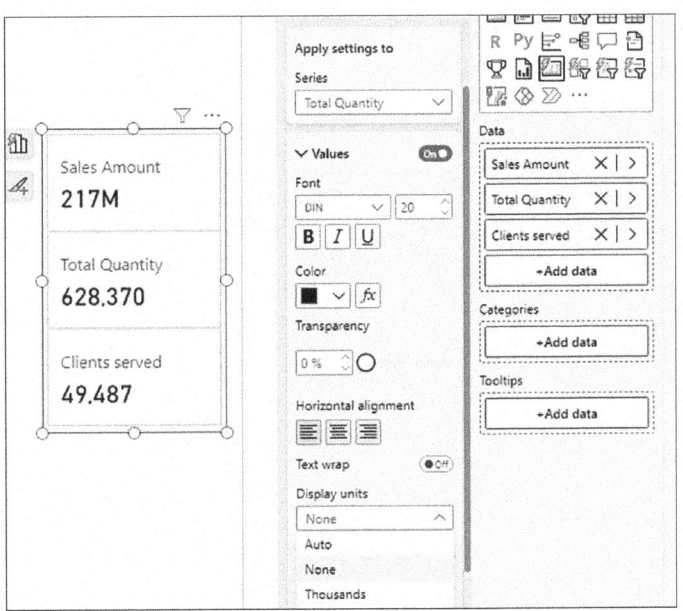

Changes can be applied individually to each series.

Now you will use a feature called *reference labels*. They allow you to add another calculation that will serve as a comparison for each of the values. In other words, it will tell you whether or not there is growth for the selected year.

To do this, you will create three measures that have the same syntax:

- Sales Amount YoY (year over year)
- Total Quantity YoY
- Clients served YoY

The only difference between the three will be the reference to the Sales Amount measure (lines 2 and 4). The others will use their corresponding measures: Total Quantity and Clients served. The format type assigned must be percentage.

```
1 Sales Amount YoY =
2 VAR CurrentYear = [Sales Amount]
3 VAR LastYear =
4     CALCULATE ( [Sales Amount], SAMEPERIODLASTYEAR ( 'Date'[Date] ) )
5 VAR Result =
6     DIVIDE ( CurrentYear - LastYear, LastYear )
7 RETURN
8     Result
```

In the Report view, the Sales Amount YoY measure provides the percentage change in sales for the selected year compared to the previous year.

Now you will use those measures as reference labels. Select the **Sales Amount** series or measure and assign it the Sales Amount YoY measure in Add label.

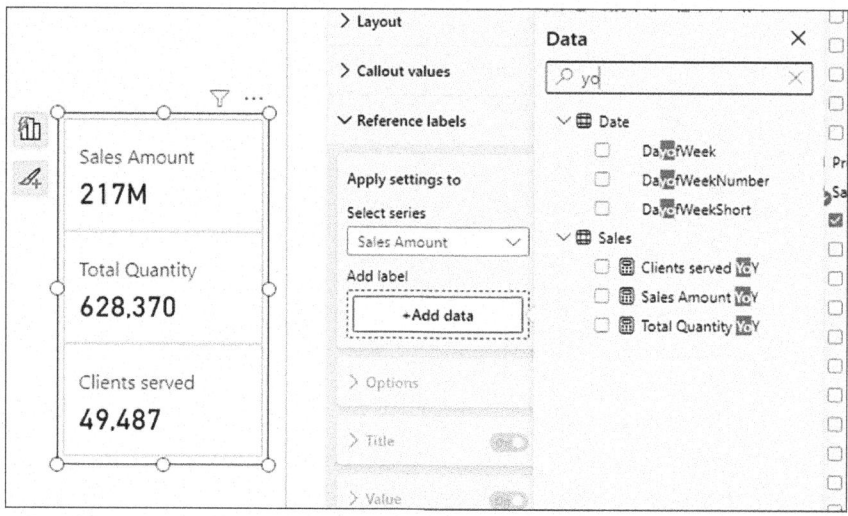

By selecting each measure individually, you can assign the label.

Repeat this operation with the other measurements. In the same way, after you disable the title of the reference labels, you will end up with something similar to the following image.

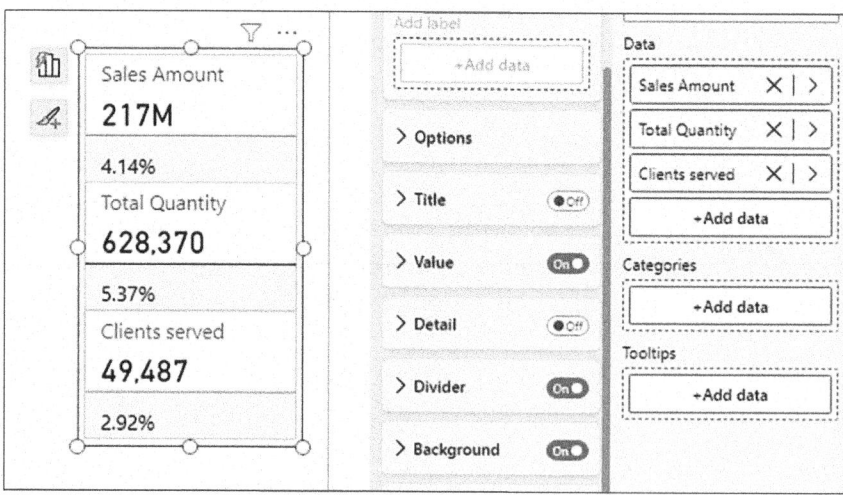

Reference labels now appear below each element.

Finally, you will create a new measure with the following syntax:

```
Card Text = "vs last year"
```

This line will allow you to reuse that text in each element. To use it, go to the **Detail** tab and assign it one by one.

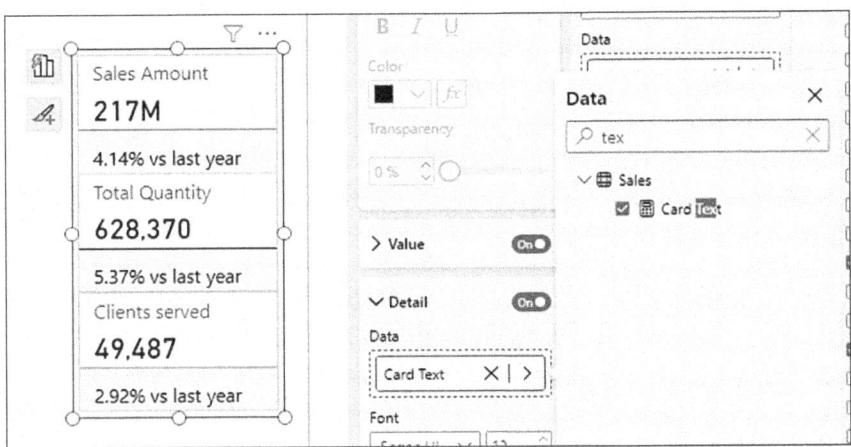

The words vs last year appear below.

The cards have many features that you can adjust. Remember that settings can be global, affecting all cards equally, or individual, requiring a specific selection.

Line chart

The line chart will show sales performance over time. You will use months as a categorical value (X-axis) and sales amount as a continuous value (Y-axis).

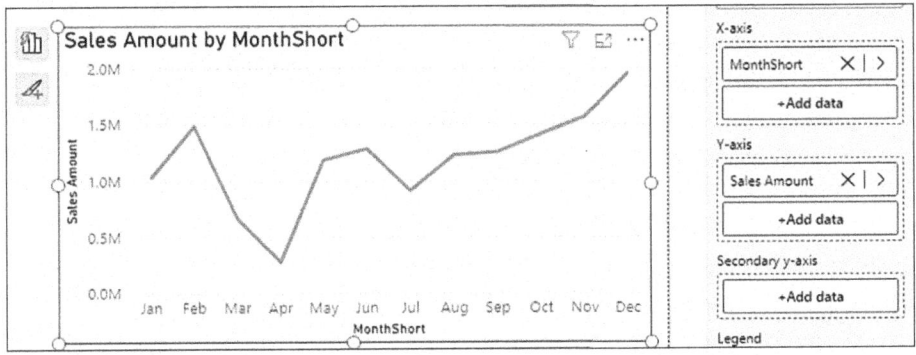

In this line chart, MonthShort is shown on the X-axis and Sales Amount is shown on the Y-axis.

You will also be able to see the percentage change or growth compared to the previous month.

To do this, you will create the measure shown in the following image.

```
1  Sales Amount MoM =
2  VAR CurrentYear = [Sales Amount]
3  VAR LastYear =
4      CALCULATE ( [Sales Amount], DATEADD( 'Date'[Date], -1, MONTH ) )
5  VAR Result =
6      DIVIDE ( CurrentYear - LastYear, LastYear )
7  RETURN
8      Result
```

In the Report view, the Sales Amount MoM (month over month) measure provides the percentage change in sales compared to the previous month.

Before activating the data labels in the line chart, you will modify the previously created measure, adding a custom format that combines the following:

- Numeric value (Sales amount)

- A triangular shape

To modify the format

1. Select the **Sales Amount MoM** measure.

2. In the format options, choose **Dynamic**.

3. In the DAX toolbar, type the following: **""""" & FORMAT([Sales Amount MoM], "▲ 0%;▼ -0%; #") & """""**

4. Select the green check mark.

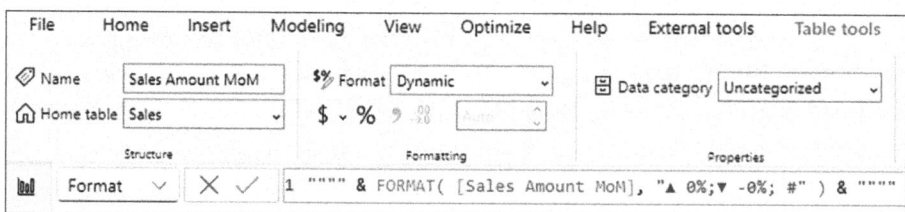

In the Report view, measures can change the format dynamically.

After you have adjusted the calculation in its format, you can activate the data labels. In the Detail pulldown menu, you will use the Sales Amount MoM measure.

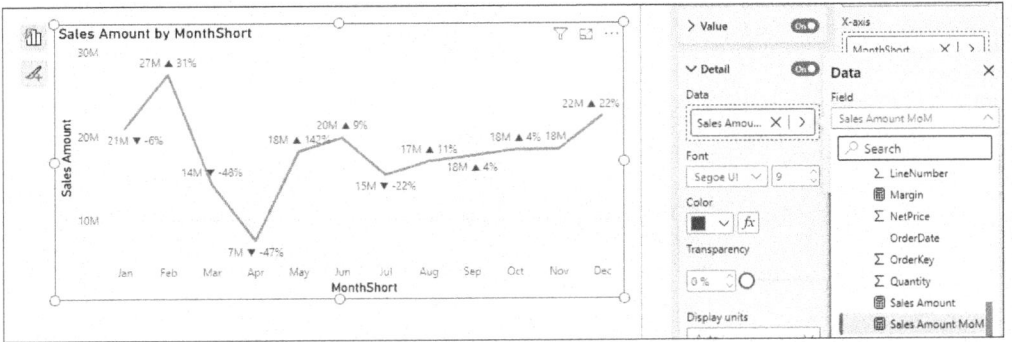

When you activate the details, the triangles are displayed in the line chart.

In addition, apply the following changes to the visual object:

- Title: **Sales over the course of the year**
- Title font: **Segoe UI Semibold (10)**
- Subtitle: **Change from the previous month**
- Subtitle font: **Segoe UI (10)**
- Divider: **on**
- Divider color: **#E6E6E6**
- Titles (X-axis/Y-axis): **off**
- Y-axis values: **off**
- Line width: **2 px**
- Line interpolation type: **smooth**
- Size of data labels and details: **8**
- Position: **above**
- Shade area: **on with area transparency at 90%**

The following line chart is the result after adjusting each of the features in the Format pane.

7

Chapter 7: Building your first report

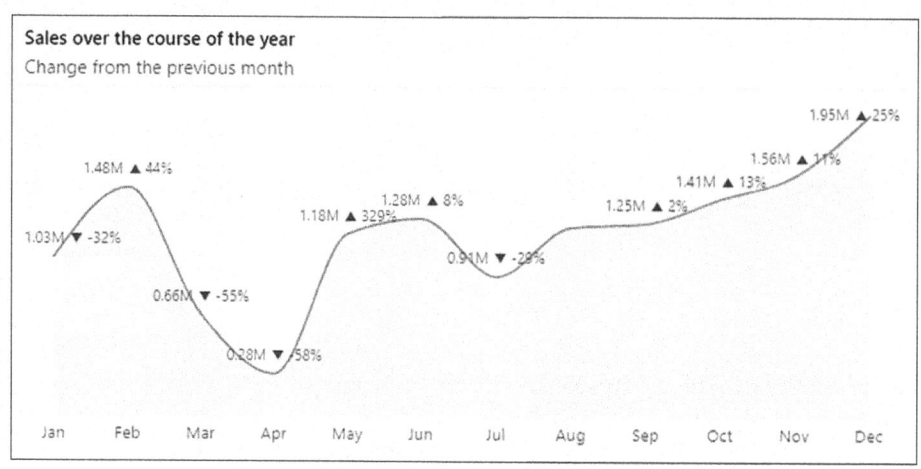

A significant visual change in the line chart is evident.

Something is missing, however. The triangles help identify whether there is an increase or decrease in sales, but ideally, a conditional color should be added to them.

To assign a conditional color

1. Select the **data labels > detail** option.

2. Select the **(fx)** button.

3. For the Format style, select **rules**.

4. For What field should we base this on?, select **Sales Amount MoM**.

5. Define two rules, as shown in the following image.

6. Select **OK**.

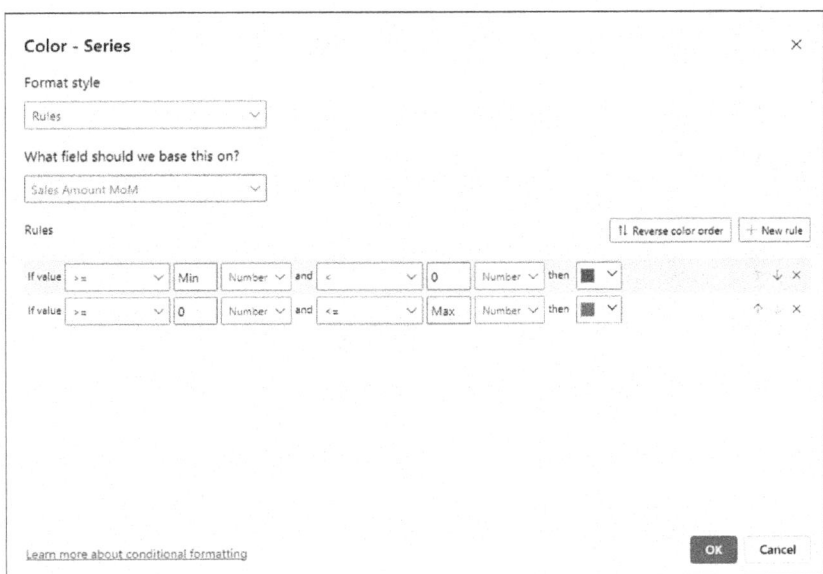

Setting rules allows you to assign colors conditionally.

Colors used (hexadecimal):

- Green: **#007F00**

- Red: **#C62126**

 TIP To remove the zero and define the minimum (Min) and maximum (Max) values, press the Backspace key. This ensures that the value will be adjusted to its extremes.

The line chart will look like the following image.

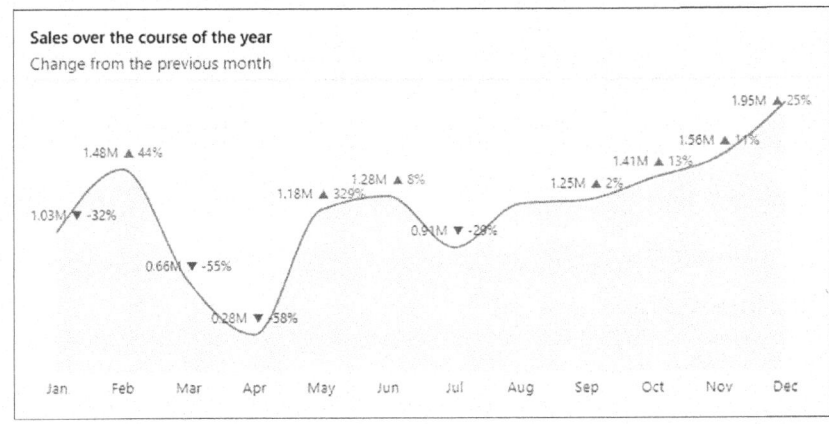

In the line chart, the triangles now have color.

As you might have noticed, with a series of adjustments, you can improve conventional labeling when combined with other visual elements.

Stacked bar chart

The stacked bar chart will display sales by continent. Here you will apply what you learned earlier by using a measure that allows you to see the relative variation (percentage) in sales.

Create the following measure and format it as a percentage

```
Continent percent =
DIVIDE (
    [Sales Amount],
    CALCULATE ( [Sales Amount], REMOVEFILTERS ( Customer[Continent] ) )
)
```

Add the continent to the Y-axis and the Sales amount to the X-axis. Then, as a second data label, add the Continent percent to the detail section.

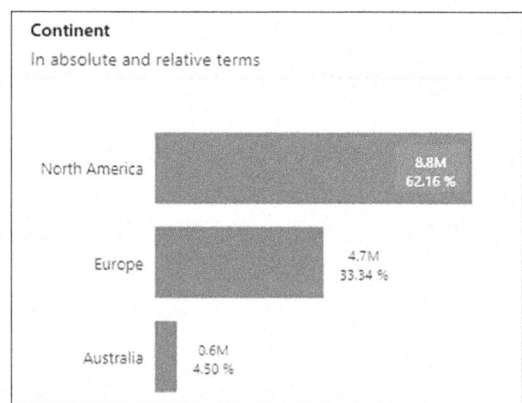

In this stacked bar chart, data labels provide absolute and relative values.

These are the changes that have been applied:

- Title: **Continent**

- Title font: **Segoe UI Semibold (10)**

- Subtitle: **In absolute and relative terms**

- Subtitle font: **Segoe UI (10)**

- Divider: **on**

- Divider color: **#E6E6E6**

- Titles (X-axis/Y-axis): **off**

- X-axis values: **off**

- Size of data labels and detail: **8**

- Detail background: **color #E6E6E6 at 90% transparency**

Ribbon chart

The ribbon chart allows you to view the behavior of categories over time.

To create the visual object

1. Add the **MonthShort** column to the X-axis.

2. Add the **Clients served** measure to the Y-axis.

3. Add the grouped **NewCategory** column as a legend.

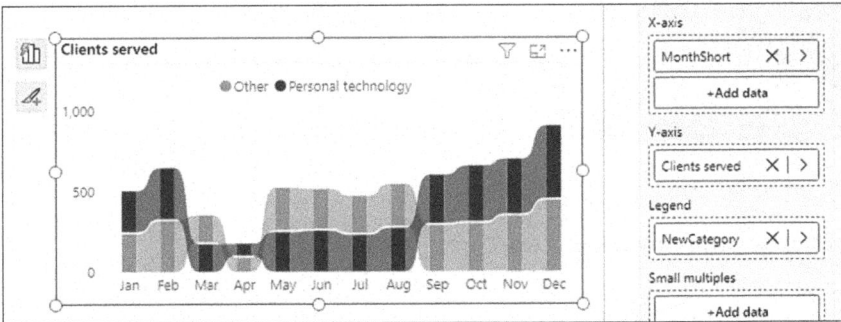

When the category is added to the legend for this ribbon chart, its behavior is displayed.

These are the changes that have been applied:

- Title: **Clients served**

- Title font: **Segoe UI Semibold (10)**

- Divider: **on**

- Divider color: **#E6E6E6**

- Legend position: **top center**

- Legend title: **off**

- Columns layout (space between series): **2 px**

Treemap

You can use a treemap to visualize the margin across different products. This chart is useful for saving space due to its compact way of presenting data.

Two measures are required to create the margin calculation:

```
Total Cost = SUMX( Sales, Sales[Quantity] * Sales[UnitCost] )
Margin $ = [Sales Amount] - [Total Cost]
```

To create the visual object

1. Add the **CategoryName** column to the category.

2. Add the **Margin** measure to the values.

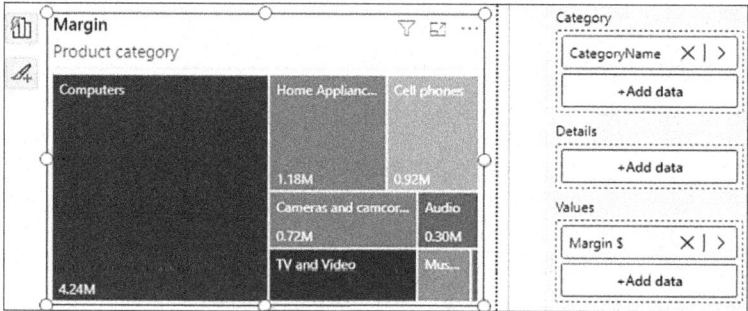

This treemap compares proportions in margin distribution.

These are the changes that have been applied:

- Title: **Margin**

- Title font: **Segoe UI Semibold (10)**

- Subtitle: **Product category**

- Subtitle font: **Segoe UI (10)**

- Divider: **on**

- Divider color: **#E6E6E6**

- Layout (space between all nodes): **2px**

- Data labels: **on**

- Size for data and category labels: **8**

Stacked column chart

Now you will add a stacked column chart to the report. The goal is to see sales grouped according to price segmentation.

Simply drag the Purchase Price Category column to the X-axis and Sales Amount to the Y-axis.

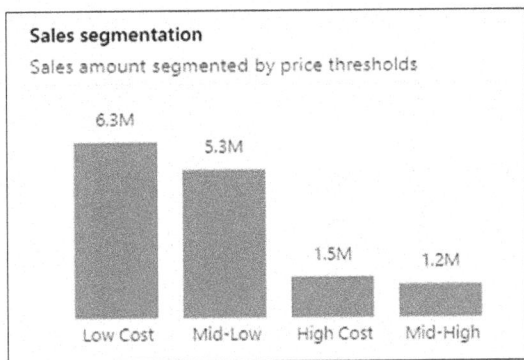

This stacked column chart shows sales segmentation by price thresholds.

These are the changes that have been applied:

- Title: **Sales segmentation**
- Title font: **Segoe UI Semibold (10)**
- Subtitle: **Sales amount segmented by price thresholds**
- Subtitle font: **Segoe UI (10)**
- Divider: **on**
- Divider color: **#E6E6E6**
- Titles (X-axis/Y-axis): **off**
- Y-axis values: **off**
- Data labels: **on**

Organize layout and apply slicers and filters

With all the visual objects designed, it's time to organize them on the canvas. Similarly, you need to add a slicer and apply filters. The report will be organized as shown in the following image.

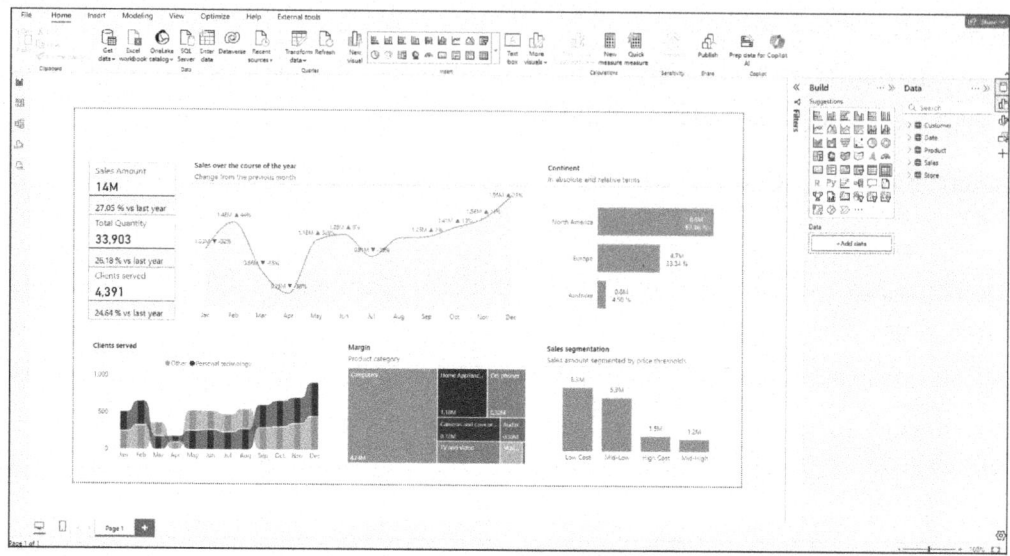

In Report view, each visual object has a different position on the canvas.

In the Format pane, you can modify the size and position of visual objects with the following data:

Visual	Height	Width	Horizontal Position	Vertical Position
Card	315	178	22	98
Line chart	315	641	227	98
Stacked bar chart	315	350	906	98
Ribbon chart	235	459	32	447
Treemap	235	350	525	447
Stacked column chart	235	350	906	447

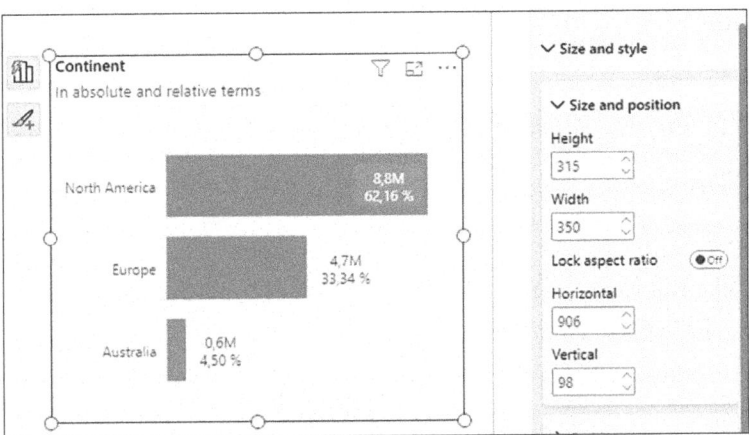

In Report view, you can adjust the size and position in the Format pane.

Now let's add a slicer that allows selection by brand.

To add a slicer

1. Select the **Button slicer** visual object.

2. Add the **Brand** column to the fields.

3. Adjust its dimensions: Height: **50**, Width: **452**, Position Horizontal: **777**, Vertical: **7**.

4. Disable the title.

5. Change the size of the values to **8**.

6. Set the horizontal alignment of the text to **Center**.

7. Expand the filter pane, and in the Filters on this visual section, select these brands: **Adventure Works**, **Contoso**, and **Wide World Importers**.

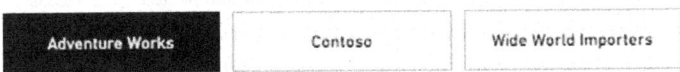

The Button slicer looks like this after being configured horizontally.

Finally, you need to add a page-level filter. It will allow you to define the year that will be used to display the report. The card's percentage calculations will also provide a comparison with the selected year.

To add a page-level filter

1. Expand the Filters pane.

2. Add the **Year** column to the Filters on this page section.

3. Select the basic filter type.

4. Choose the year **2017**.

The report would look like the following image after you select the Adventure Works brand and have a page filter where the year is 2017.

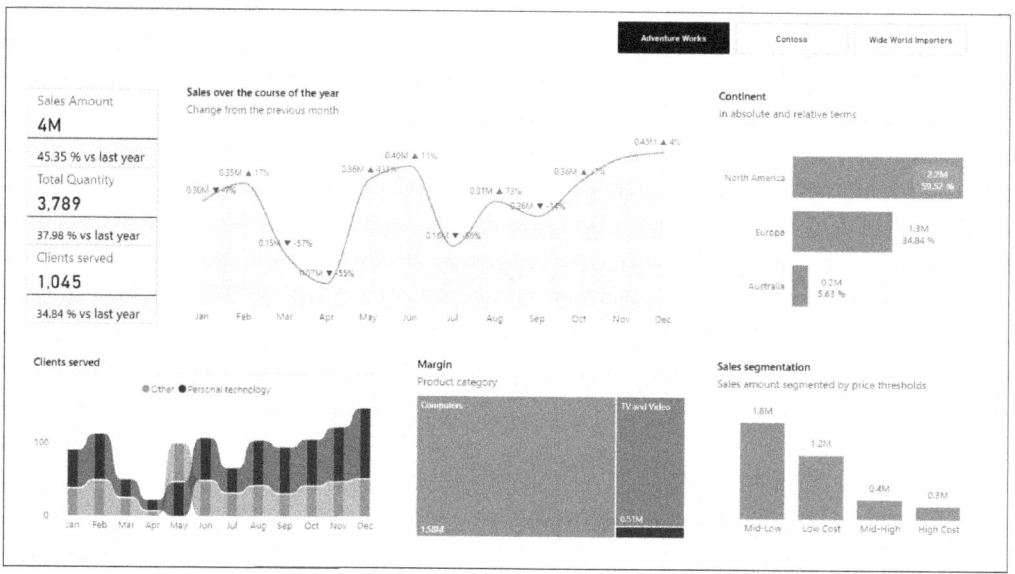

In Report view, a slicer allows you to reduce the number of records.

Creating a report in Power BI can be extremely quick. Simply dragging and dropping the necessary fields into each visual object is enough to get started. What you have learned in this chapter could be defined as not just sticking with the default settings, but taking advantage of the vast array of features that can be modified to improve the report design.

Skills review

In this chapter, you learned how to

- Explore the Report view and configure canvas size, orientation, and layout.

- Identify and understand the main visual objects and their analytical purpose.

- Insert and customize visual objects using formatting, labels, and reference measures.

- Organize layout and apply slicers and filters to enhance report interactivity.

7

Practice tasks

Before you can complete these tasks, you must copy the book's practice files to your computer. The practice files for these tasks are in the PowerBISBS\C07 folder.

Explore the Report view

Configure the report canvas:

1. Open Power BI Desktop and switch to Report view.

2. Change the canvas size from the default 16:9 to another format, such as **Letter**.

3. Adjust the vertical alignment to **Top**.

4. Reflect: How does changing canvas size or alignment affect the layout of your visuals?

Understand types of visual objects

Insert and compare different chart types:

1. Add a 100% Stacked column chart to the canvas and assign **CategoryName** to the X-axis and **Sales Amount** to the Y-axis.

2. Add a treemap with **CategoryName** as Category and **Sales Amount** as Values.

3. Reflect: When comparing proportions, does a 100% Stacked column chart or a treemap make interpretation clearer?

Insert and customize visual objects

Format and refine a pie chart visual:

1. Insert a pie chart onto the canvas.

2. Add **Continent** to the Legend field and **Sales Amount** to the Values field.

3. Change the title to **Sales Amount by Continent**, align it to the center, and set the font to **Segoe UI Semibold**, size **10**.

4. Disable the legend.

5. In the Slices section, enable the border, set the border color to **white**, and increase the border width to **2 px**.

6. In the Detail labels section, set the option to **All detail labels**.

Organize layout and apply slicers and filters

Assign filters at the page level:

1. Open the previously created report in Power BI Desktop.

2. In the Filter pane, locate the Filters on this page section.

3. Drag the **Year** column into this section.

4. Set the filter type to **Basic filtering** and select value **2024**.

5. Drag the Continent column into the section and select the values **North America** and **Australia**.

6. Drag the CategoryName column into the section and select the values **Computers** and **Cell phone**.

7. Review how all visuals on the page update according to the combined filter conditions.

Designing advanced visualizations

Practice files

You will need to use the practice files provided with this chapter to complete the practice tasks.

Visualizations are considered advanced when visual objects are modified using visual design techniques that enhance what the data is offering. It is noteworthy that, in the same way, some less common visual objects could be classified as advanced because they require greater effort to understand how they work.

This combination of the use and application of techniques is what allows you to take them to another level, starting from the simple and gradually adjusting them to improve analytical visual communication.

In this chapter, you will learn about other visual objects and features that will allow you to design advanced reports in Power BI.

In this chapter

- Visualize geographic data using maps
- Compare variables and reveal patterns with scatter charts
- Break down measures and explore categories with decomposition trees
- Display multiple comparisons using small multiples
- Analyze trends, forecast values, and detect anomalies using line charts
- Summarize key metrics using narrative text

Visualize geographic data using maps

Maps allow you to represent geographic data, which is useful when you want to analyze behavior by location. However, before you start using them, *you must categorize their fields (columns) individually* so that they are displayed correctly.

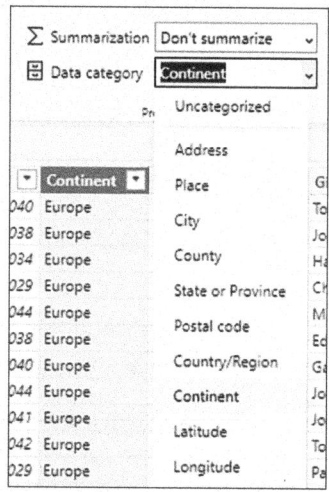

Under the Data category, different categories can be assigned depending on the type of data.

Among all categorizations, coordinates (latitude/longitude) offer the highest level of spatial accuracy within a map. Some maps available in Power BI, such as the Azure map, use them.

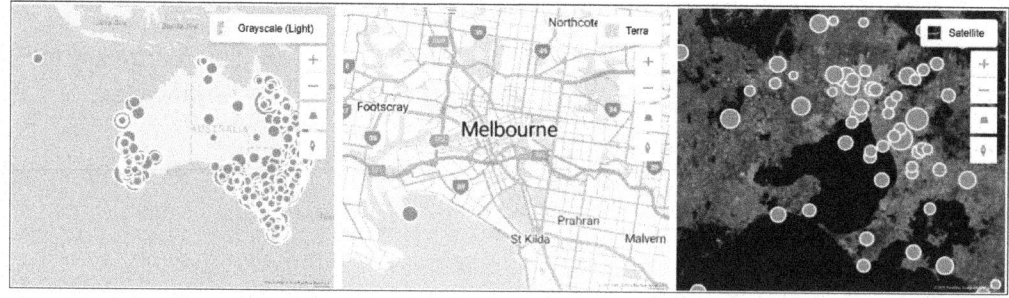

This Azure map visual object shows various map styles: grayscale (light), terra, and satellite.

As with other visual objects, you can assign fields in the legend to group each of the bubbles that are represented—in this case, based on the Sales Amount measure.

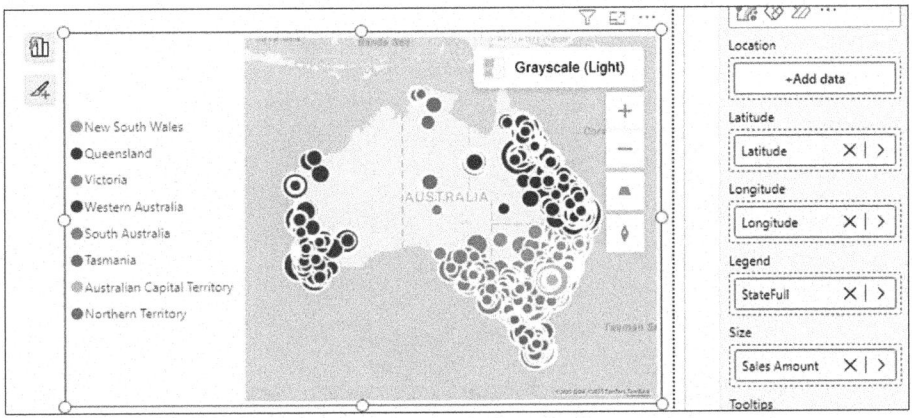

This Azure map visual object shows sales by state.

By default, each location will be assigned a bubble, but you can also group them according to their proximity by activating the **Cluster bubbles** option.

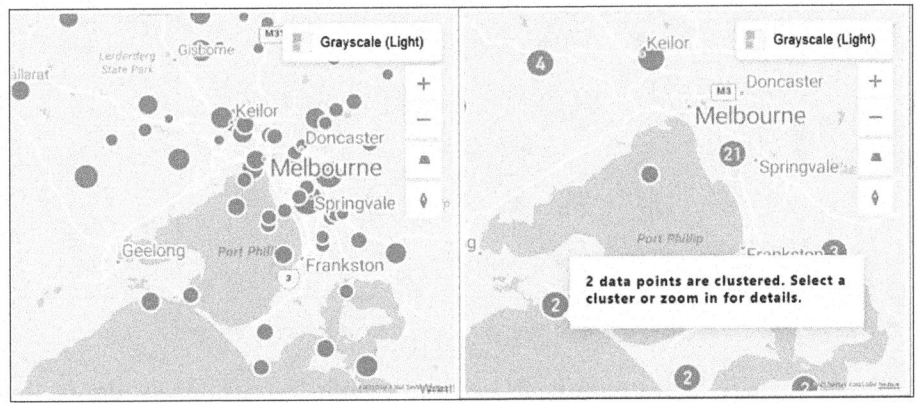

In this Azure map visual object, note the differences between bubbles (default) and clustered bubbles.

Another notable feature is the ability to draw polygons and perform research based on a range determined by time or distance. To do this, you must select **Map settings > Controls** and then enable the **Selection** option.

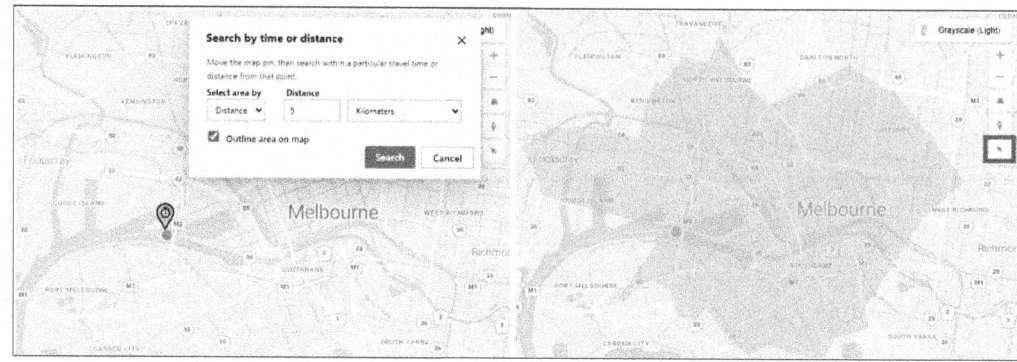

In this Azure map visual object, when you do a search within 5 km, a polygon is generated.

When using other types of fields, such as cities, you can activate the filled map. Doing so will delimit the location, providing an alternative to displaying a single point (bubble).

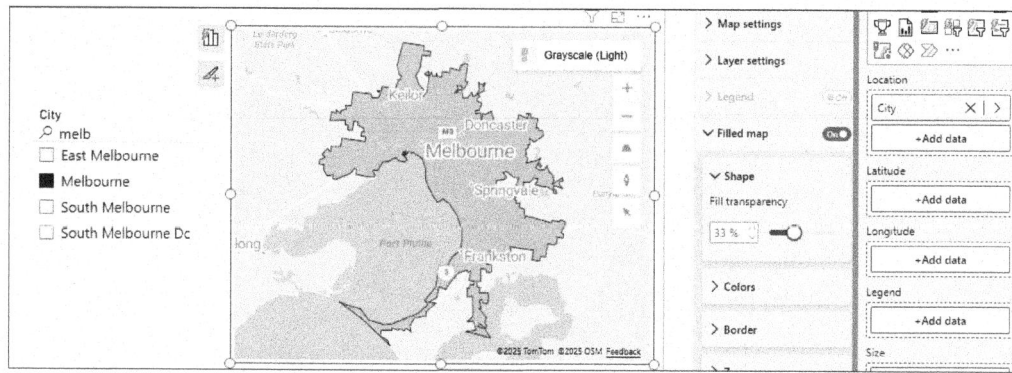

In this Azure map visual object, activating the filled map generates a location boundary.

The maps also allow you to activate traffic layers that provide live data on incidents. These maps can be used simultaneously with bubbles and fill layers.

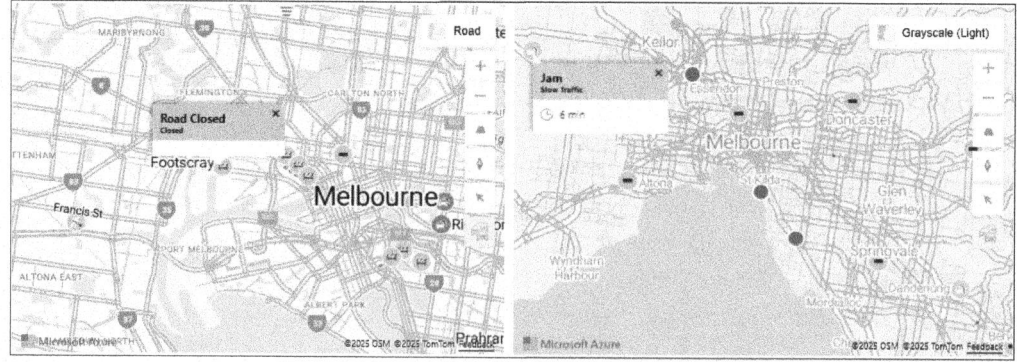

In this Azure map visual object, when the traffic layer is activated, live alerts are displayed.

Among all the maps available in Power BI, the Azure map is one of the most comprehensive, combining the accuracy of coordinates, locations, and the assignment of reference layers.

Compare variables and reveal patterns with scatter charts

The scatter chart could be classified as an abstract visual object because it requires quantitative values on both axes (X-axis/Y-axis) and, in turn, a categorical order that will position the values on the Cartesian plane.

This chart is obtained by using the Sales Amount (X-axis) and Margin (Y-axis) measures and the CategoryName column as values. At first glance, the most obvious feature is its markers, which you can modify in terms of size, rotation, and colors in the Markers section.

In this scatter chart visual object, product categories are located according to margin and sales amount.

 TIP Activating the titles on the axes (X-axis/Y-axis) helps to identify the values on each axis.

When values are widely dispersed, displaying them using the linear scale (default) can group them toward the extremes. In these cases, you can activate the logarithmic scale in the axis properties.

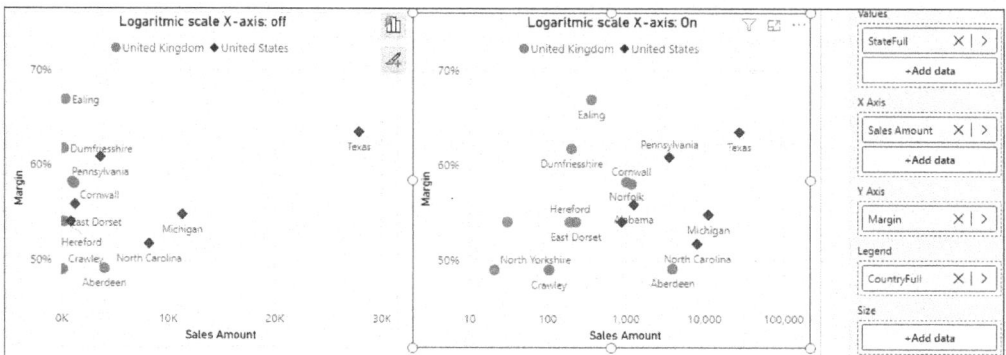

In this scatter chart visual object, note the difference in the distribution of the data when the logarithmic scale is activated on the X-axis.

Setting a reference point can help you find values faster. In the Reference line section, you can set different types of lines and decide which series (X-axis/Y-axis) they should be assigned to.

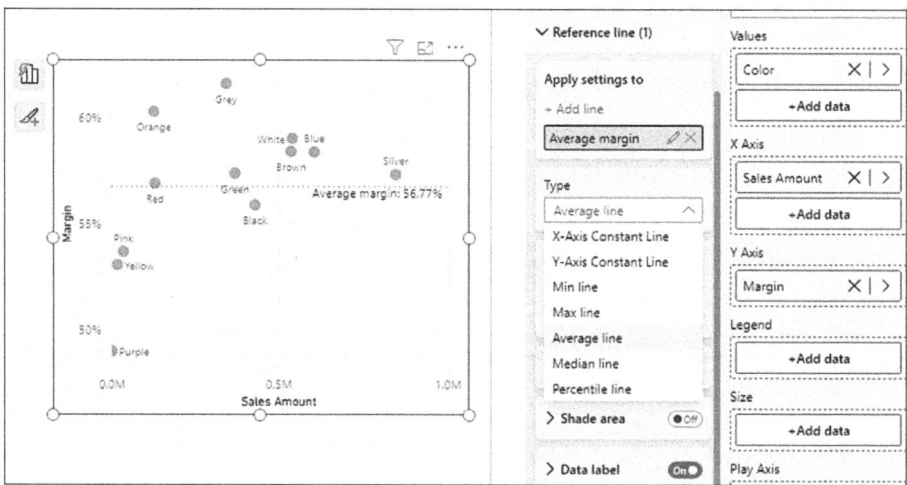

In this scatter chart visual object, an average line has been activated according to the margin measure.

In the same section, you can activate a shade area before or after the reference line to emphasize and separate the boundaries using color as a distinguishing feature.

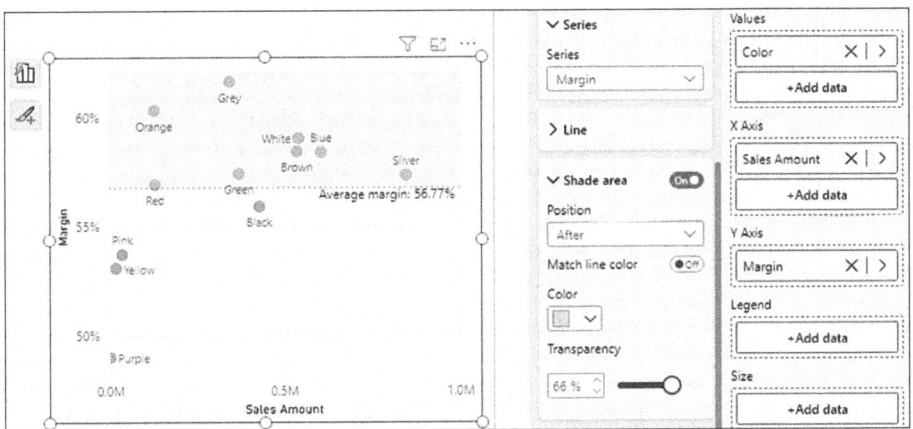

In this scatter chart visual object, a shade area has been activated after the reference line.

A unique feature of the scatter chart is the play axis. It allows you to visualize how the points in the chart change over time. All you have to do is add a field (column) in the Play axis section of the visual object.

In this scatter chart visual object, adding the year activates the play axis.

Another element that can be used as a third variable is the size of the bubbles. Adding a quantitative field (column or measure) in the size option will assign an independent size to each one. You can also use the same value that assigns bubbles as a legend (fourth variable) to differentiate them by color.

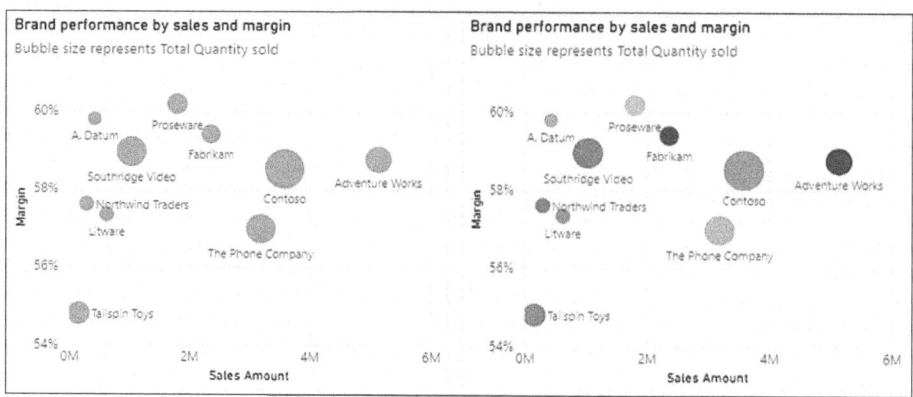

In this scatter chart visual object, the size of the bubbles is affected by the quantities sold.

 TIP When different variables are used in the same chart, titles and subtitles help to identify each element.

The scatter chart allows you to reveal patterns that would not be evident with more conventional visual objects. Its ability to combine numerical axes, size, color, and animation makes it a tool for comparative analysis and exploration of relationships between data.

Break down measures and explore categories with decomposition trees

The decomposition tree allows you to break down a measure into multiple dimensions without following a fixed hierarchy. Its branched structure is built dynamically, showing how each category contributes to the total value.

When adding a measure and a categorical value, you can choose how the data will be separated: high value, low value, and according to the column used, in this case, Brand.

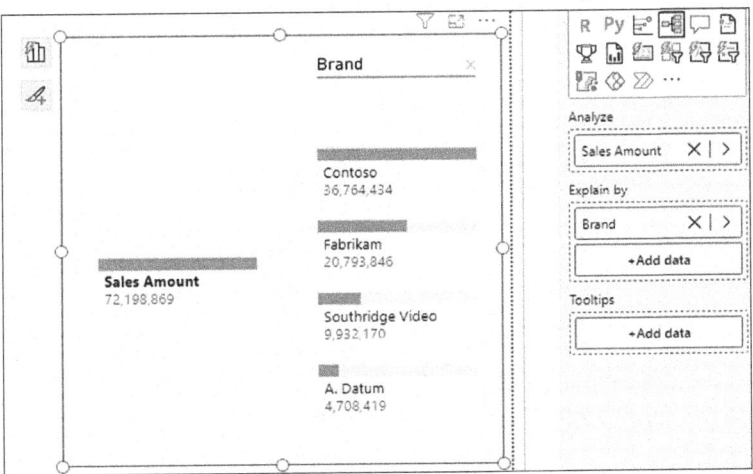

In this decomposition tree visual object, the Sales Amount metric is analyzed by brand.

As you add new fields in the Explain by section, you can expand the measurement results. For example, select the Fabrikam brand to view the categories.

8

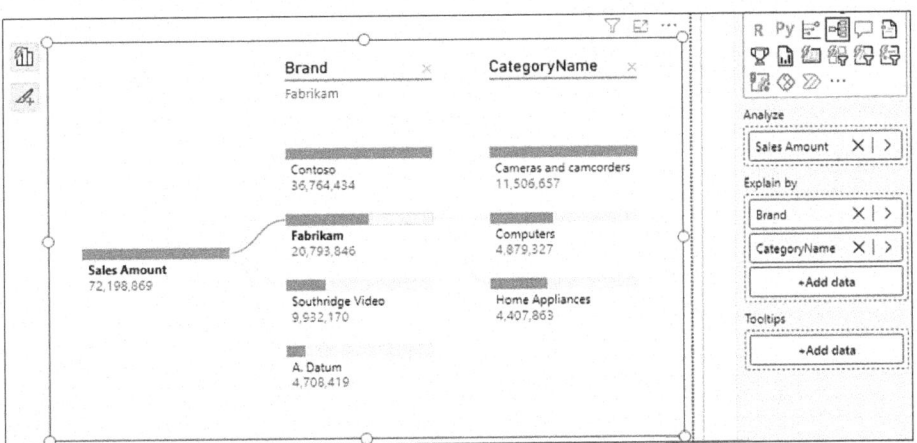

In this decomposition tree visual object, with each new categorical value, the hierarchy can be further expanded.

The following image shows what a selection based on the highest value would look like compared to a selection by category.

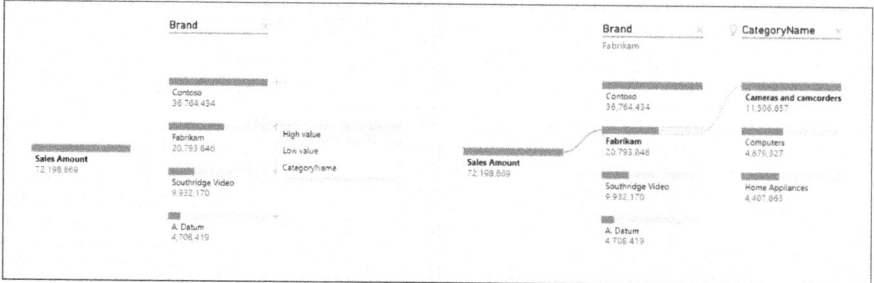

In this decomposition tree visual object, note the emphasis on the lines to follow the highest value.

Like other visual objects, the decomposition tree also allows you to set conditional formats so that the bars are colored according to the condition.

To define a conditional format

1. Select the **Conditional formatting** option.

2. Select the **fx** button.

3. Under format style, select **Rules**.

4. For the measurement, select **Margin**.

5. Define a rule as shown in the following image.

6. Select **OK**.

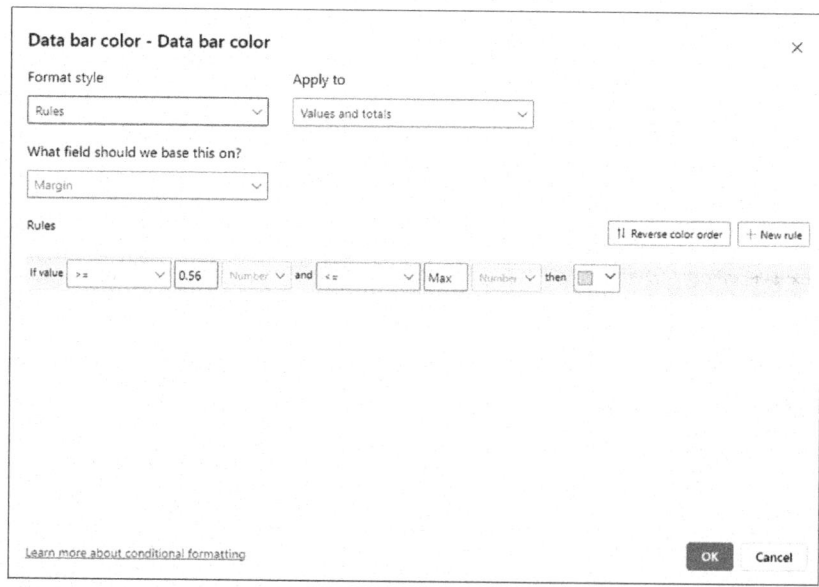

With conditional formatting, setting rules allows you to assign colors conditionally.

The following image shows how the decomposition tree will look under a rule that establishes if the Margin measure is greater than or equal to 56%, it will be colored gray.

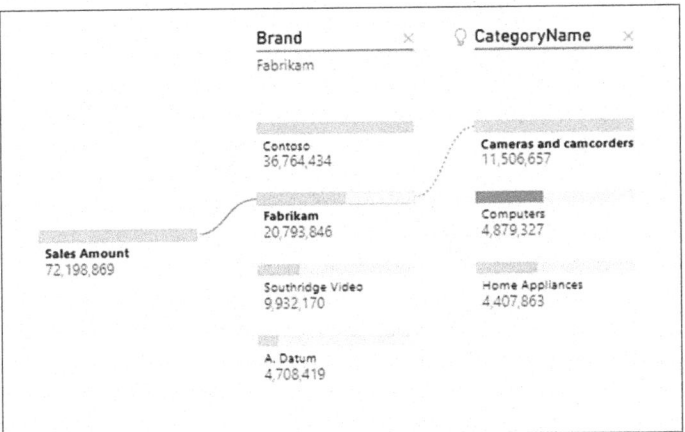

In this decomposition tree visual object, when conditional formatting is applied, the bars are differentiated.

The decomposition tree becomes an ideal visual object for exploratory analysis, leading to the identification of causes, comparison of segments, and deeper insight into data behavior.

Display multiple comparisons using small multiples

The small multiples feature allows you to divide certain visual objects into repeated panels according to a categorical field. Each panel retains the same type of graph, making it easy to compare categories side by side.

All you have to do is drag a field (column) into the visual object in the Small multiples option. In the following example, you can see the brands being separated by country.

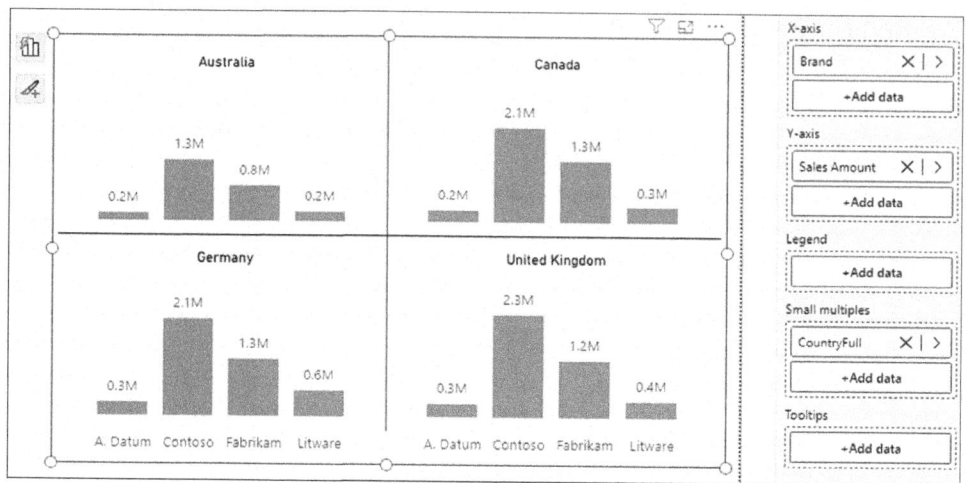

In this stacked column chart visual object, when the Countryfull column is added, the countries are divided.

When you're using them, a section called Small multiples is enabled. In this section, you can modify the layout, borders, title, and background.

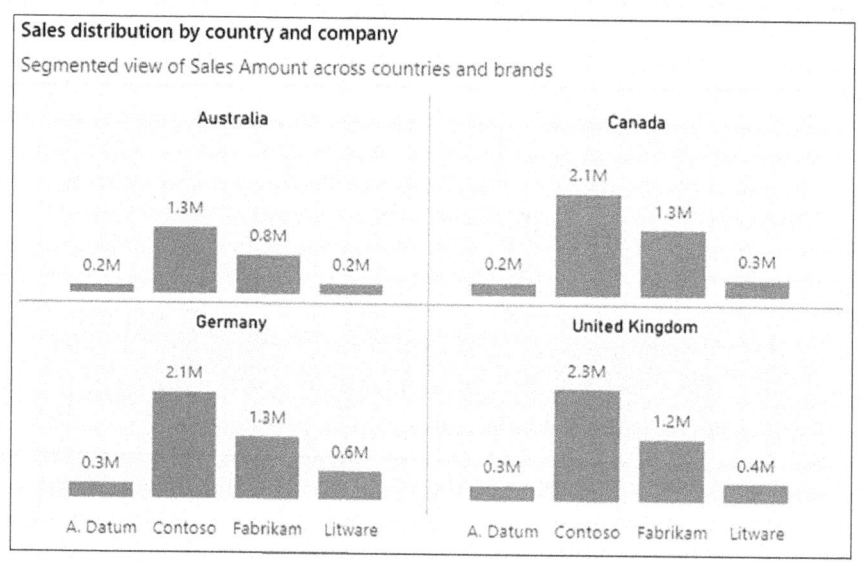

This stacked column chart shows the result after adjustments are made to small multiples.

Changes applied in the small multiples section:

- Layout (all padding): **6**
- Border color: **#999999**
- Background color: **#F7F7F7**

By default, the Y-axis shares the scale between each of the panels, but you can disable it if you need it to be independent, as you can see in the following image (the area chart). You can configure this setting by selecting **Y-axis > Range > Shared Y-axis & Scale to fit**.

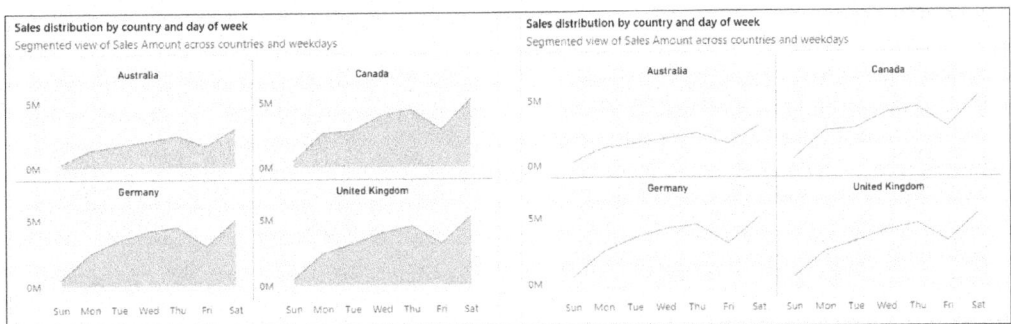

In these area chart and line chart visual objects, note that the Shared (Y-axis) option is disabled for the area chart.

In summary, small multiples allow categories to be compared in a clear and structured way, maintaining visual consistency and offering design options that enrich the interpretation of the data.

Analyze trends, forecast values, and detect anomalies using line charts

Trend lines, forecasting, and anomalies are analytical tools that enrich line charts with predictive and explanatory information, helping to identify patterns, project future values, and detect irregular behavior in time series.

Trend lines

A trend line is an automatically calculated line that summarizes the overall behavior of data over time. Power BI generates it using a statistical model (linear regression) to show whether values tend to *rise, fall, or remain stable*.

8

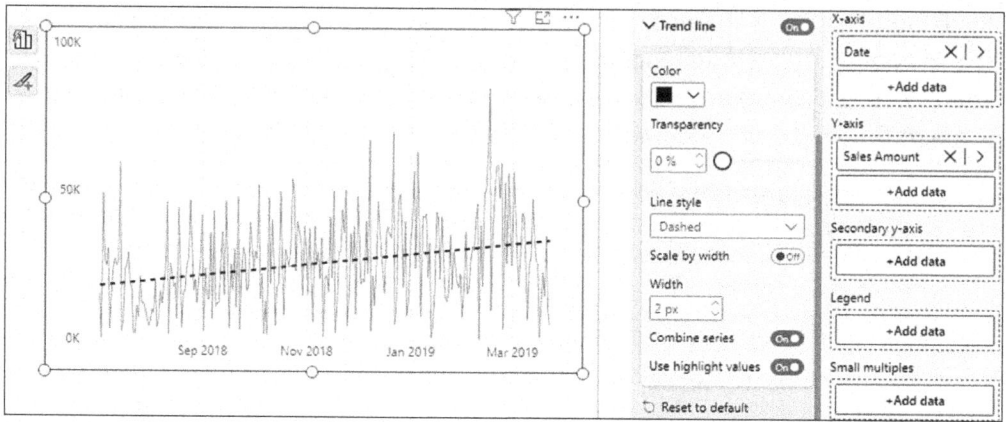

This line chart visual object shows the evolution of the Sales Amount metric over time, with a trend line.

You can customize the style of the trend line by adjusting its color, transparency, line style, and thickness.

> **IMPORTANT** To enable the trend line option in the line chart, you must define the X-axis as continuous.

Forecast

The Forecast option allows you to make automatic predictions about future trends based on historical data. It is a useful feature for anticipating behavior and exploring what might happen if current trends continue. Note that the X-axis must be defined as continuous for the forecast to work properly.

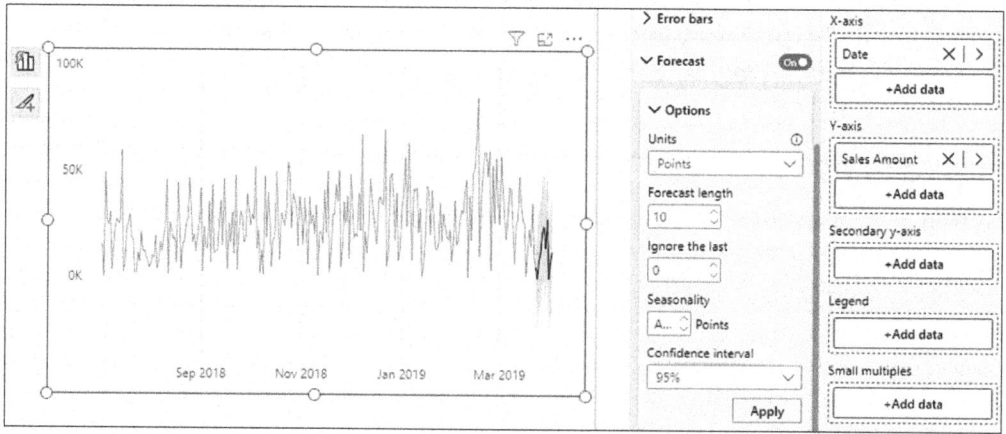

This line chart visual object shows the evolution of the Sales Amount measure over time, with a forecast line that projects future values.

The forecast parameters are adjusted in the Options section. For example, you can set how many points will be projected, whether the latest data should be ignored, how to detect seasonal patterns, and the level of certainty.

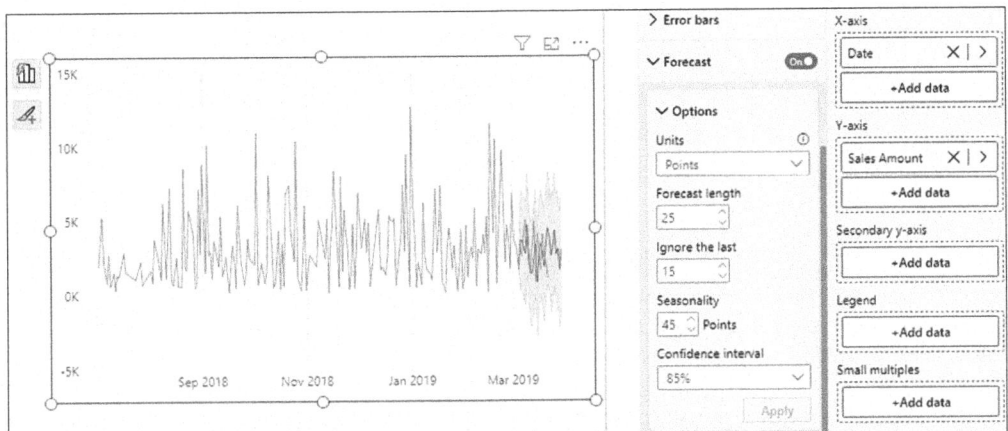

This line chart visual object shows the evolution of the Sales Amount measure over time, with a forecast line that projects values 25 points forward and omits the last 15 points of the history.

In the preceding image, 25 points are projected forward, allowing an extended trend to be visualized. The last 15 points of the historical data are omitted to avoid distortions if recent data is incomplete or atypical. Seasonality is set at 45 points (useful if the cyclical pattern is known), and finally, a range of uncertainty with 85% confidence is shown. *Ultimately, the forecast is not exact, but rather an estimate.*

Anomalies

Anomalies are observations that deviate significantly from expected behavior. Detecting them allows you to identify unusual events or structural changes that could affect the analysis.

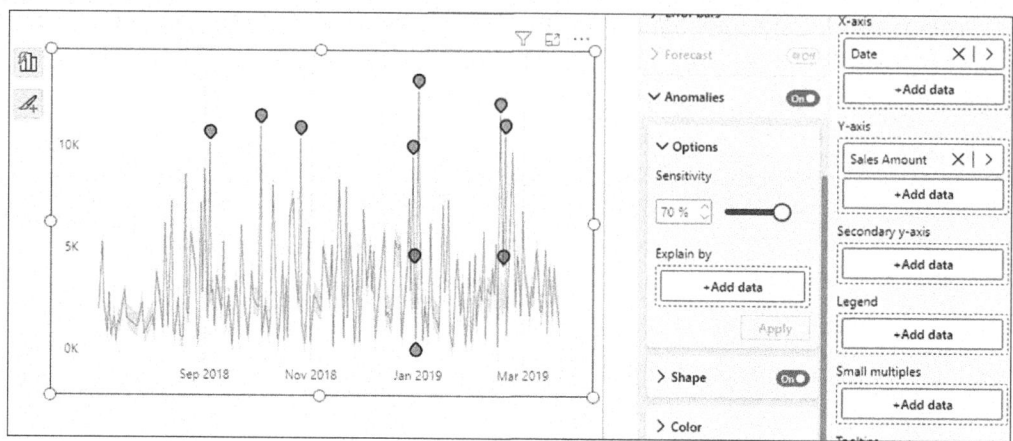

This line chart visual object shows the evolution of the Sales Amount metric over time, with anomalies enabled to identify points with significant deviations in the series.

You can modify the sensitivity; for example, reducing it to 50% makes the analysis more stringent, highlighting only more pronounced deviations. It is also possible to disable the expected ranges, which are shown as soft edges above or below the line.

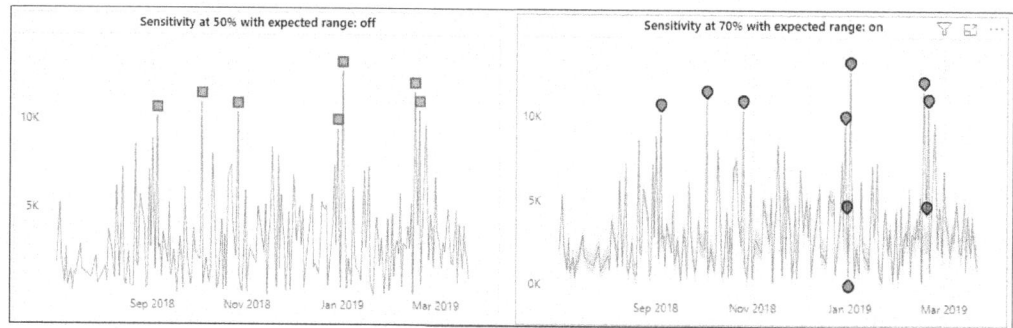

This line chart visual object shows the evolution of the Sales Amount metric over time, with anomalies enabled, and both sensitivity and expected range at their minimum values and disabled.

This example shows how sensitivity and expected range settings influence anomaly detection within a time series.

Summarize key metrics using narrative text

The narrative visual object allows you to write text directly on the canvas, using columns and measures from the semantic model. It is useful for summarizing key elements and communicating results in a contextual and accessible way.

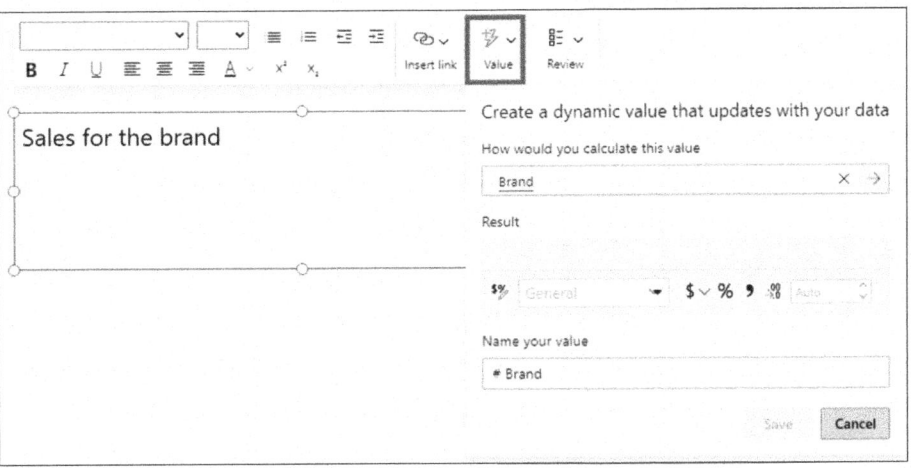

This narrative visual object combines text with dynamic values from the model.

As you write the text, you can insert dynamic values that are updated with report interactions. For example, when entering **Sales for the brand**, you can add the Brand column and then a measure such as Sales Amount, combining static content with data from the model.

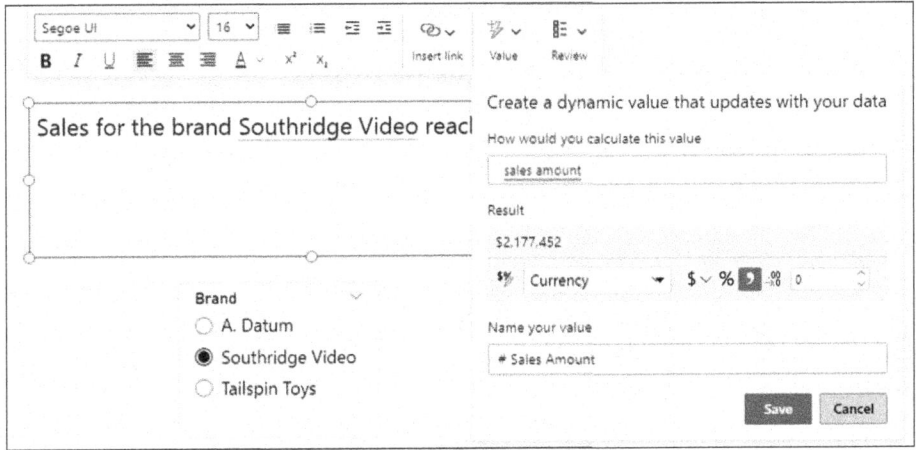

For this narrative visual object, a measure with a currency format and custom name is added, making it easy to reuse.

To identify which values come from dynamic attributes, simply look at the underline that appears under each word inserted from the semantic model, whether it is a column or a measure.

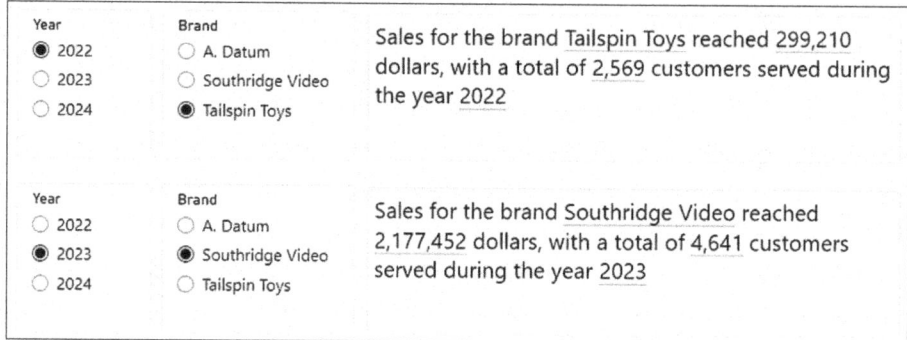

In this narrative visual object, note how the narratives are updated when selecting different years and brands.

 IMPORTANT Slicers must be set to single select for the narrative to correctly reflect dynamic values.

This visual object enriches reports with dynamic narratives, facilitating the interpretation of results without losing connection with the underlying data.

Skills review

In this chapter, you learned how to

- Use maps to visualize geographic data by configuring data categories, applying styles and layers, and enabling features like clustered bubbles, polygons, and traffic overlays to enrich spatial analysis.

- Compare variables with scatter charts by combining quantitative axes, customizing markers, and using reference lines, shaded areas, and play axes to reveal patterns and relationships across multiple dimensions.

- Break down measures with decomposition trees by dynamically exploring contributions across categories, applying conditional formatting, and identifying key drivers without relying on fixed hierarchies.

- Display multiple comparisons using small multiples by segmenting visuals into panels that maintain consistency while allowing side-by-side analysis, with layout and scale adjustments to support cognitive flow.

- Analyze trends, forecast values, and detect anomalies with line charts by enabling statistical tools that summarize behavior, project future outcomes, and highlight deviations, using configurable parameters for precision.

- Summarize key metrics using narrative text by integrating dynamic values into written explanations, allowing contextual storytelling that adapts to user selections and complements visual reporting.

8

Practice tasks

Before you can complete these tasks, you must copy the book's practice files to your computer. The practice files for these tasks are in the PowerBISBS\C07 folder.

Visualize geographic data using maps

Configure data categories for geographic fields:

1. Go to Table view and select the **State** column from the Customer table.

2. In the Columns tools tab, set Data category to **State** or **Province**.

3. Select the Latitude and Longitude columns and set their Data category to **Latitude** and **Longitude**, respectively.

4. Reflect: Why is it important to set the correct data category before adding to a map?

Compare variables and reveal patterns with scatter charts

Create a scatter chart with multiple variables:

1. Add a scatter chart visual to the report.

2. Assign **Sales Amount** to the X-axis and **Margin** to the Y-axis.

3. Add **CategoryName** to the Values field.

4. In the Format pane, change marker shape to **diamond** and color to **green**.

5. Enable **Average line** for the Margin (Y-axis).

6. Enable **Data label**, set their horizontal orientation to **right**, and label style to **both**.

7. Reflect: How does the average line help interpret scatter chart data?

Break down measures and explore categories with decomposition trees

Build a decomposition tree by category:

1. Add a decomposition true visual to the report.

2. Use **Sales Amount** as the Analyze field.

3. Add **Continent** and **Countryfull** to the Explain by section.

4. Select **Europe** and expand it by **Low** value.

5. Drill down to CountryFull to see which countries contribute the least to sales.

6. Reflect: How does this visual help pinpoint underperforming regions?

Display multiple comparisons using small multiples

Create small multiples by country:

1. Add a stacked column chart to the report.

2. Place **Monthshort** on the X-axis and **Sales Amount** on the Y-axis.

3. Add **CountryFull** to the Small multiples field.

4. Adjust the layout: columns to **4**, padding to **6**, border color to **#CCCCCC**, and background color to **#F2F2F2**.

5. Reflect: How does using small multiples help compare performance across countries while maintaining visual consistency and reducing cognitive load?

Analyze trends, forecast values, and detect anomalies using line charts

Add a trend line to a line chart:

1. Add a line chart visual to the report.

2. Place **Date** on the X-axis and **Sales Amount** on the Y-axis.

3. Enable **Trend line**.

4. Add a Slicer visual to the report, place **Year** in the slicer field, and select **2024**.

5. Reflect: With the slicer set to 2024, what does the trend line reveal about the overall direction compared to the month-by-month values?

Summarize key metrics using narrative text

Create a narrative with dynamic values:

1. Add a narrative visual object to the report.

2. Enter **For the occupation [Occupation – dynamic value], the margin reached [Margin – dynamic value], with total sales of [Sales Amount – dynamic value] achieved in [Year – dynamic value]**.

3. Select **Format Margin** as a percentage and **Sales Amount** as currency.

4. Rename them to **#Margin** and **#Sales Amount** for reuse.

5. Add slicers for Occupation and Year, and set both to **Single select**.

6. Select different occupations and years in the slicers and observe how the narrative updates.

7. Reflect: How can a dynamic text narrative convey key insights differently from a visual chart?

Enhancing reports

Practice files

You will need to use the practice files provided with this chapter to complete the practice tasks.

When you're creating reports in Power BI, much of your attention is focused on each of the visual objects that make up the report. And yes, together they allow you to capture your findings or what you are trying to communicate. But that's not all. Complementary features help improve the design from a functional and aesthetic point of view, as well as the user experience when interacting with them.

This stage is not limited to creating visualizations but also to designing reports that invite exploration, guide the user, and adapt to their needs—from applying custom themes, contextual pages to provide details, interactivity using buttons, tooltips to increase data comprehension, bookmarks that fix behaviors, and slicers that dynamically modify calculations in visual objects, to adapting layouts for mobile experiences. These techniques form the core of what you will learn in this chapter.

In this chapter

- Apply themes to shape visual identity

- Navigate into details using drillthrough pages

- Trigger actions via buttons, shapes, and images

- Show insights with tooltips and field parameters

- Control report behavior by applying bookmarks

- Adapt layouts for mobile experiences

Apply themes to shape visual identity

Themes allow you to modify the visual appearance of a report. They are useful when you need to apply immediate, quick changes and adopt a previously configured design. In Power BI Desktop, you can adjust the main items, but if you require more detailed, granular control, you can also adjust them through a JSON format document.

To set a theme in the report, just select the **View** ribbon and choose the theme you prefer.

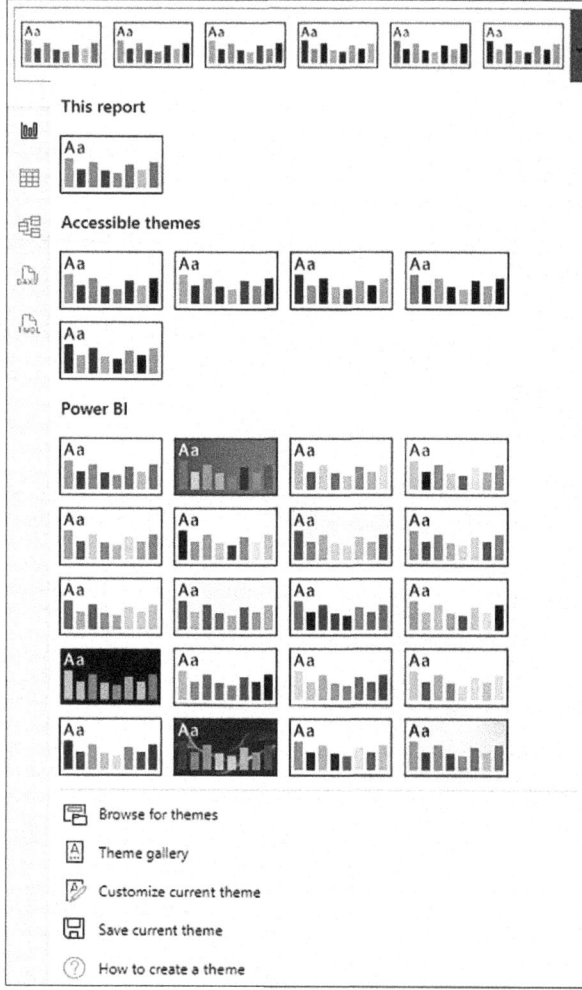

Themes are available for use with a single click.

When you select a theme, various items are automatically modified, such as colors, fonts, report background, visual object borders, and the filter pane, to name a few.

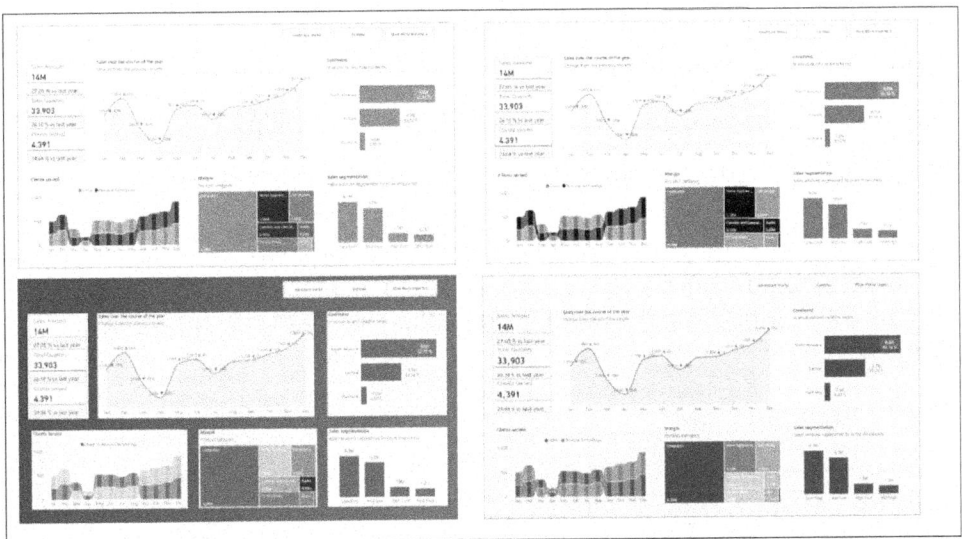

The same report is shown with different themes.

9

However, in some situations you might need to adjust a theme. To do this, in the list of available themes, select **Customize current theme**.

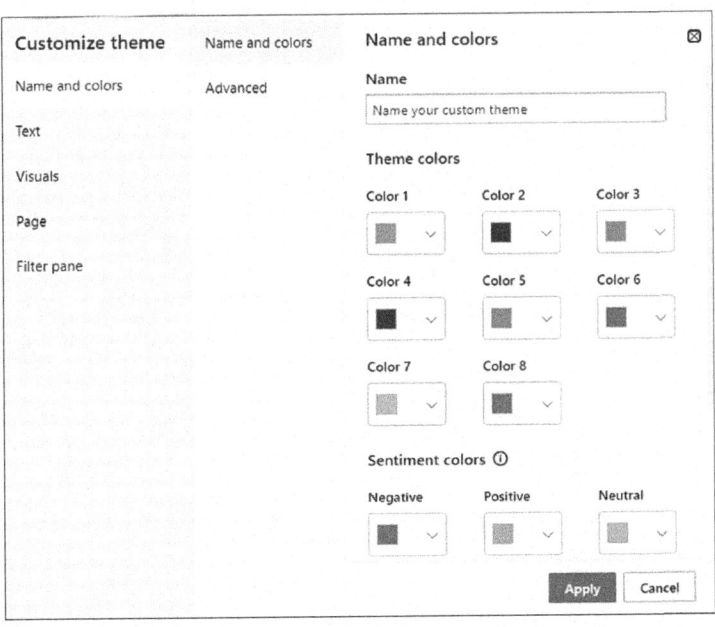

The Customize theme panel.

The settings are as follows:

- **Name and colors:** Assigns the theme name and color settings for the theme, sentiment colors, divergent colors, and structural colors.

- **Text:** Includes font family, size, and color.

- **Visuals:** Includes backgrounds, borders, header, and tooltips.

- **Page:** Includes page elements such as wallpaper and background.

- **Filter pane:** Includes settings for background color, transparency, font, color, size, and cards.

Now, do the following: Using the report you created in Chapter 7, apply the following changes:

- Name: **Arctic Executive**

- Theme Colors: **Color 1: #7093B8, Color 2: #6083C5, Color 3: #96B8DB, Color 4: #0096C7, Color 5: #00A3D1, Color 6: #00B4D8, Color 7: #67C7FF, Color 8: #80D0FF.**

- Visuals: **Background color: #FCFBFA, Border Color #F0F0F0 (Radius: 3 px).**

- Page: **Wallpaper color #FEFBF6 at 75% transparency, Page background color #FEFBF6 at 0% transparency.**

You will get the result shown in the following image.

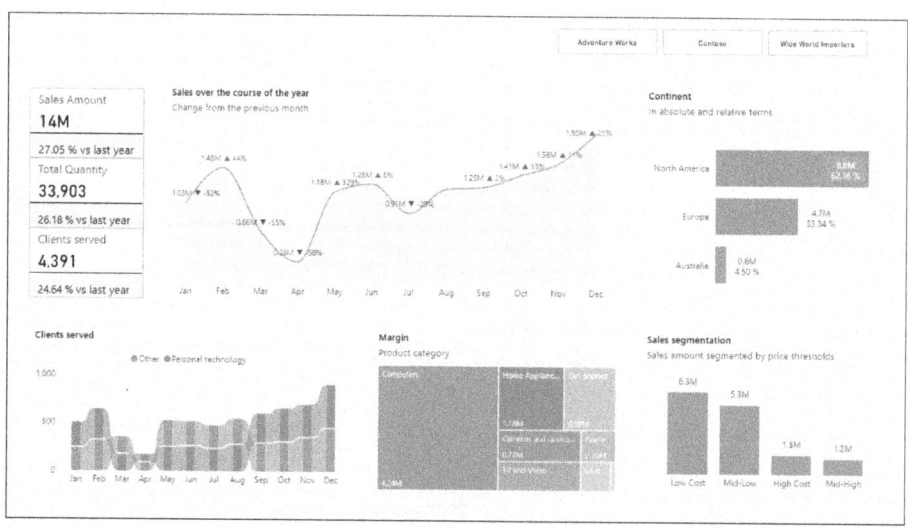

The report will look like this after you make changes to the theme.

The settings you applied have been saved in a new theme called Arctic Executive. It now will appear in the list of themes.

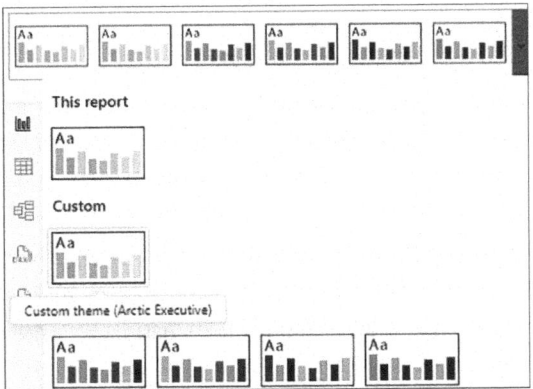

The report now uses the Arctic Executive custom theme.

> ✅ **TIP** If you want to apply this theme to other reports, you can export it using the **Save current theme** option, which will create a file with a JSON extension. You can then import that file into another report by selecting **Browser** for themes.

Another alternative is to use themes from the community. In the Themes Gallery, you will find a variety of designs that allow you to streamline the process.

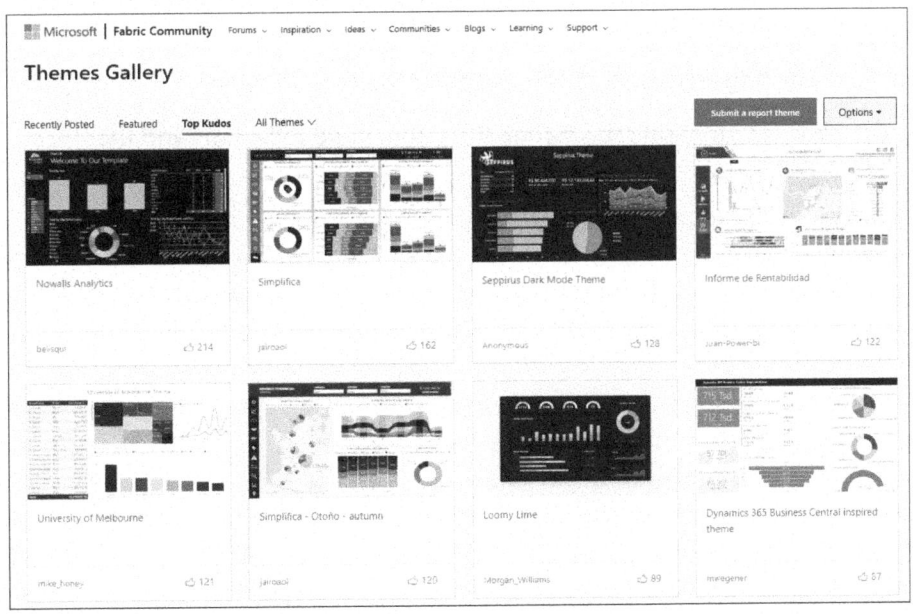

The Themes Gallery on the Microsoft website provides a showcase of custom themes.

9

Using themes not only offers an advantage when speed and default settings are required to streamline design times but also reveals the variety of modifiable elements within a report.

Navigate into details using drillthrough pages

A report can have one or multiple pages. This is common because not all visual objects fit on a single page and, in other cases, because each page functions as a conceptual separation of what is being displayed, allowing each set of visuals to respond to a specific intention.

Drillthrough pages is a feature that converts a report page into a landing page, *while maintaining the filters applied to the source page*. These pages are usually hidden and activated by user interactions with visual objects; they are not pages that are visited or activated like conventional pages.

To create a drillthrough page

1. Create a new page.

2. Choose the table visual object and add the following columns and measures: **Date**, **ProductName**, **Sales Amount**, and **Total Quantity**.

3. Without selecting any visual objects, expand the Format pane.

4. On the Page information tab, change the page name to **Details** and the Page type to **drillthrough**.

5. In the Drill through from section, add the **Purchase Price Category** column.

The Format pane shows the Drillthrough page configuration.

When you define a report page as drillthrough, a left arrow button will appear in the upper-left corner of the report. Its function is to allow you to return to the source page. This button is automatically configured to perform a back action.

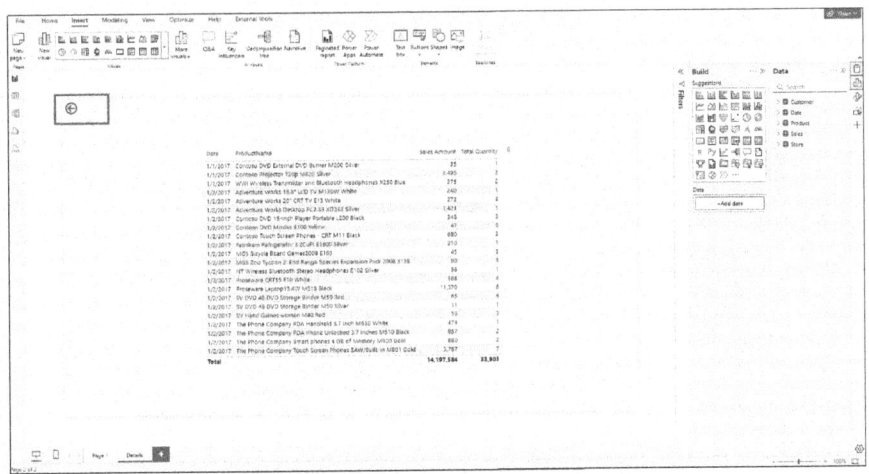

Note the button in the upper left corner of the Report view.

From the source page (Page 1), select the **Adventure Works** brand; then place the cursor over the **Mid-Low** column of the stacked column chart. In less than one second, a floating box, or *tooltip*, will appear where you can select **Drill through > Details**.

9

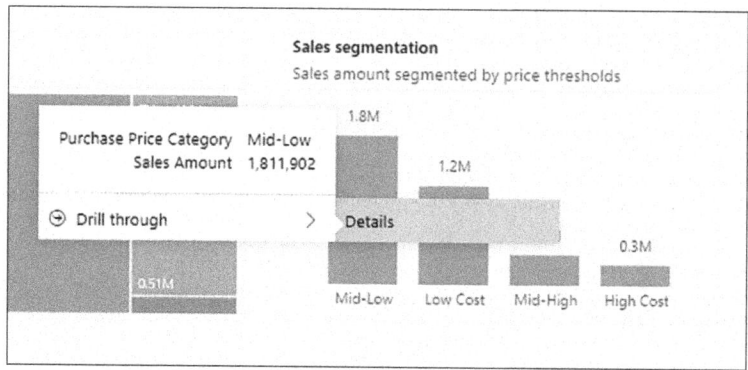

When you hover the cursor over one of the columns in Report view, a tooltip will appear.

The action will take you to the previously created page—in this case, Details. At first, it may seem as though nothing has happened, but when you expand the Filters pane, you will see that the applied filters (Adventure Works, Purchase Price Category Mid-Low, year 2017) are present on the Details page.

 TIP You can also access the drillthrough options by right-clicking the column.

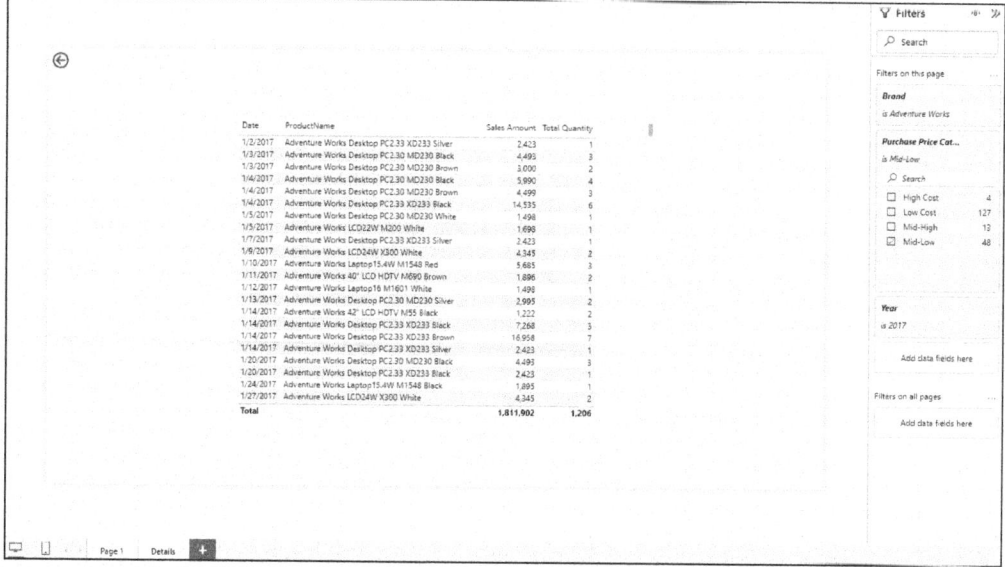

The Details page maintains the filters applied on the source page in the Report view.

A drillthrough page adapts to the context of the filters from the source page. To finish, right-click the name of the Details page and select the **Hide** option. This selection will hide the page when viewing the report in the cloud, but the page will still be available to end users when they activate the drillthrough.

Trigger actions via buttons, shapes, and images

What buttons, shapes, and images have in common as complementary elements in report design is their ability to trigger actions. An action can return to the previous page, as you saw when adding a left arrow when assigning a page as a drillthrough. In other cases, the action can be going to a web page, removing applied filters, or moving to a specific page in the report.

You can find each of these actions by selecting **Insert > Elements**.

This list of buttons shows available elements.

9

Do the following, add the information icon, and apply the following changes:

- Position: **Horizontal: 838 / Vertical: 457**
- Size and style: **Height: 30 / Width: 30**
- Visual border: **off**
- Button style: **Icon > Weight 1 px**
- Action: **on**
- Type: **Web URL**
- Web URL: **https://learn.microsoft.com/en-us/power-bi/support/**
- Tooltip: **on**
- Text: **Need more details? Reach out to our support team.**

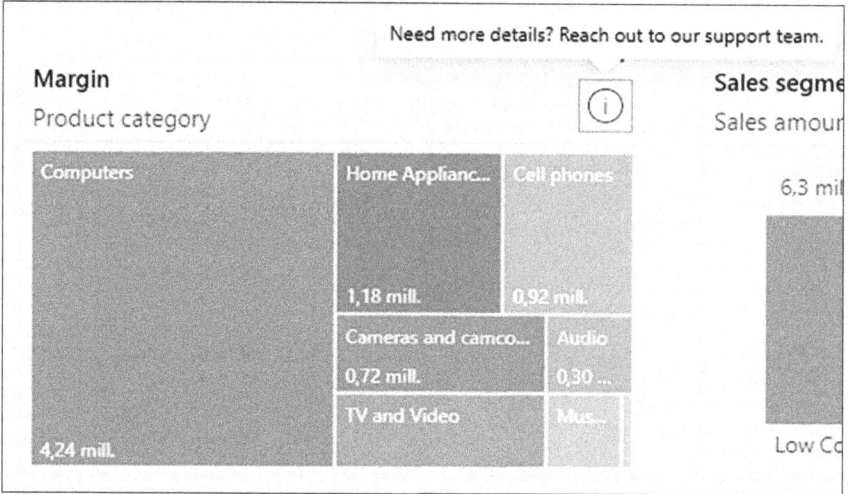

This information icon displays text when the cursor is hovered over it, and when clicked, directs the user to a web page.

Now add a rectangle and apply the following changes:

- Position: **Horizontal: 0 / Vertical: 0**
- Size: **Height: 69 / Width: 1280**
- Shape style: **Fill Color: #FCFBFA, Border: off**
- In the Format menu, select **Send to back** (optional).

And finally, add a text box with the following changes:

- Title: **Business Analysis**

- Font: **Segoe (Bold) 18 px**

- Color: **#666666**

- Subtitle: **Management summary**

- Font: **Segoe UI 11 px**

- Size: **Height: 76 / Width: 259**

- Position: **Horizontal: 22 / Vertical: 4**

- Background: **off**

- Visual border: **off**

- In the Format menu, select **Bring to front** (optional).

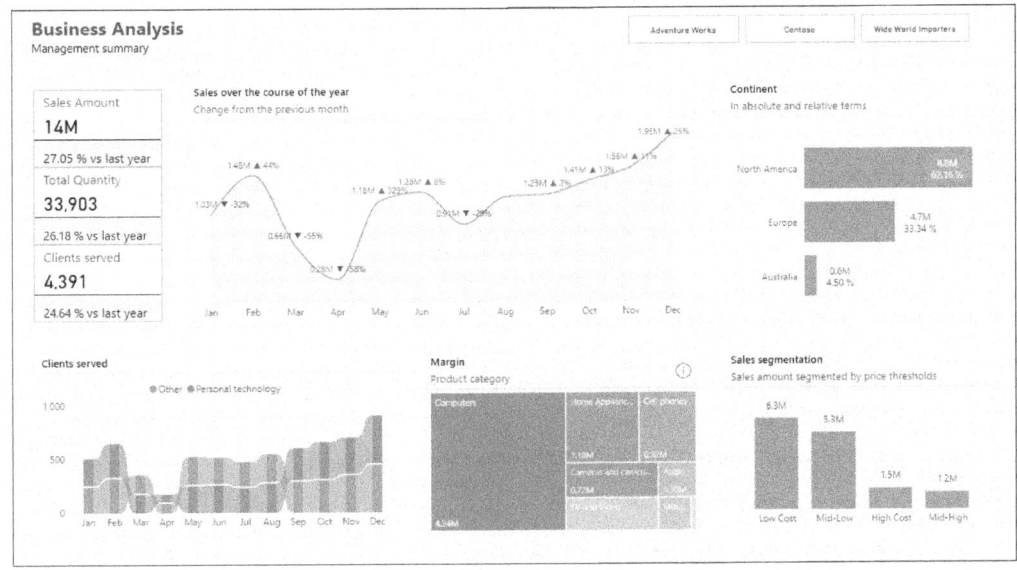

The report now contains a title, subtitle, and a rectangle separating the top elements above the visual objects.

Each of these changes helps improve the user experience. The use of complementary elements and their actions allows for minor adjustments, but together they make a big difference.

Show insights with tooltips and field parameters

You are already familiar with tooltips, which are the pop-up boxes that automatically appear when you hover your cursor over the elements of a visual object. They show the results of the intersection between categorical and continuous values. They also allow you to activate drillthrough functions.

Most visual objects have a specific section where you can add measures or quantitative elements to be displayed in the tooltip.

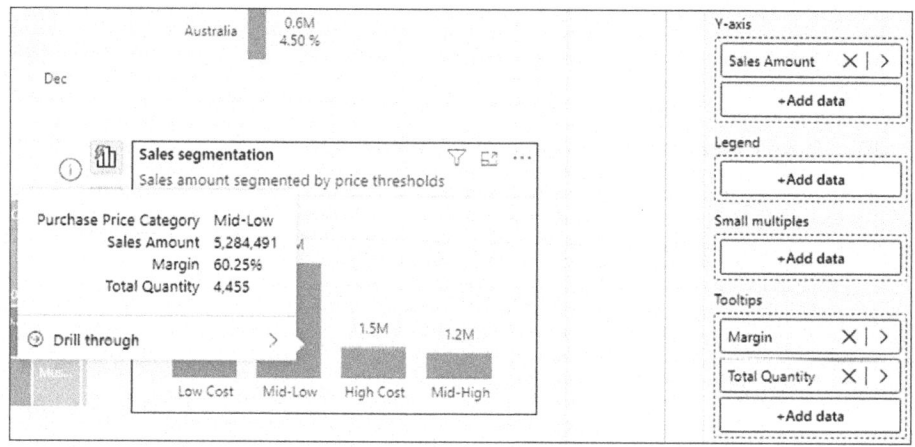

When the cursor is on the Mid-Low classification showing the Sales Amount measure, the resulting tooltip shows the Margin and Total Quantity measures.

However, tooltips can be created from scratch, customized, and adapted to the unique context of each visual object. This adaptability makes them an ideal feature when you need to provide more context for a result without having to use other visual objects.

To create a custom tooltip

1. Create a new page.

2. In the Page information section of the Format pane, change the page name to **Tooltip MoM**, and change the Page Type to **Tooltip**.

3. Adjust the page zoom in the lower right corner (optional).

4. Add a Stacked bar chart and assign the **CategoryName** column (Y-axis) and the **Sales Amount** measure (X-axis).

5. Enable data labels and details with the **Sales Amount MoM** measure.

6. Change the color of the Sales Amount MoM measure using the same conditional formatting applied to the line chart seen in Chapter 7.

7. Expand the Filter pane, select **CategoryName**, and assign a Top N filter showing the **Top 5 by Sales Amount** value.

8. On the initial page, select the line chart and in the Format pane, select **Properties > Tooltips > Type: Report page > Page: Tooltip MoM**.

The result will look like the following image:

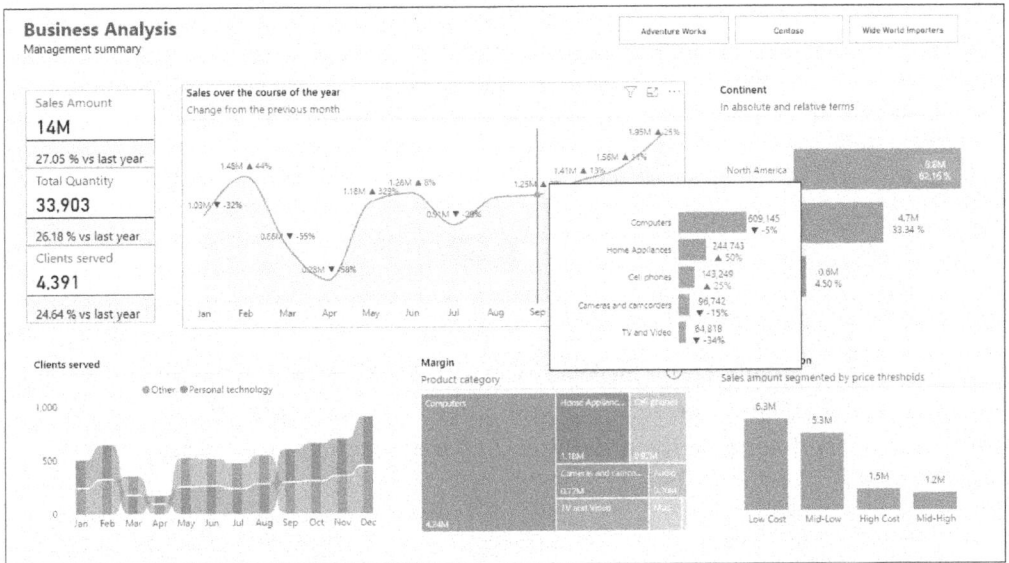

The line chart features a custom tooltip for each month, showing the top five product categories according to the Sales Amount metric and detailing the Sales Amount MoM metric with conditional colors.

Now let's make a slight change to the stacked bar chart containing sales by continent. *Field parameters* are another feature that offers dynamism and prevents you from having to duplicate a visual object when you need to show different calculations under the same structure.

To create a field parameter, select **Modeling > New parameter > Fields**.

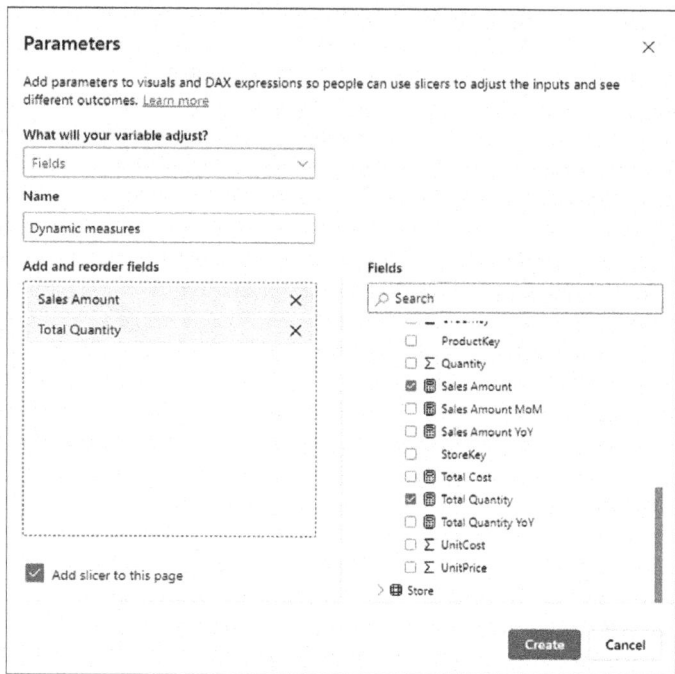

The Field Parameters configuration panel is based on the Sales Amount and Total Quantity measurements.

Name the field parameter **Dynamic Measures** and drag the Sales Amount and Total Quantity measures. When you select **Create**, a new table is generated in the model with columns that determine the order and source of the measures. This column is used as a field in the slicer.

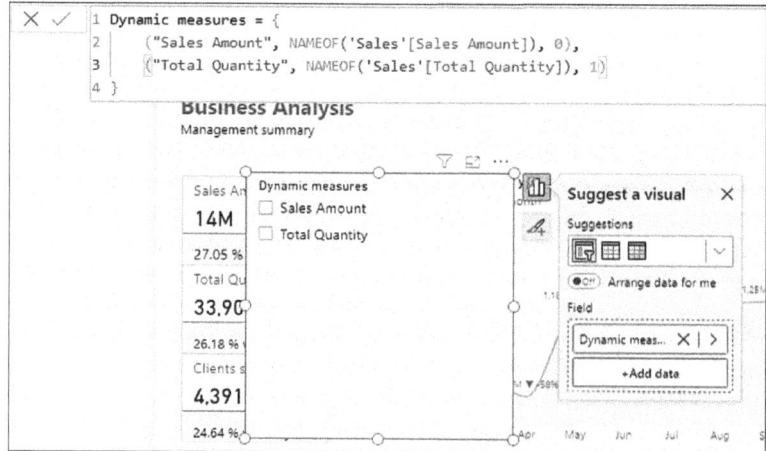

A slicer is automatically created with the selected measures. Note the syntax generated in DAX from the measures.

Adjust the slicer with the following changes:

- Size: **Height: 46 / Width: 127**
- Position: **Horizontal 1129 / Vertical 98**
- Background: **off**
- Visual border: **off**
- Slicer settings: **Style: Dropdown / Selection: Single select**
- Slicer header: **off**
- Values: **Font 8**

The slicer is then positioned as shown in the following image:

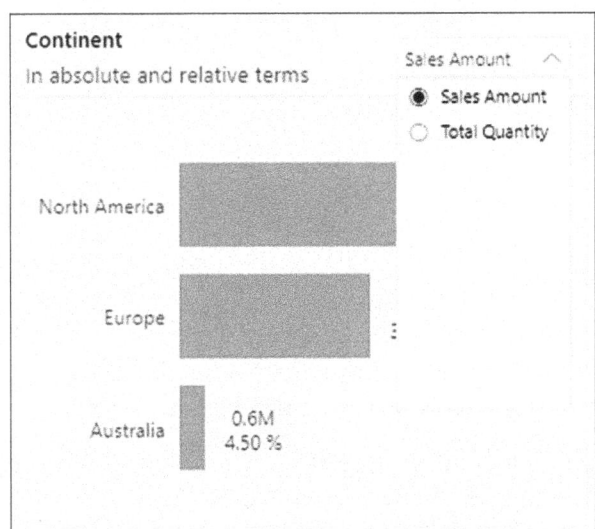

The slicer is configured under a single selection with values from the field parameter.

Finally, for the visual object to change its results according to the slicer, you must replace the Sales Amount measure with the same column that contains the slicer. In this case, it is Dynamic Measures.

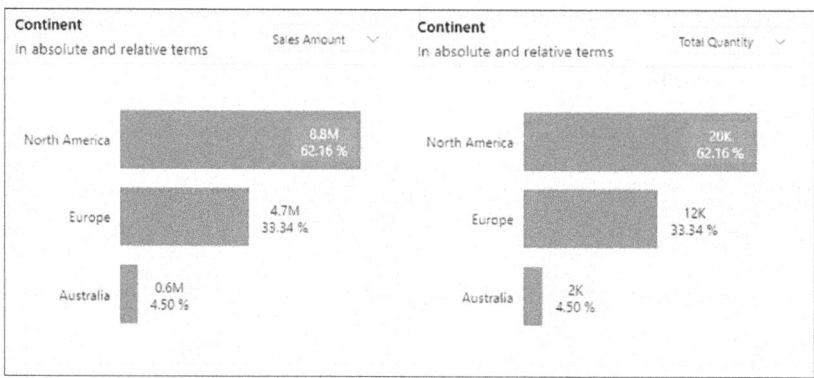

The same visual object—a stacked bar chart—now responds to the selection of the measure from the slicer. Note the different results between Sales Amount and Total Quantity.

The strength of field parameters is not limited to use with measurements, which are quantitative values. They can also be used on categorical elements such as brands, categories, and years. When combined, these parameters open the door to intersections so that a single visual object can have multiple facets.

Control report behavior by applying bookmarks

Bookmarks add an extra layer of customization to reports by saving the layout of visual objects, complementary elements, and applied filters. They are activated through any element that allows an action to be assigned to it, avoiding the need to repeatedly perform the same number of clicks. You can think of them as predefined shortcuts.

To create a bookmark, enable the tab by selecting **View > Bookmarks**.

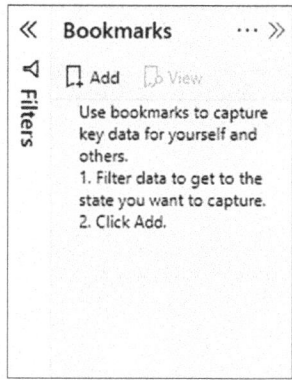

Bookmarks are created and managed in this section of the Bookmarks tab.

Then, add a new bookmark by selecting **Add**. Change the name by right-clicking or double-clicking **Line chart Spotlight**.

A new bookmark called Line chart Spotlight has been created in the Bookmarks tab.

To define the report status that will be assigned to the bookmark

1. Select the **Contoso** brand in the top slicer.

2. Then, in the Stacked column chart, select **Low Cost** and **Mid-Low** by Ctrl+clicking.

3. In the top tab of the line chart, you will see an ellipsis. Select it and then select the **Spotlight** option.

4. Go to the Line chart Spotlight bookmark and select the ellipsis that appears to its right.

5. Select **Update**.

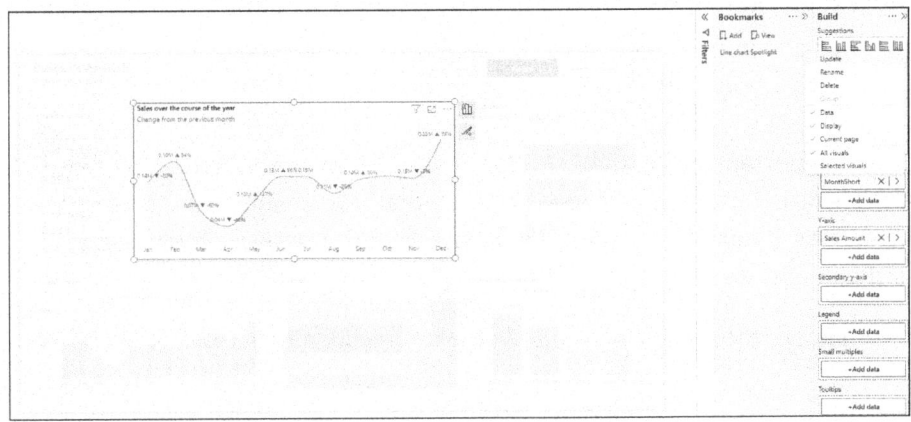

The bookmark isolates the line chart using Spotlight mode.

After the bookmark is configured, it must be assigned to an element. To do this, add a new Bookmark button with the following settings:

- Size: **Height: 35 / Width: 30**

- Position: **Horizontal 1241 / Vertical 14**

- Visual border: **off**

- Button Style: **Icon > Weight 1 px**

- Action: **Type > Bookmark > Bookmark: Line chart Spotlight**

- Tooltip: **on**

- Text: **Spotlight line chart**

The resulting bookmark will look like the following image:

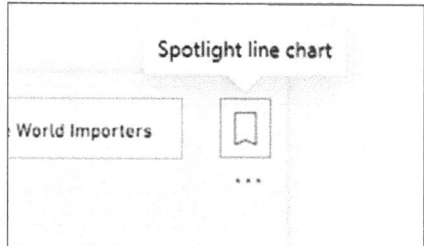

The Bookmark button has been assigned as an action.

When you Ctrl+click, the assigned bookmark will be activated, and you will see the behavior where the line chart is in Spotlight mode, affected by the Contoso mark and the multiple selection of the Low Cost and Mid-Low columns of the Stacked column chart. Note that in Power BI Service, you only need to click to activate the bookmark.

Adapt layouts for mobile experiences

Adaptability is important in design because not all users will necessarily view reports on the same devices. It is important to emphasize that if you want to design a report for mobile devices, it must first exist in the design from the Desktop layout view present in the Report view.

At the bottom left of the screen, you will see the mobile icon to access the Mobile layout view.

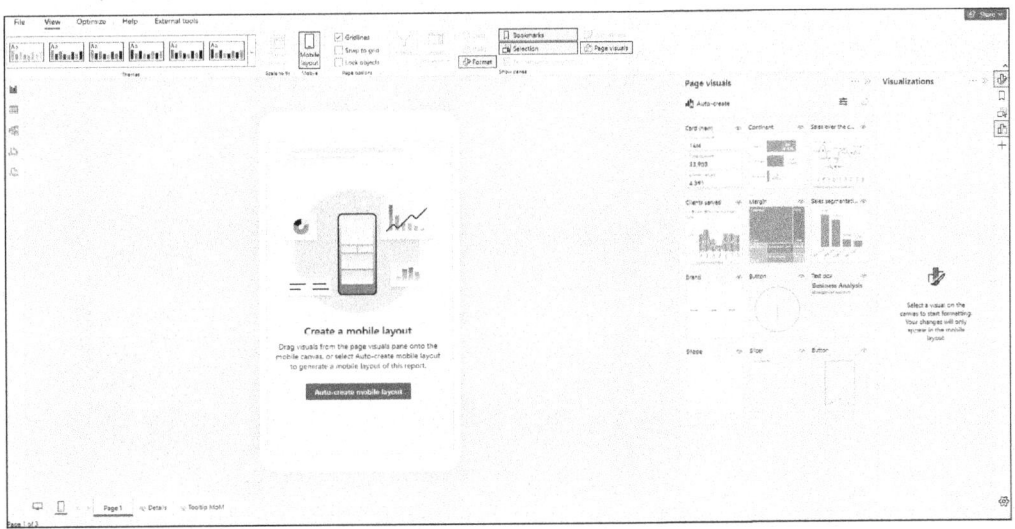

The Mobile layout view displays all visual objects used.

One adjustment option is to select the **Auto-create mobile layout** button, adjusting the visual objects hierarchically based on the original design.

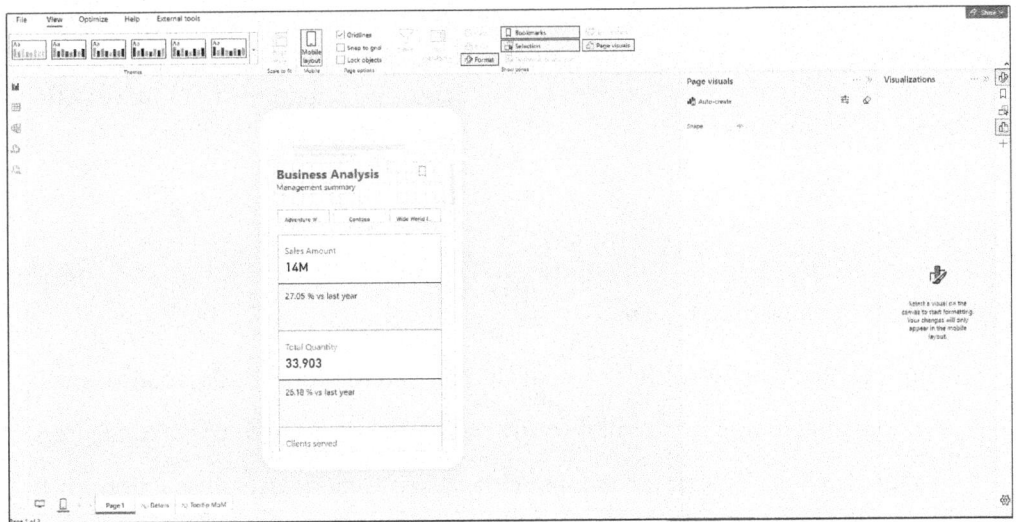

*When you select **Auto-create mobile layout**, the visual objects and elements used are added automatically.*

However, you might need to apply style changes, such as omitting elements, changing cards to a horizontal view, modifying the font size in visual objects, and making other subtle adjustments that help organize elements better for a vertical reading experience.

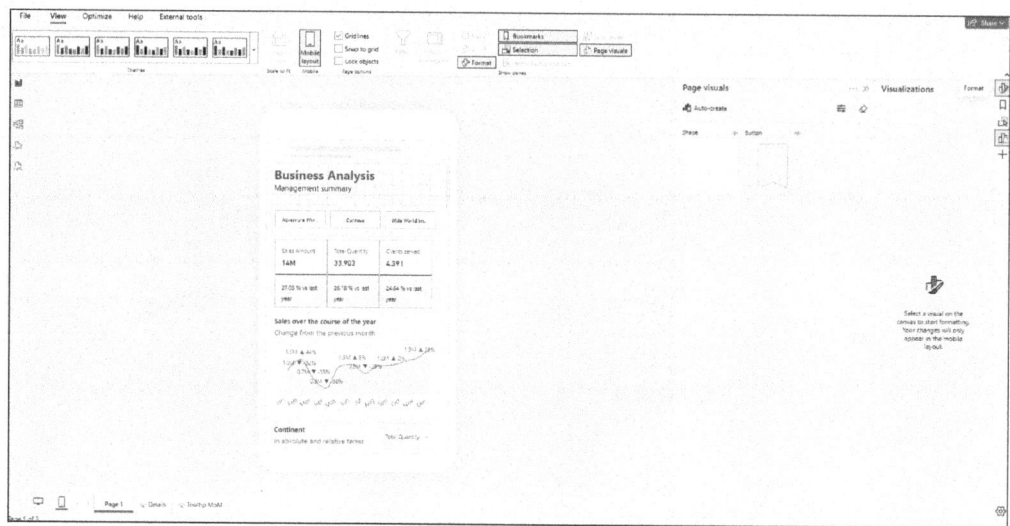

This result will look like this with some changes to orientation and font size.

> **IMPORTANT** Changes applied in the Mobile layout view are independent; they do not affect the original design from the Desktop layout view.

Mobile design has become a structural necessity, and with the tools offered by Power BI Desktop for designing adaptive experiences, it is often one of the final stages when you're designing a report.

Skills review

In this chapter, you learned how to

- Apply report themes to shape visual identity and reinforce design consistency.

- Navigate into detail using drillthrough pages that respond to contextual filters.

- Trigger actions via buttons, shapes, and images to guide user interaction.

- Reveal insights with tooltips and field parameters for dynamic, contextual exploration.

- Control report behavior by applying bookmarks to manage navigation and visibility.

- Adapt layouts for mobile experiences using Power BI responsive design tools.

Practice tasks

Before you can complete these tasks, you must copy the book's practice files to your computer. The practice files for these tasks are in the PowerBISBS\C09 folder.

Apply themes to shape visual identity

Refine the report's appearance by adjusting visual borders:

1. Go to a table's View tab and expand the list of themes.

2. Select **Customize current theme** from the bottom of the list.

3. In the Visuals > Border section, set the border color to **#b2cce0**.

4. Select the brand slicer and disable its border in the Format pane.

5. Reflect: How does switching from a subtle light gray to a more saturated blue affect the visual balance and user perception of the report?

Navigate into details using drillthrough pages

Enable drillthrough from multiple contexts by adding a new field:

1. Go to the Details page already configured for drillthrough.

2. In the Format pane, under Page information, add the **Continent** column in the Drill through from section.

3. Test the drillthrough by right-clicking a continent in the stacked bar chart and selecting **Drill through > Details**.

4. Note: You can use more than one column or attribute to activate drillthrough from different visuals.

Trigger actions via buttons, shapes, and images

Insert a button to reset slicers using a bookmark:

1. Create a bookmark with all slicers cleared and visuals in the default state.

2. Insert the Clear all slicers button from the Insert > Buttons menu, adjust its style to your visual criteria, and position it where it best fits the layout.

3. In the Action section of the Format pane, set the action type to **Bookmark** and choose **Clear all slicers**.

4. Note: Bookmarks can be used to restore the report to its default state, helping users avoid multiple clicks and recover clarity with a single action.

Show insights with tooltips and field parameters

Add contextual detail and expand dynamic measure options:

1. In the Ribbon chart, go to the Tooltip section and add the **Clients served YoY** measure.

2. Modify the DAX syntax of the Dynamic measures table to include the new entry: **Dynamic measures = { ("Sales Amount", NAMEOF('Sales'[Sales Amount]), 0), ("Total Quantity", NAMEOF('Sales'[Total Quantity]), 1), ("Margin", NAMEOF('Sales'[Margin $]), 3) }**

3. Note: Each visual can have its own tooltip configuration, and updating the field parameter table automatically adds the new measure to the slicer.

Control report behavior by applying bookmarks

Create a bookmark with specific selections applied:

1. Select the brands Adventure Works and Contoso from the top slicer.

2. Create a bookmark and name it **Adventure & Contoso View**.

3. Select **Update** in the Bookmark pane to save the current filter state.

Adapt layouts for mobile experiences

Design a mobile layout that fits without scrolling:

1. Go to the View tab and select **Mobile layout**.

2. Add only the title, subtitle, Card (New) visual, and the line chart.

3. Resize and position the elements to fit the vertical canvas, avoiding scroll and preserving readability.

Publishing and sharing reports

Practice files

No practice files are necessary to complete the practice tasks in this chapter.

After you finish building your report in Power BI Desktop, the next step is to make it accessible to others in your organization. To do so, you might consider sending them the .pbix file. Although this method may seem practical, it is not recommended, especially if the report contains sensitive data or if you plan to update it and collaborate on the report regularly.

Sharing .pbix files can lead to version control issues and limit access to key features such as a scheduled refresh, data security, collaborative workspaces, or mobile access. For these reasons, publishing to the Power BI Service is considered a best practice to ensure control, consistency, and scalability across the organization.

In this chapter, you will learn how to publish reports from the Power BI Desktop to the Power BI Service, manage permissions, configure scheduled data refreshes, and explore different methods for sharing and collaborating within the Power BI Service.

In this chapter

- Explore the Power BI Service
- Schedule data refreshes
- Collaborate and share in the Power BI Service

Explore the Power BI Service

The Power BI Service is a cloud-based platform where reports, dashboards, and semantic models can be securely stored, accessed, and shared. It allows business users to consume data through a browser or mobile app without needing Power BI Desktop.

Publishing to the Power BI Service enables you to

- Secure sharing with role-based access and row-level security.
- Schedule automatic data refreshes.
- Collaborate with others in shared workspaces.
- Build dashboards that combine multiple reports.
- Have mobile access from anywhere using the Power BI mobile app.
- Monitor usage and audit report access.

Key Power BI Service concepts

Before you begin publishing and sharing reports, it is important to understand three key Power BI concepts: licenses, capacities, and workspaces. These elements determine what you can do in Power BI, whom you can share content with, and how your content is stored and accessed.

Licenses and subscriptions

To publish and collaborate in the Power BI Service (now part of Microsoft Fabric), you need a Power BI account with the appropriate license. Three main licensing options are available:

- **Power BI Pro:** This license is required to publish reports to shared workspaces, collaborate with others, and access content shared by colleagues.

 TIP All users involved in collaboration must have a Pro license.

- **Power BI Premium Per User (PPU):** This license includes all Pro capabilities, plus access to premium features such as larger models, advanced AI, higher refresh rates, and other capabilities.

 TIP All users accessing PPU content must also have a PPU license.

- **Microsoft Fabric capacity (F SKUs):** A capacity is a pool of dedicated resources that provide enhanced performance, scalability, and sharing capabilities across Power BI and other Microsoft Fabric workloads.

 TIP If your organization has a Premium capacity subscription (Fabric capacity of SKU F64 or higher), Pro and PPU users can invite free users to workspaces hosted in that capacity. With the appropriate permissions, free users can also create, collaborate, share, and use advanced Power BI features.

⚠ **IMPORTANT** As of January 1, 2025, Power BI Premium SKUs have been retired. Premium functionality is now fully integrated into Microsoft Fabric. The equivalent of Power BI Premium capacities is a Fabric capacity SKU of F64 or higher.

10

Capacities

A *capacity* is a collection of resources, such as memory and processing power, which determines the amount of computation power available:

- **Shared capacity:** Used across multiple organizations; suitable for Pro and PPU scenarios

- **Reserved capacity:** Dedicated to a single organization; required for free users to access shared content

Workspaces

Workspaces are collaborative containers where you can store and manage content such as reports, dashboards, semantic models, and paginated reports.

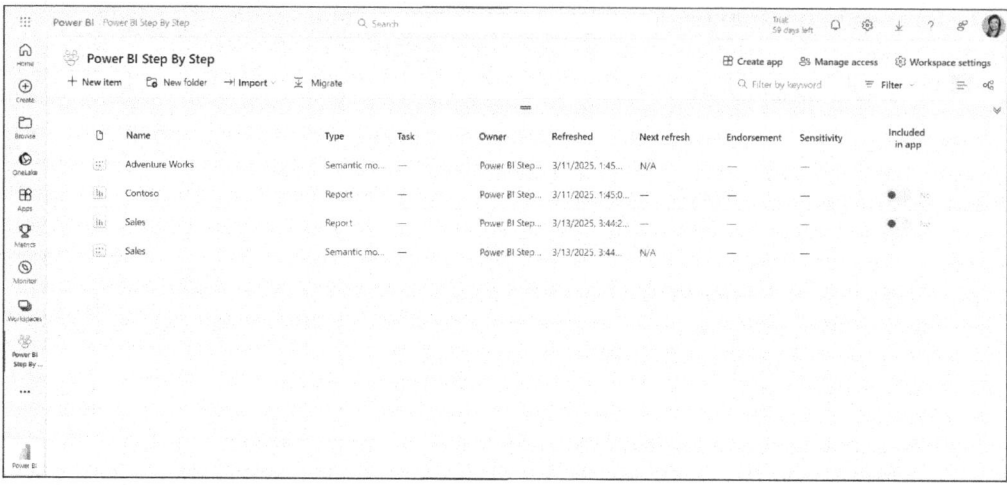

A workspace in the Power BI Service.

The two types of workspaces are

- **My workspace:** This workspace is your personal area for private content. Only you have access.

- **Shared workspaces:** In collaborative environments, you can work with teammates on shared content.

Set up an account in the Power BI Service

To use the Power BI Service, you need to sign in with a work or school account that has been enabled for Power BI. This account allows you to access shared content, publish reports, collaborate with others, and manage workspaces and dataflows.

Power BI does not support personal email accounts (like Gmail or Outlook.com) for creating organizational workspaces. You must use an account associated with Microsoft Entra ID.

 TIP If your organization already uses Microsoft 365, you likely have access to Power BI. If not, you can sign up for a free trial of Power BI Pro or Power BI Premium Per User.

To sign in to the Power BI Service

1. Open a web browser and go to https://app.powerbi.com.

2. On the sign-in page, enter your work or school email address.

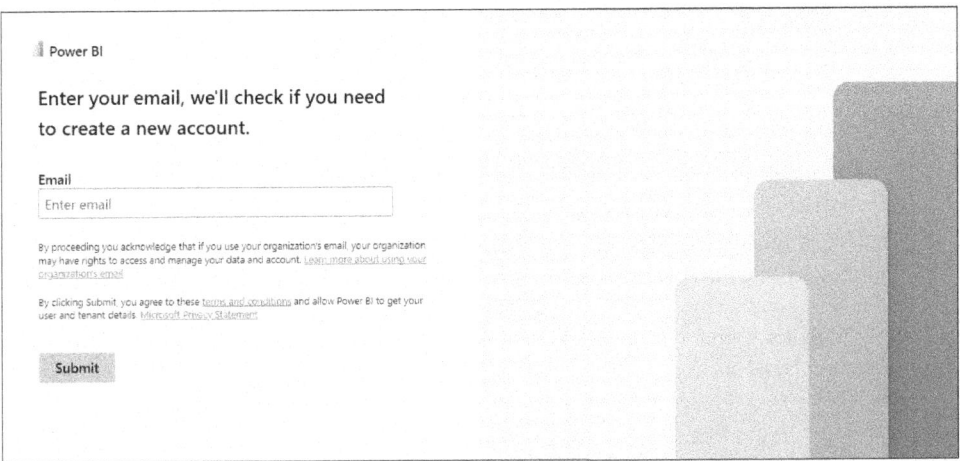

Power BI sign-in page.

3.   Select **Submit**.

4.   Enter your password and then select **Sign in**.

5.   If your organization uses multifactor authentication (MFA), follow the required verification steps.

6.   After you're signed in, you will be redirected to the Power BI Home page.

Publish reports from Power BI Desktop

To publish a report from Power BI Desktop

1.   Open the .pbix report you want to publish.

2.   On the Home ribbon, select **Publish**.

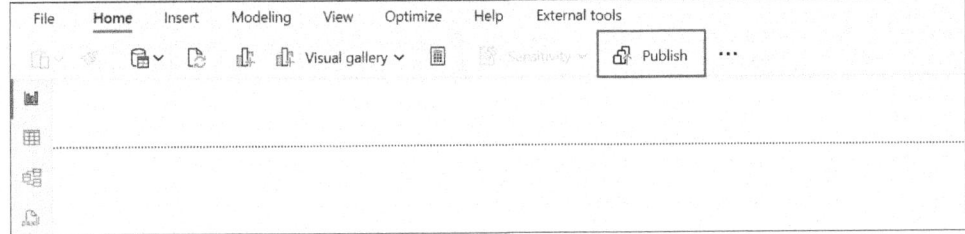

The Power BI Desktop interface with the Publish button highlighted on the Home ribbon.

3.   If prompted, sign in with your Power BI account credentials.

4.   In the Select a destination dialog, choose the target workspace (for example, **My workspace** or a shared workspace).

5. Choose **Select**.

6. Wait for the confirmation message indicating the report was successfully published.

7. Select the link provided to open the report in the Power BI Service.

> **TIP** Perform all data modeling and transformations in Power BI Desktop before publishing. After the report is published to the Power BI Service, you won't be able to fully modify the semantic model or Power Query steps directly in the service. Although a preview feature allows limited model editing in the Power BI Service, most transformations still require Power BI Desktop.

Navigate the Power BI Service

Now that you understand licenses, capacities, workspaces, and how to publish reports, let's take a brief tour of the Power BI Home page in the Power BI Service.

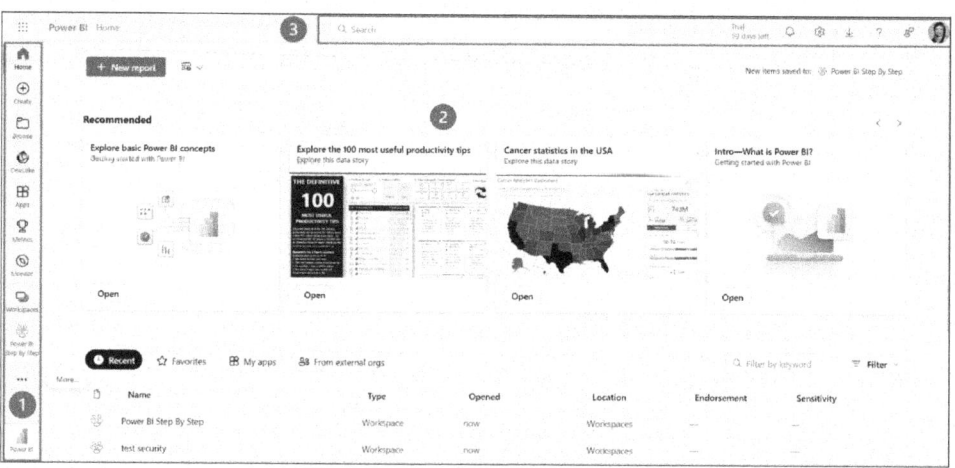

The Power BI Service Home page.

Left Navigation pane: Use the navigation pane in the Power BI Service to quickly access and switch between different components such as workspaces, reports, dashboards, apps, and semantic models.

- Select **Create** to add new content.

- Use **Browse** to find recent, favorite, or shared content.

- Open the **OneLake** data hub to explore organizational data models.

- Access apps, metrics, or your workspaces (both shared and personal).

Below that, the user's personal or selected workspace is pinned for quick access. This vertical menu remains visible throughout the session, making it easy to move between different parts of the platform without losing context.

Canvas area: The canvas area is the central and most dynamic part of the Home page. It displays personalized content such as recommended reports, dashboards, and learning resources based on user activity and organizational preferences.

Top Bar: This area of the Home page provides access to essential global controls, which include a search bar at the center for quickly locating reports, dashboards, or semantic models by name or keyword. On the right side, users can view the remaining days of their trial license, access notifications, open the Help menu, and manage their profile settings.

Schedule data refreshes

After your report is published to the Power BI Service, keeping the data up-to-date is essential. You can configure a scheduled refresh so that Power BI automatically connects to your data source and refreshes your semantic model at regular intervals.

To use a scheduled refresh, your semantic model must be connected to a supported data source and stored in a workspace—either an organizational workspace or My workspace. If the data source is on-premises, you'll also need to set up and configure a data gateway.

10

 IMPORTANT Power BI Pro licenses allow up to 8 refreshes per day on shared capacity. If your workspace resides on a Premium capacity, this limit increases to 48 refreshes per day.

Configure a scheduled refresh

To configure a scheduled refresh

1. In the Power BI Service, select **Workspaces** and then select the workspace where your semantic model is published.

2. Hover over your semantic model and then click the **More options** (•••) button.

3. Select **Settings** from the menu.

4. In the Semantic models settings page, expand the **Refresh** section.

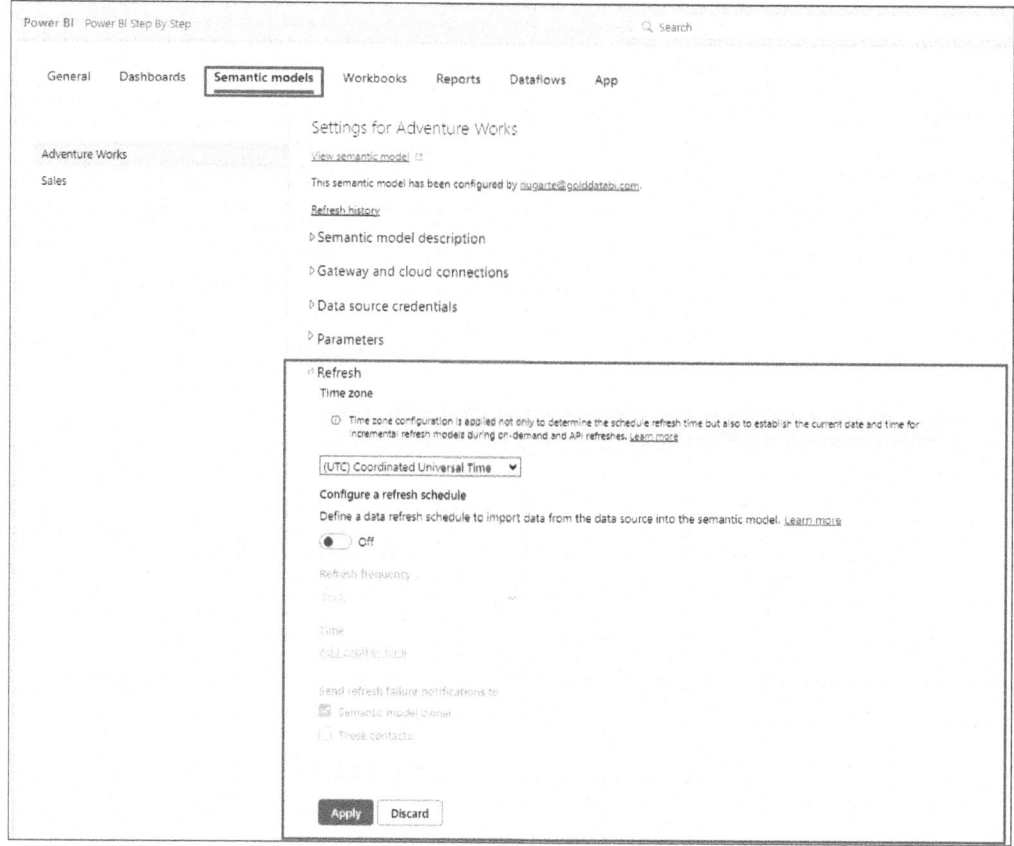

The Refresh section in the Power BI Service semantic model settings.

5. Select your time zone.

6. Turn on the **Configure a refresh schedule** toggle.

7. Under Refresh frequency, choose **Daily** or **Weekly** and then select the time(s) you want the semantic model to refresh.

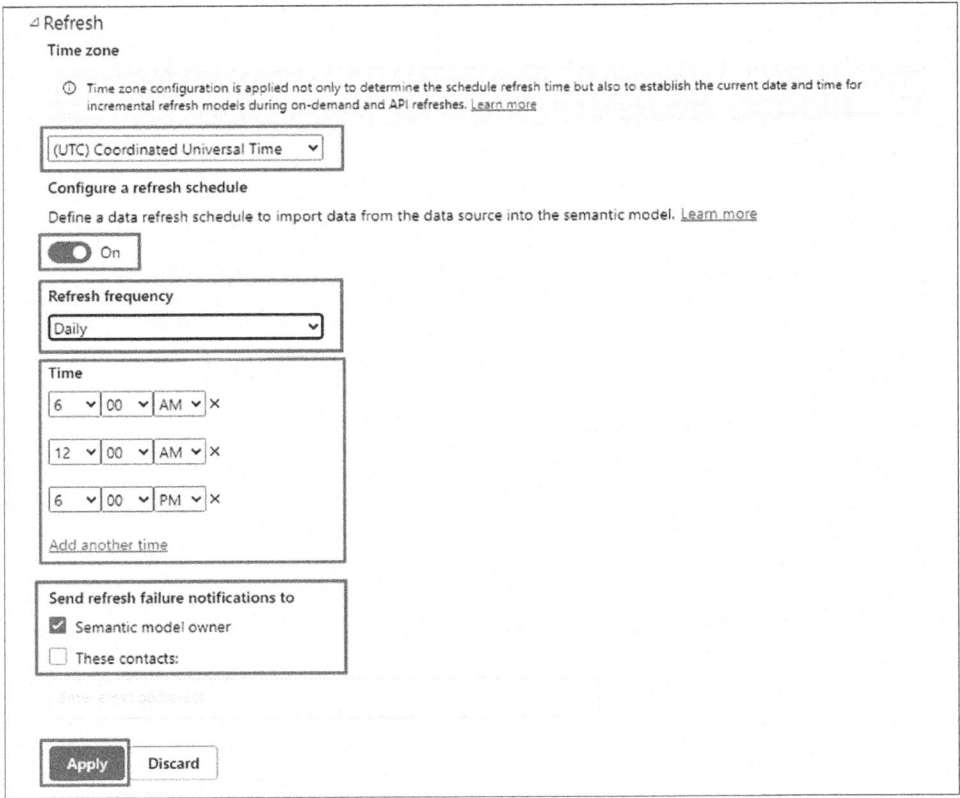

Scheduled refresh settings in the Power BI Service.

8. If needed, enable **Send refresh failure notifications** to receive an email if the refresh fails.

9. Scroll down and select **Apply** to save your settings.

> **TIP** If a semantic model remains inactive (no one opens a report or dashboard using it) for more than two months, Power BI will pause its refresh schedule. Also, Power BI will disable a scheduled refresh after four consecutive failures or if credentials expire.

Collaborate and share in the Power BI Service

Power BI provides several options for securely sharing reports, dashboards, and semantic models, both inside and outside your organization. Depending on the audience and purpose, you can choose from various sharing and collaboration methods.

Share reports and dashboards

You can share Power BI content directly from workspaces or individual items. This way, selected users or groups can view or interact with reports, dashboards, or apps.

To share a report

1. In the Power BI Service, open the report or dashboard you want to share.

2. Select the **Share** icon.

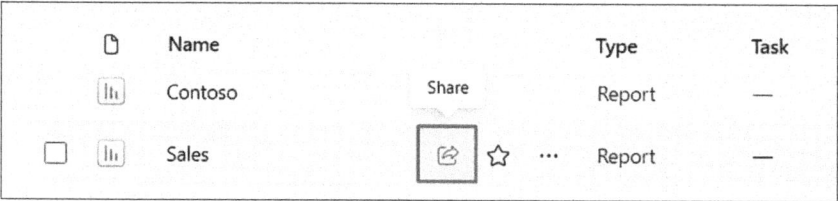

The Share icon next to a Power BI report in a workspace.

3. Copy the link or send it directly via email, Teams, or PowerPoint.

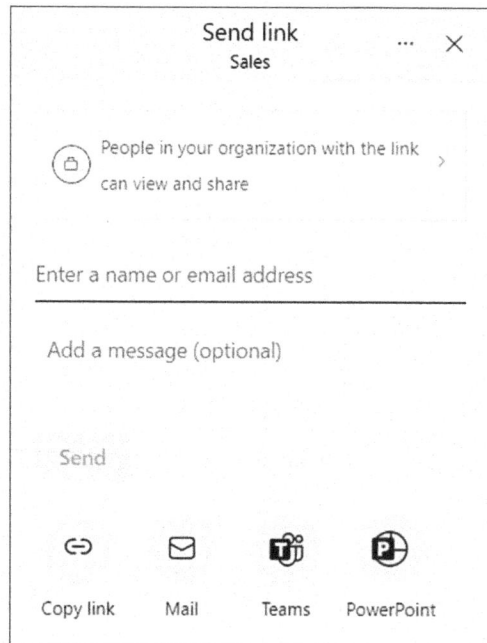

The Send link window in the Power BI Service.

4. Alternatively, select the **Send link** option to open the dialog, and then choose one of the following options:

- People in your organization (broad internal access)

- People with existing access (resend the link)

- Specific people (direct access, including external users)

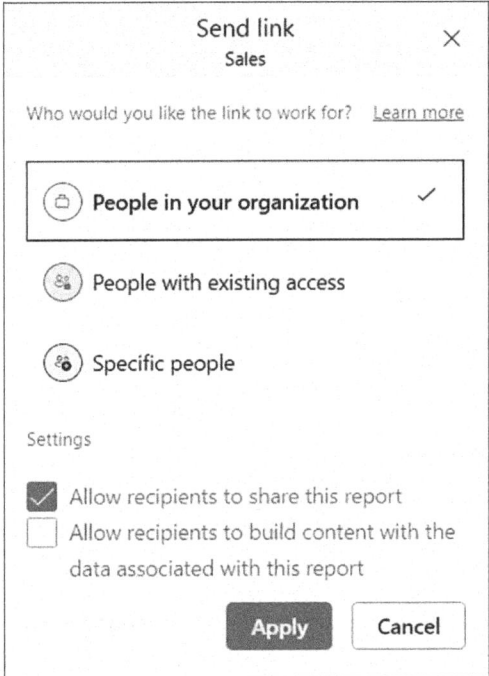

The Send link sharing options in the Power BI Service.

5. Set permissions:

- **Allow recipients to share this report** (recipients can share with others).

- **Allow recipients to build content with the data associated with this report** (recipients can create their own reports from the semantic model).

 IMPORTANT Both sender and recipients must have a Power BI Pro or PPU license, unless the content is hosted in a Premium capacity.

10

Collaborate in workspaces

Workspaces are collaborative environments where teams manage reports, dashboards, and dataflows. To control access and editing, assign one of the following roles:

- **Admin:** This role provides full control over content and permissions.

- **Member:** This role can create, edit, and share content.

- **Contributor:** This role can edit and publish content but cannot manage access or permissions.

- **Viewer:** This role can view all content but cannot make changes.

 TIP Use workspace roles strategically to ensure proper governance and avoid accidental changes or unauthorized sharing.

To add users and assign roles in a Power BI workspace

1. Go to https://app.powerbi.com and sign in.

2. In the left navigation pane, select **Workspaces**.

3. Hover over the workspace where you want to add users and then select the **More options** (•••) button.

 TIP You can also select the workspace name to open it and then select **Manage access** from the ribbon.

4. Select **Workspace access**.

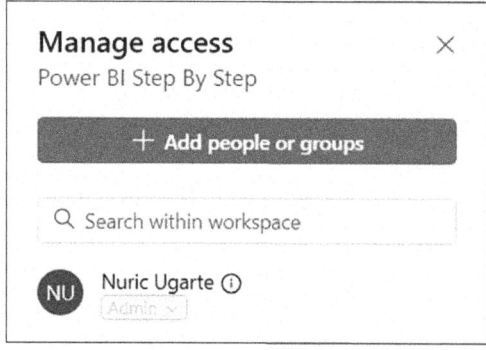

Manage access settings for a workspace in Power BI.

5. Select **Add people or groups**.

6. Enter the names, email addresses, or Microsoft Entra ID groups you want to add.

7. From the dropdown, select the appropriate role (**Admin**, **Member**, **Contributor**, or **Viewer**).

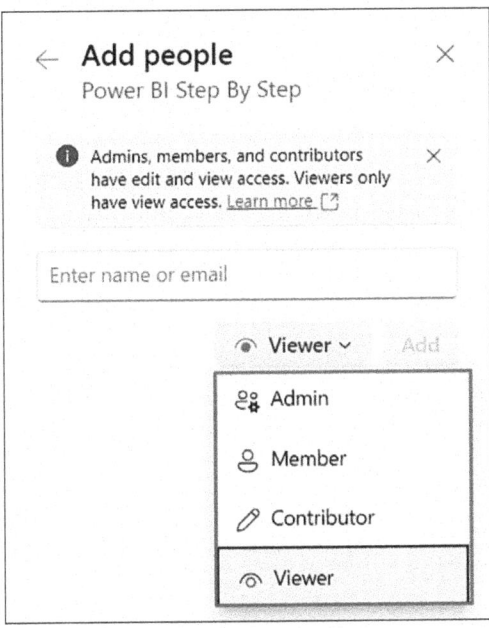

The BI Add people dialog shows workspace role options.

8. Select **Add** to grant access.

Publish and distribute a Power BI app

An *app* is a packaged collection of reports and dashboards that you can publish to a broad audience. It can be available to your whole organization or only to specific people or groups.

> ✓ **TIP** You can define multiple audiences for a Power BI app and customize the content each audience sees. This feature helps report creators and admins manage permissions more efficiently by showing or hiding specific content depending on the audience.

To create and publish an app

1. Go to the workspace that contains the reports and dashboards you want to publish.

2. At the top-right corner of the workspace, select **Create app**.

The Create app button in a Power BI workspace.

3. On the Setup tab, enter a name and description for the app. You can also add a logo and choose a color theme. In Advanced options, you can allow users to save copies of reports.

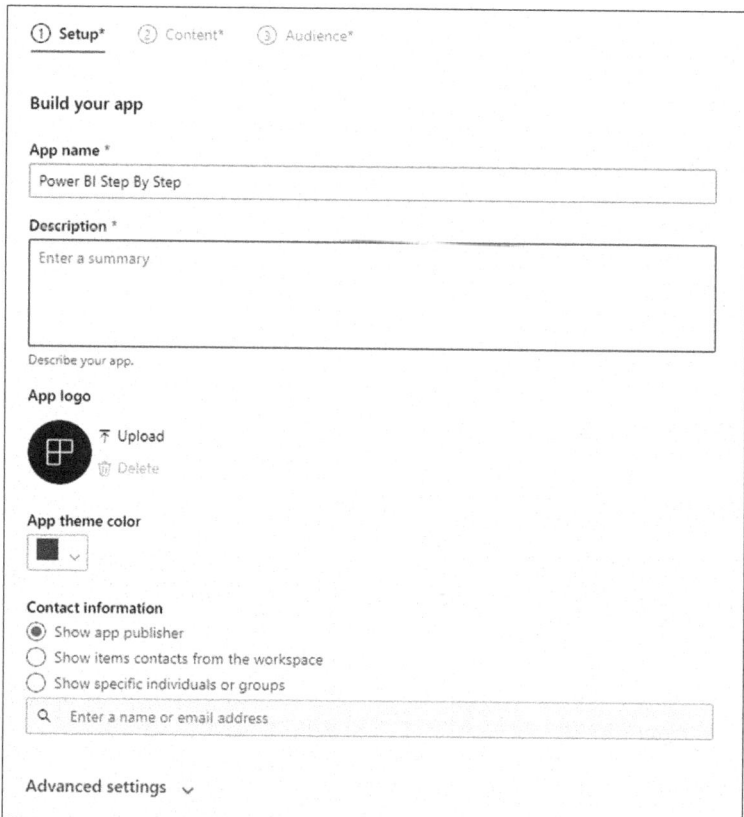

Power BI app setup page.

4. On the Content tab, select **Add content** and select the dashboards and reports you want to include in the app. You can rearrange the order as needed.

5. On the Audience tab, click **New audience** to define different user groups. For each audience, choose which items to show or hide depending on what they need to see.

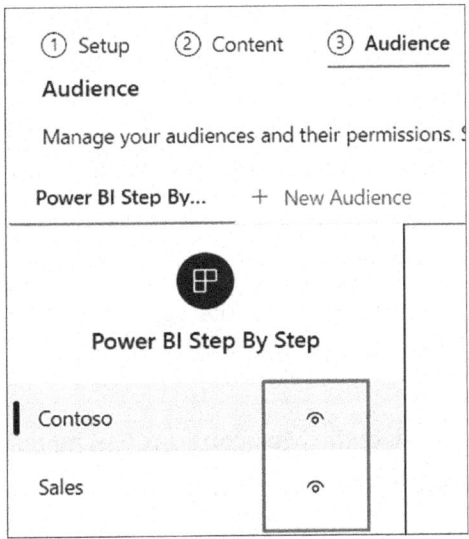

The Audience tab in the app publishing flow.

6. For each audience, specify who can access the app: specific users, groups, or the entire organization. Use Advanced settings if you want users to build or share content based on the app's semantic models.

7. Once everything is configured, select **Publish app**.

Share with external users

Power BI allows secure external sharing using Microsoft Entra B2B (Business-to-Business) accounts. You can enter the guest's email directly in the sharing dialog. External users must sign in to Power BI.

To share externally

1. Invite the external user through Entra B2B.

2. Assign permissions on the report or workspace.

3. Ensure the user has at least a free license (for content in Premium capacity) or a Pro/PPU license otherwise.

10

IMPORTANT Only the specified recipient will have access. Forwarding the link will not grant others access.

Manage permissions

From the sharing dialog or the workspace content list, you can review and update who has access to a report or dashboard.

To manage sharing permissions

1. In the Power BI Service, navigate to the semantic model, report, or dashboard you want to manage.

2. Open the Manage permissions pane using one of the following methods:

   • *Option A:* Select the **Share** button; then in the Send link dialog, select the **More options** (•••) menu in the top-right corner and select **Manage permissions**.

   • *Option B:* In the workspace content list, select the **More options** (•••) menu next to the item, then select **Manage permissions**.

3. In the Manage permissions pane, you can copy or modify existing links, grant or remove direct access, view pending access requests, and explore related content.

 TIP Each report can have a maximum of 1,000 shareable links. To avoid reaching this limit, use direct access for specific users instead of sharing links individually.

Skills review

In this chapter, you learned how to

- Recognize the role of the Power BI Service in report distribution and collaboration.

- Publish reports from Power BI Desktop to the service and identify licensing requirements for sharing content.

- Navigate the Power BI Service interface.

- Configure scheduled data refreshes for semantic models.

- Explore different methods for sharing and collaborating securely within the Power BI Service.

Practice tasks

No practice files are necessary to complete the practice tasks in this chapter.

Explore the Power BI Service

These questions will help you reflect on the key differences between Power BI Desktop and the Power BI Service, as well as understand workspaces and licensing requirements for sharing content:

1. What are the main benefits of using the Power BI Service instead of only working in Power BI Desktop?

2. What are the main risks of distributing reports manually instead of using the Power BI Service?

3. How does My workspace differ from a shared workspace?

4. Which license do you need to publish a report and share it with colleagues in a shared workspace?

Schedule data refreshes

In this task, you'll walk through the steps to configure a scheduled refresh for a semantic model in the Power BI Service:

1. Navigate to the workspace and locate the semantic model for your report.

2. Select **Settings > Refresh** and turn on **Configure a refresh schedule**.

3. Choose an appropriate frequency and time zone.

Collaborate and share in the Power BI Service

These questions are designed to reinforce your understanding of the different sharing methods in Power BI and to help you evaluate collaboration strategies based on common real-world scenarios:

1. List three different ways to share a report in the Power BI Service.

2. Think of a real or hypothetical team scenario: How would you decide between sharing a report directly, adding users to a workspace, or publishing a Power BI app?

3. What risks can arise if workspace roles are not assigned properly?

Creating
dashboards

Practice files

There are no practice files for this chapter.

Dashboards in the Power BI Service are designed to provide a high-level, at-a-glance view of your most important business metrics. They help you monitor data from multiple reports and datasets in a single, consolidated canvas, making it easy to track key performance indicators (KPIs) and trends over time.

Unlike reports, which offer multipage layouts and interactive filtering, dashboards provide curated snapshots of visuals that can be pinned from different reports and semantic models. They are especially useful for executives and decision-makers who need a quick overview of key indicators.

Build a dashboard from a report

Power BI dashboards are powerful tools designed for data monitoring and storytelling. Unlike reports, which offer deep exploration through multiple pages and filters, dashboards provide a high-level, consolidated view of the most important business metrics, pulled from one or more reports or datasets.

In this chapter

- Build a dashboard from a report
- Add comments to a dashboard
- Set data alerts on dashboard tiles
- View insights on dashboard tiles

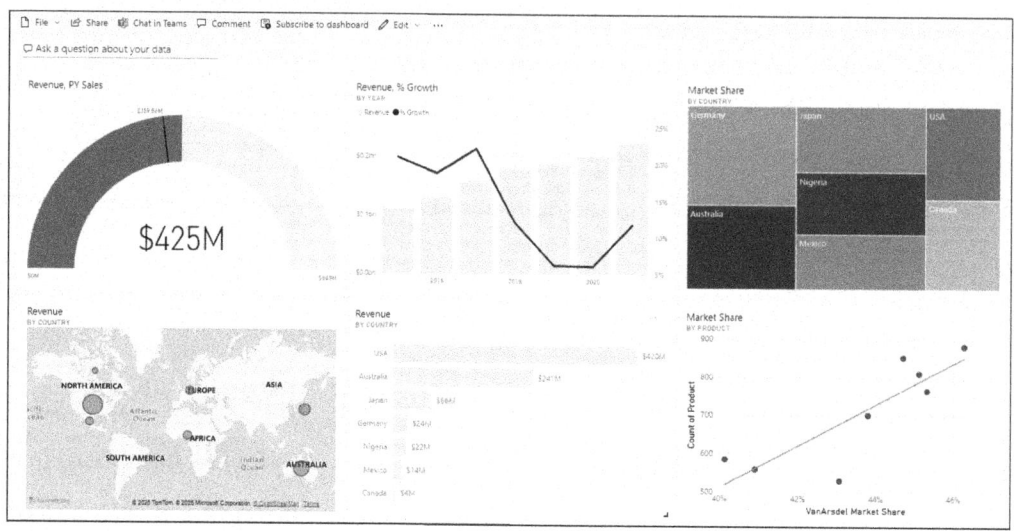

A dashboard in the Power BI Service.

Use dashboards to

- Monitor the health of your business in real time.

- Combine insights from multiple sources.

- Collaborate with colleagues through comments and alerts.

- Enrich storytelling with images, videos, or natural language queries.

> ⚠ **IMPORTANT** Dashboards are a feature of the Power BI Service. You cannot create dashboards in Power BI Desktop or on mobile devices. However, you can view and share dashboards using the Power BI mobile apps.

Understand dashboard tiles

Each item added to a dashboard is called a tile. A *tile* is a snapshot of the data at the time it was pinned. When the underlying dataset refreshes, the tile updates automatically.

Tiles can be pinned from

- Reports

- Excel workbooks on OneDrive for work or school

- Other dashboards

- Power BI Q&A
- Paginated reports in Power BI Report Server
- Quick Insights
- Streaming datasets

You can also add standalone tiles such as images, text boxes, videos, and web content by selecting **Add a tile** from the dashboard menu.

> ⚠ **IMPORTANT** If the visual type used to create the tile changes (for example, from a line chart to a bar chart), the data refreshes, but the visualization type does not. Always verify visuals after pinning.

To pin a tile

1. Open a report in the Power BI Service.

2. Select **Edit** from the ribbon to enter editing mode.

The Edit option in the Power BI Service toolbar.

3. Hover over a visual and select the **pin** icon.

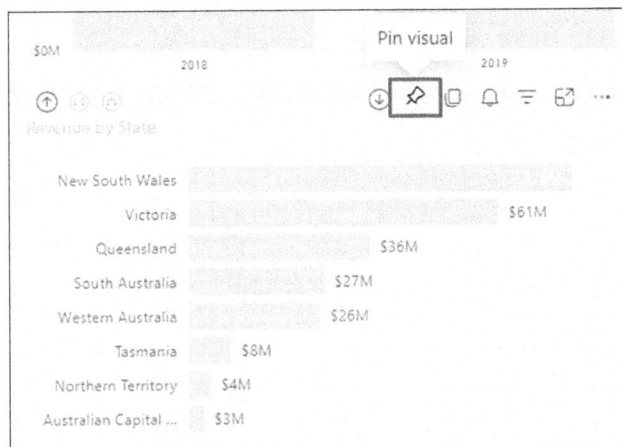

The pin visual icon on a bar chart within a report.

4. In the Pin to dashboard dialog, select **New dashboard** and enter a name. To pin to an existing one, choose **Existing dashboard** and select it from the list.

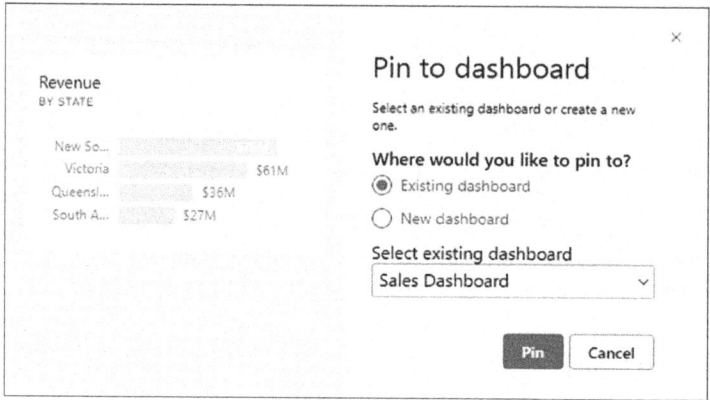

The Pin to dashboard dialog enables you to pin a visual to a dashboard.

5. Select **Pin** and go to the dashboard to view the tile.

6. Pin additional visuals to this dashboard by returning to the report and selecting **Existing dashboard** when prompted.

> ✅ **TIP** Dashboard tiles may not preserve all report formatting, and visuals are resized automatically. To prevent layout issues or rendering problems, avoid using large background images and keep visual formatting simple.

To pin an entire report page

In addition to pinning individual visuals, you can pin an entire report page to a dashboard.

1. Open the report page you want to pin in Editing view.

2. Select the **pin** icon from the top bar. Make sure no visual is selected.

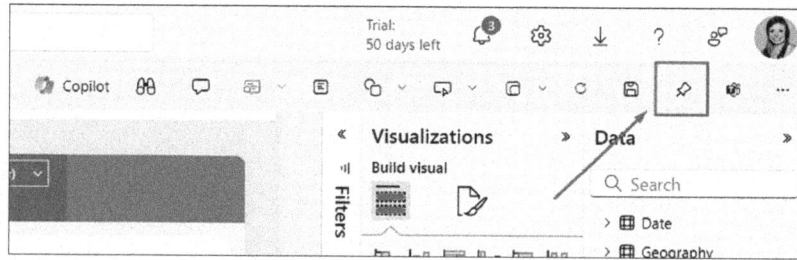

Selecting the option to pin a report page to a dashboard in the Power BI Service.

3. Pin the tile to an existing dashboard or to a new dashboard.

4. Select **Pin live**. A success message will appear near the top-right corner confirming the tile was added.

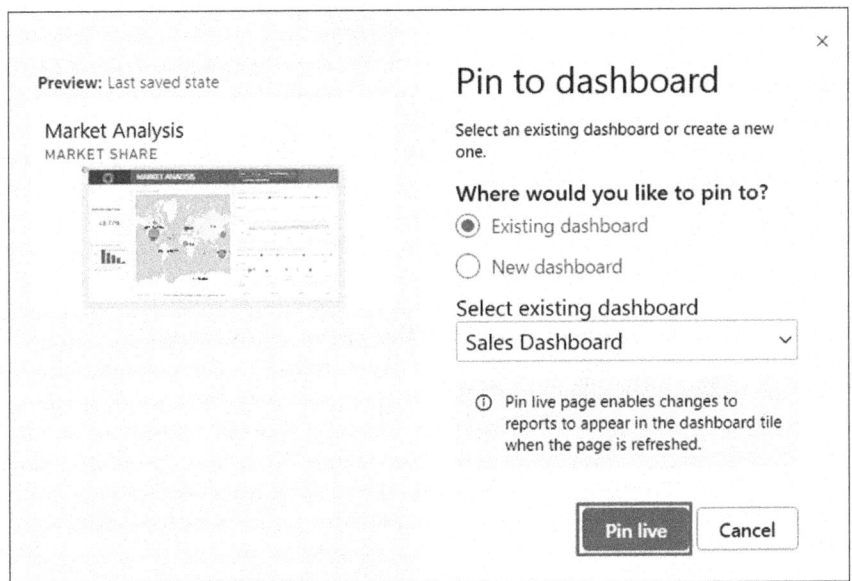

The option to pin a report page as a live tile to a dashboard.

5. Open the dashboard with the new live tile to rename, resize, link, or move it.

 TIP You can interact with the tile directly. Selecting elements like bars or slices will cross-filter and highlight related visuals within the same tile.

 IMPORTANT Report tiles can be viewed on the Power BI mobile apps, but they are not interactive.

Customize tiles

After you have created a dashboard and pinned tiles to it, you can customize its layout and behavior by interacting with the individual tiles. This includes moving, resizing, formatting, and navigating tiles.

11

To move a tile

1. Open a dashboard.

2. Select a tile and drag it to a new location on the dashboard canvas.

To resize a tile

1. Open a dashboard.

2. Hover over the bottom-right corner of the tile. Then drag the diagonal resize handle (a small arrow pointing down and to the right) to adjust its size.

To customize a behavior tile

1. Open a dashboard.

2. Hover over the tile to display the ellipsis (...) in the upper-right corner.

3. Select the ellipsis to open the tile actions menu.

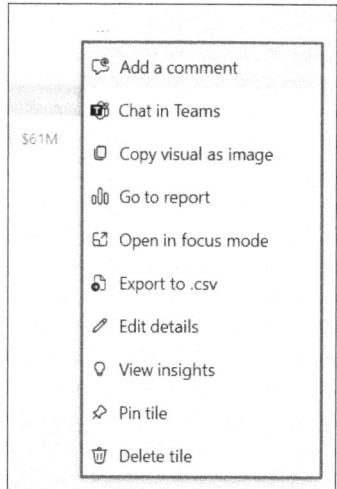

The Tile actions menu in the Power BI dashboard.

From here you can

- Add comments to the dashboard.

- Open the report that was used to create this tile.

- View in focus mode.

- Export the data used in the tile.

- Edit the title and subtitle and add a hyperlink.

- Run insights.

- Pin the tile to another dashboard.

- Delete the tile.

 IMPORTANT These options apply mainly to tiles pinned from individual visuals. Some options may be unavailable for tiles created from entire report pages or other sources.

4. Close the action menu by selecting a blank area in the dashboard.

Add comments to a dashboard

Collaboration is an essential part of working with data in Power BI. One simple but powerful way to collaborate is by adding comments to dashboards and reports. You can leave personal notes, start a conversation, and even tag specific colleagues to draw their attention to important insights.

 IMPORTANT To use the comment feature, you need a Power BI Pro license or access to content hosted in Power BI Premium capacity.

You can add comments in several places:

- Entire dashboards

- Individual dashboard visuals (tiles)

- Report pages

- Individual report visuals

- Paginated reports (general comments only, not on specific visuals)

You can post general comments or tag specific colleagues using the @ symbol. When others are mentioned, they receive an email and, if they use the Power BI mobile app, a push notification.

 IMPORTANT Each comment can contain up to 2,000 characters, including spaces and @mentions.

11

To add a comment to a dashboard or report

1. Open the dashboard or report in the Power BI Service.

2. On the top menu bar, select the **Comment** icon.

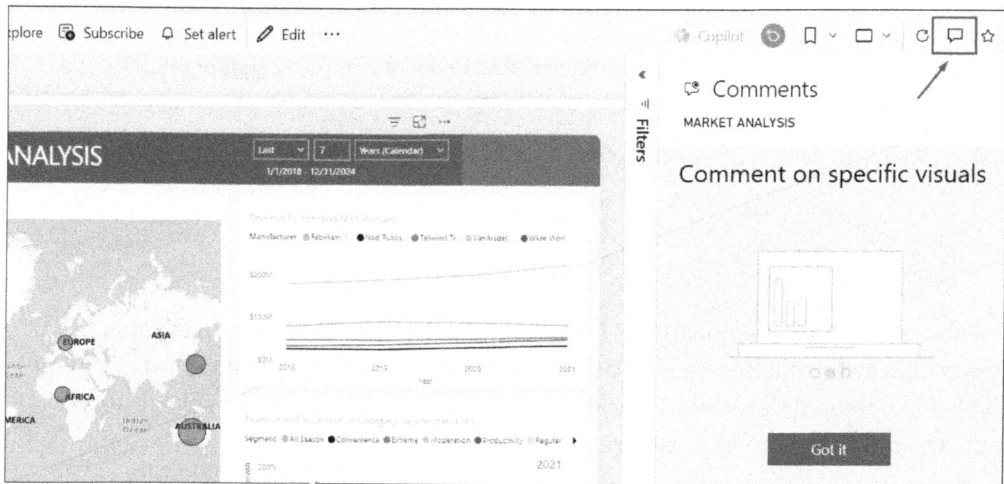

The Comment icon in the Power BI Service menu bar.

3. In the Comments pane, type your message.

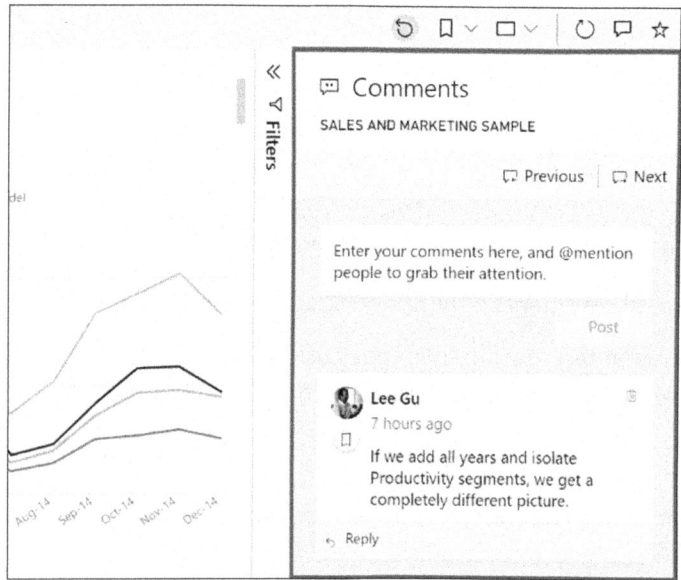

The Comments pane in the Power BI Service.

4. To respond to a thread, select **Reply**, enter your response, and select **Post**.

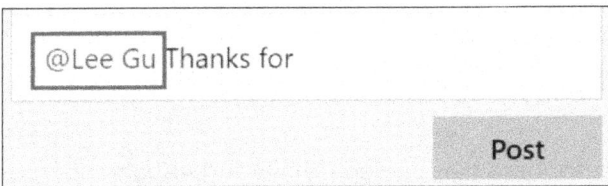

A reply in the Comments pane in the Power BI Service.

> ⚠ **IMPORTANT** All users with access to the dashboard or report can view and respond to comments.

> ✓ **TIP** If someone filters the report before commenting, Power BI saves those filters as a bookmark. When others view or respond to the comment, the page will show the same filter context, helping them understand the insight.

Add a comment to a visual

In addition to adding comments to an entire dashboard or report page, you can also comment on individual dashboard tiles and report visuals. The process is similar in both cases, allowing you to provide targeted feedback on specific elements.

To comment on a specific visual in a dashboard or report

1. Hover over the visual and select **More options (...)**.

2. Select **Add a comment** from the dropdown menu.

3. Enter your message and select **Post**.

> ✓ **TIP** Use @mentions to notify your teammates directly. This approach is ideal for asking questions, requesting feedback, or highlighting something that needs immediate attention. Power BI sends an email (and mobile push notification if applicable) so the person can respond quickly.

11

Set data alerts on dashboard tiles

In the Power BI Service, you can set up data alerts to receive notifications when values on your dashboard exceed thresholds you define. This feature is especially useful for monitoring key metrics in real time.

Alerts can be configured only on dashboard tiles pinned from report visuals and *only for cards, KPIs, or gauges*. You cannot create alerts on tiles created directly from streaming datasets or on tiles pinned from shared dashboards where you don't have the necessary permissions.

To set a data alert

1. Open a dashboard in the Power BI Service.

2. Hover over a card, KPI, or gauge visual and select **More options (...)**.

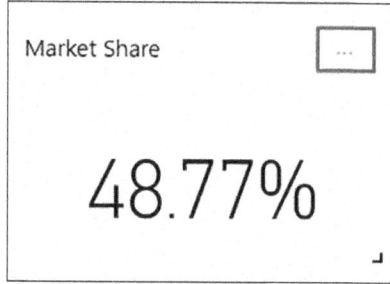

A KPI tile with ellipsis highlighted to set a data alert.

3. Select **Manage alerts** from the menu.

4. Select **+ Add alert rule**. Make sure the Active toggle is set to **On** and enter a clear title for your alert

The Manage alerts panel in the Power BI Service.

5. Scroll down and enter the alert logic:

- Choose whether the alert triggers when the value rises above or falls below a threshold.

- Set the threshold value.

- Choose the frequency: once per hour or once per day.

Optionally, select the **Send me email, too** checkbox.

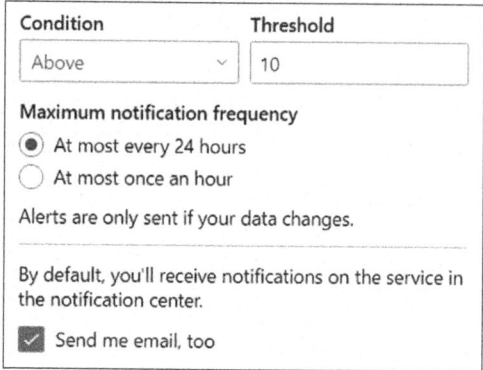

Condition	Threshold
Above ⌄	10

Maximum notification frequency

◉ At most every 24 hours

◯ At most once an hour

Alerts are only sent if your data changes.

By default, you'll receive notifications on the service in the notification center.

☑ Send me email, too

The Alert configuration panel in the Power BI Service.

6. Select **Save and close**.

 TIP Power BI sends you a notification (and optionally an email) when the data value reaches the threshold you set, but only after the data is refreshed.

Make sure your dataset has a scheduled or manual refresh so the alerts can work as expected.

⚠ **IMPORTANT** Alerts are personal: Only you can see the alerts you create, even if you share the dashboard. If your mobile device is lost or stolen, consider disabling your alert rules through the Power BI Service to prevent sensitive notifications from being exposed.

View insights on dashboard tiles

The Quick Insights feature in the Power BI Service uses advanced machine learning algorithms to automatically scan your entire imported semantic model and uncover interesting patterns, trends, and outliers without requiring any setup.

This capability is especially useful when

- You don't know where to start building your dashboard. Quick Insights is perfect for brainstorming during the early stages of analysis or when reviewing a dataset shared with you.

- You want to explore new angles or double-check for insights you might have missed manually.

IMPORTANT Quick Insights works only with imported data, not with DirectQuery, and it's available only in the Power BI Service (not in Desktop).

To run insights on a dashboard tile

1. In the Power BI Service, open a dashboard.

2. Hover over the tile to display the ellipsis (...) in the upper-right corner.

3. Choose **View insights** from the dropdown menu.

 IMPORTANT Quick Insights is available only for tiles pinned from individual visuals. It does not work with tiles created from entire report pages.

4. The tile opens in Focus mode, and insight cards appear on the right side. Select the **pin** icon to save any of these insight tiles to your dashboard.

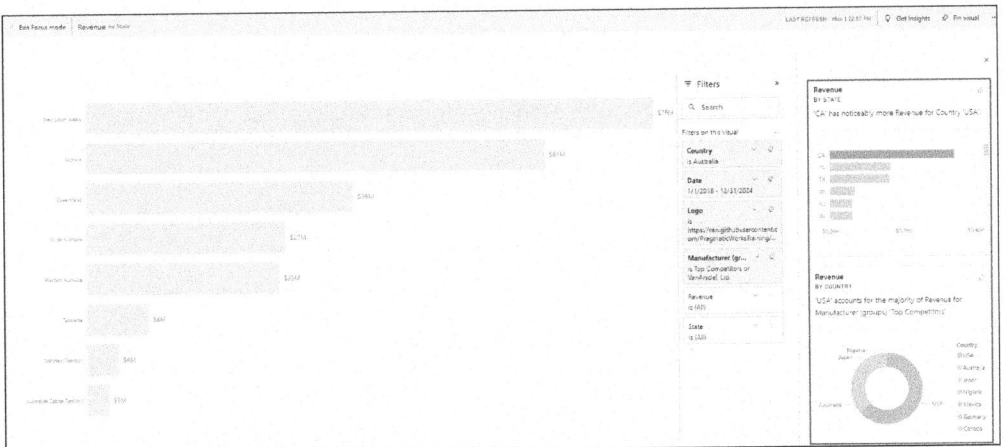

Insight cards of a dashboard tile.

5. Select any insight card to explore it in more detail.

6. Use the Filters pane to adjust the view and dig deeper into the data.

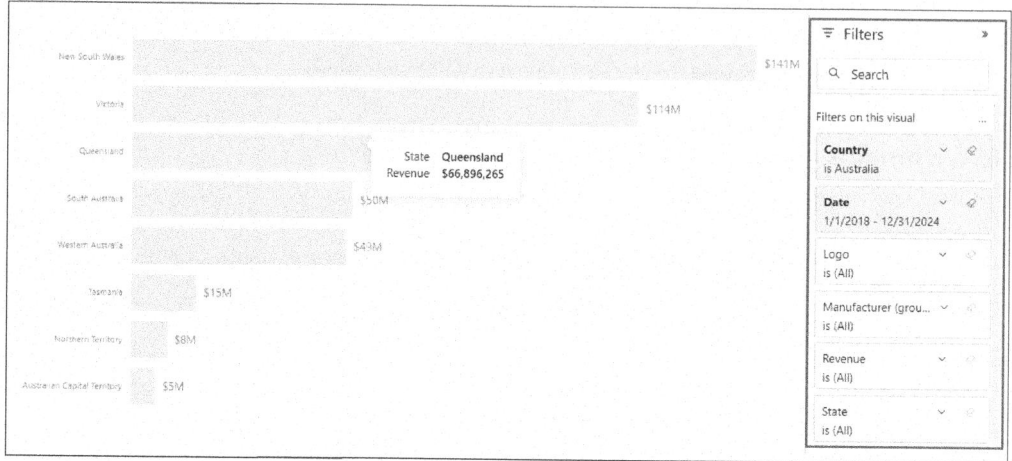

The Filters pane showing data-filtering options.

7. To return to the dashboard, select **Exit Focus mode**.

> ✅ **TIP** You can run insights on an existing insight card; this is called *related insights*. Just select an insight card to activate it. Power BI will generate new insight cards based only on the data in that insight, giving you an even more focused analysis. You can also apply filters to explore the data further.

Skills review

In this chapter, you learned how to

- Create a Power BI dashboard in the Power BI Service.
- Pin visuals or entire report pages to a dashboard.
- Use live tiles to reflect real-time data changes.
- Customize tiles by editing details, resizing, or changing their behavior.
- Set up and manage data alerts on KPI and gauge visuals.
- Collaborate using the Comments pane to discuss insights with others.
- Discover insights in your data using the View insights feature available on dashboard tiles.

Practice tasks

No practice files are necessary to complete the practice tasks in this chapter.

These tasks will help you reinforce the concepts introduced in this chapter. You will create and customize dashboards, add comments for collaboration, configure alerts, and explore AI-generated insights using the Power BI Service.

Build a dashboard from a report

Use the Power BI Service to create a dashboard and practice customizing tiles:

1. Open an existing report and pin one visual to your dashboard.

2. Pin another visual to the same dashboard.

3. Pin an entire report page using the **Pin live page** option.

4. Rearrange and resize the tiles in your dashboard layout.

5. Open the tile options (ellipsis) and edit the title or subtitle.

6. Add a custom tile with a text box to describe the dashboard's purpose.

Reflect on the following questions:

1. Why is it helpful to pin visuals from different reports into a single dashboard?

2. How does the layout and formatting affect the user's experience and understanding?

Add comments to a dashboard

Use the comment feature to add notes, tag team members, and start discussions:

1. Open the dashboard or report and select the **Comment** icon on the top menu.

2. Post a general comment explaining the purpose of the visual.

3. Use **@mention** to tag a teammate and ask for feedback.

4. Reply to an existing comment to simulate a discussion thread.

5. Add a comment directly on a specific tile or visual by using **More options (…)** > **Add a comment**.

Reflect on the following questions:

1. Where can you add comments in Power BI?

2. How can using comments and @mentions improve collaboration within your team?

Set data alerts on dashboard tiles

Practice configuring and managing data alerts on KPI visuals:

1. Locate a KPI or card tile on your dashboard.

2. Open the **More options (…)** menu and select **Manage alerts**.

3. Create a new alert rule and set the title, threshold, and frequency.

4. Enable email notifications for the alert.

5. Save and test your alert by manually updating the dataset (if possible).

6. Return to Manage alerts and disable or delete the alert.

Reflect on the following questions:

1. Which tile types support data alerts in Power BI?

2. In which business scenarios could data alerts be useful?

View insights on dashboard tiles

Use Power BI's View insights feature to explore patterns in your data:

1. Open a dashboard and hover over a visual tile.

2. Open the **More options (…)** menu and select **View insights**.

3. Review the insight cards that appear in Focus mode.

4. Pin one insight card back to your dashboard.

5. Select an insight card and run related insights on it.

6. Use the Filters pane to explore specific dimensions in the data.

7. Exit Focus mode to return to the main dashboard view.

Reflect on the following questions:

1. What does Power BI generate when Quick Insights are run?

2. How can View insights help you discover trends you may have missed?

Applying advanced topics and best practices

Practice files

There are no practice files for this chapter.

After you have built your reports and models in Power BI, the next step is to ensure they are secure, scalable, and efficient. This chapter explores advanced capabilities and techniques that go beyond building reports, focusing on how to optimize your solutions for performance, security, and usability in real-world deployments.

You will start by learning how to implement row-level security (RLS) to restrict data access dynamically based on the user's identity, an essential feature when publishing reports to a broad audience.

Then you'll explore performance tuning strategies and best practices that apply across the data preparation phase, the semantic model, DAX calculations, and visualization layout, helping you build faster, leaner, and more responsive reports. These practices help reduce refresh time, improve model efficiency, and create clearer and more maintainable solutions.

In this chapter

- Implement row-level security (RLS)
- Apply Power Query best practices
- Optimize the semantic model
- Write efficient DAX expressions
- Apply data visualization best practices

Implement row-level security (RLS)

When you're publishing reports to a wide audience, it's essential to restrict access to sensitive data. Row-level security in Power BI allows you to filter data dynamically so that users see only the data that's relevant to them.

You can implement RLS either by defining static rules, where each role is hardcoded to a specific value (like a country or region), or by using dynamic security, which filters data based on the current user's identity. This feature is essential in scenarios where the same report is used by multiple users who should see only their own data.

Define roles in Power BI Desktop

To restrict data access in your Power BI reports, you first need to define roles and filters that limit which rows a user can see.

You can define roles and their corresponding rules directly in Power BI Desktop. The Manage roles dialog allows you to create and edit roles either by using a guided interface or by writing DAX expressions. When you publish the report to the Power BI Service, the role definitions are published along with the dataset, making them available for assignment to users.

> **TIP** You can configure RLS in Power BI for both imported and DirectQuery models.

> ⚠ **IMPORTANT** When you use a live connection to Analysis Services or Azure Analysis Services, RLS must be configured directly in the external model. The Power BI Service does not show the Security option for these connections.

> **TIP** In the Power BI Service, RLS applies only to users with Viewer permissions. Users with Admin, Member, or Contributor roles in a workspace can see all the data, regardless of the RLS filters defined.

To define a security role

1. Open your report in Power BI Desktop.

2. On the Modeling tab, select **Manage roles**.

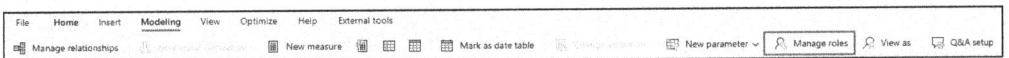

Select the Manage roles option to configure row-level security.

3. In the Manage security roles window, select **New** to create a new role.

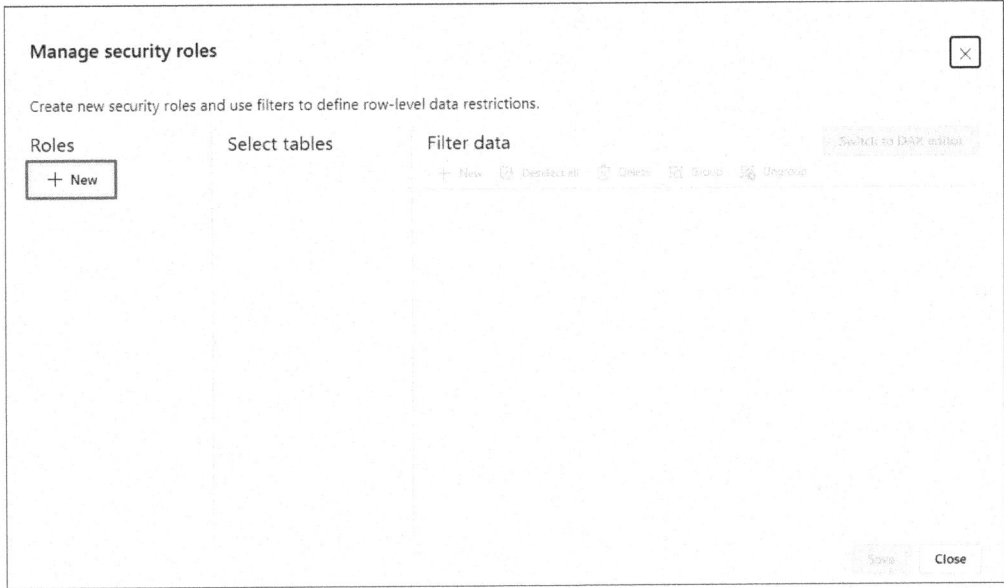

The Manage security roles window in Power BI Desktop.

4. Under Roles, assign a name to the role and press Enter.

5. Under Select tables, select the table where you want to apply a row-level security filter.

12

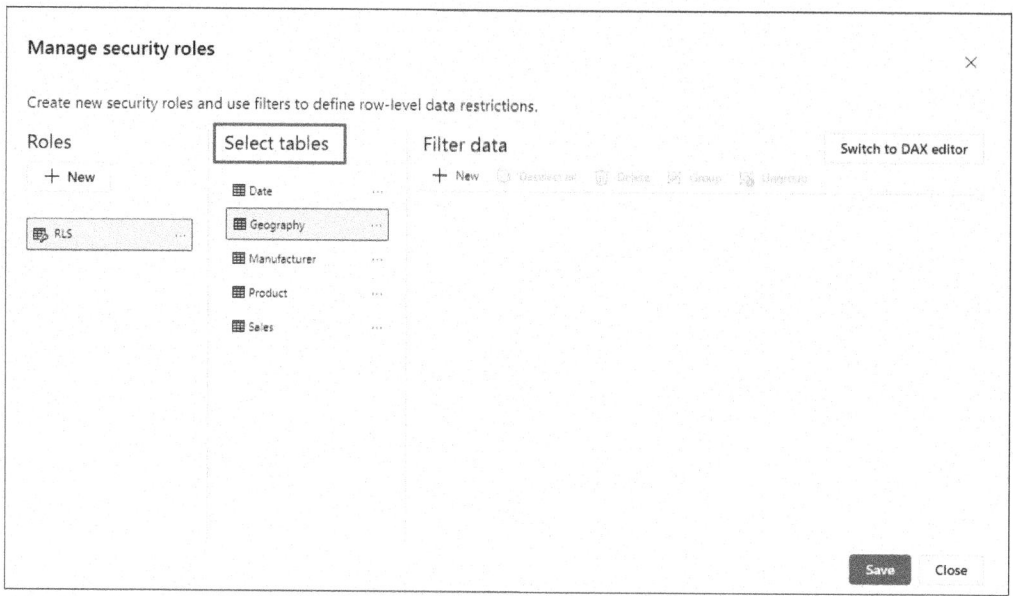

The Manage security roles window.

6. Define your filter using one of the following options:

    •   Use the default editor for simple Boolean filters, allowing you to create basic comparisons.

    •   Use the DAX editor for advanced or dynamic rules such as USERPRINCIPALNAME() or USERNAME().

    You can switch between editors. If the DAX expression is too complex for the default editor, Power BI will warn you before switching.

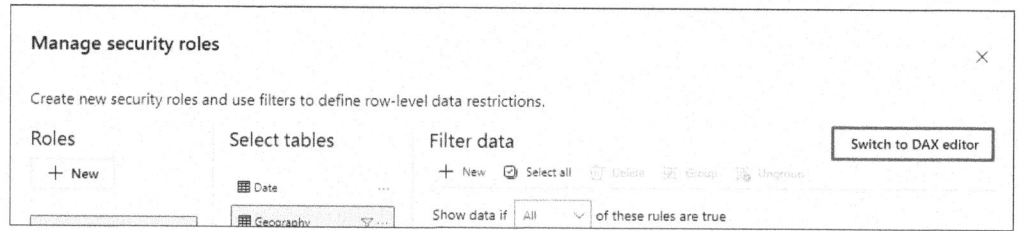

Select the Switch to DAX editor option to switch editors.

7. In the default editor, under Filter data, select **New** to create one or more conditions and use the Column, Condition, and Value dropdowns to define your filter.

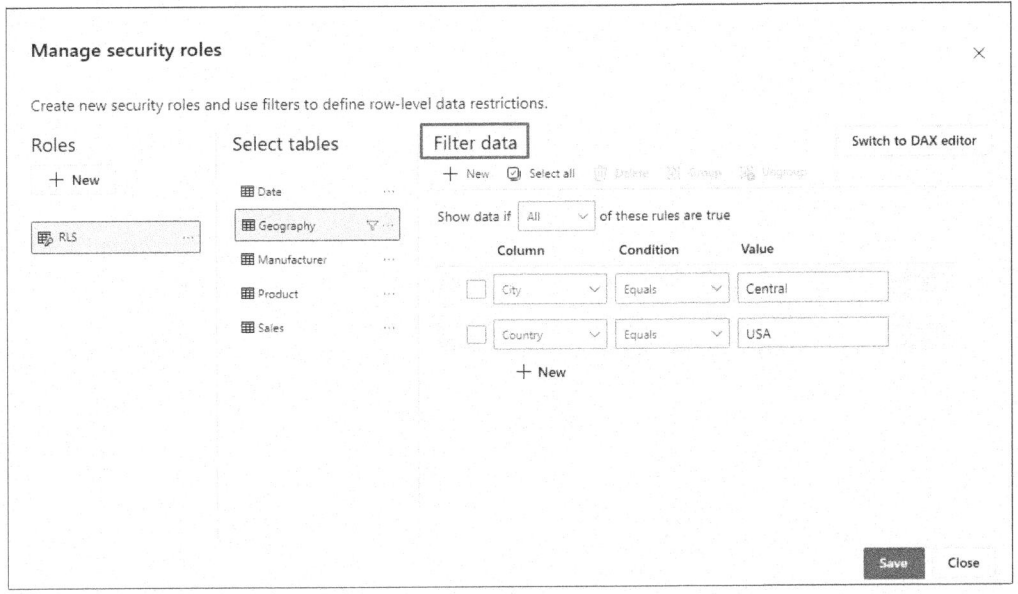

Define row-level filters based on column values.

8. To create dynamic security based on the signed-in user, select **Switch to DAX editor** and write your filter using the full DAX formula editor, which includes autocomplete (Intellisense) and validation tools.

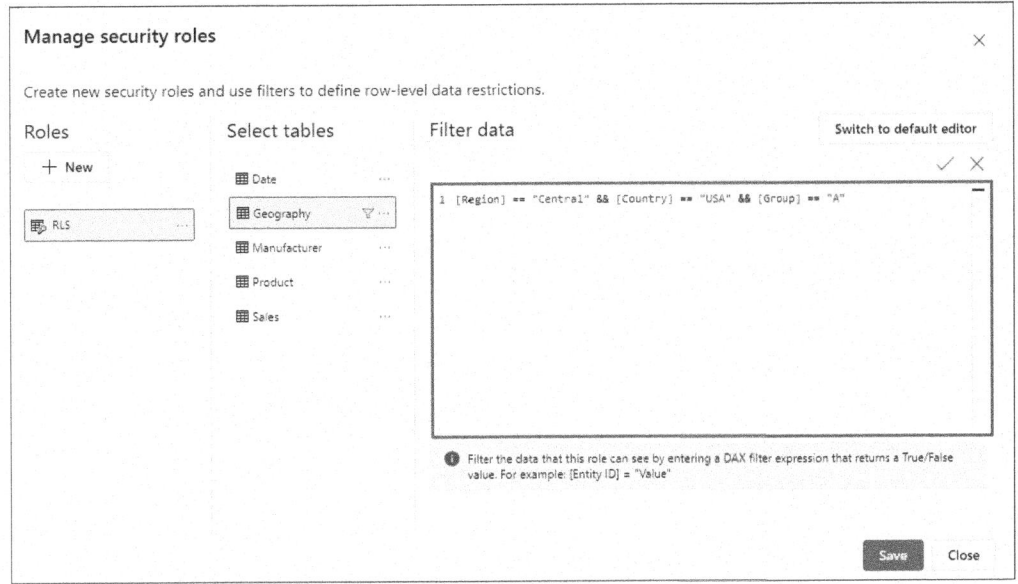

Create a complex row-level security filter based on multiple column conditions.

TIP Always use commas (,) to separate arguments in DAX, even if your locale uses semicolons.

 IMPORTANT USERNAME() returns DOMAIN\username in Power BI Desktop and the User Principal Name (UPN) (such as user@domain.com) in the Power BI Service.

 TIP Ensure your data model includes proper relationships for dynamic filters to work.

By default, RLS applies single-direction filters. To apply filters in both directions, edit the relationship and enable **Apply security filter in both directions**.

Test roles in Power BI Desktop

After defining the roles, you can simulate what each user would see by using the View as role feature.

To test a role

1. On the Modeling tab, select **View as**.

The View as option in the Modeling tab in Power BI Desktop.

2. In the View as dialog, choose a defined role or enter a test user. For dynamic roles, enter the username of the person you want to test and then select the role.

3. Validate the data restrictions as expected.

Assign users to roles

After publishing your report to Power BI, in the Power BI Service (Fabric) you can assign users or groups to the security roles you defined.

To assign users to roles

1. Publish the report to a workspace in Power BI Service.

2. In the workspace, select **More options (...)** for the dataset and then select **Security**.

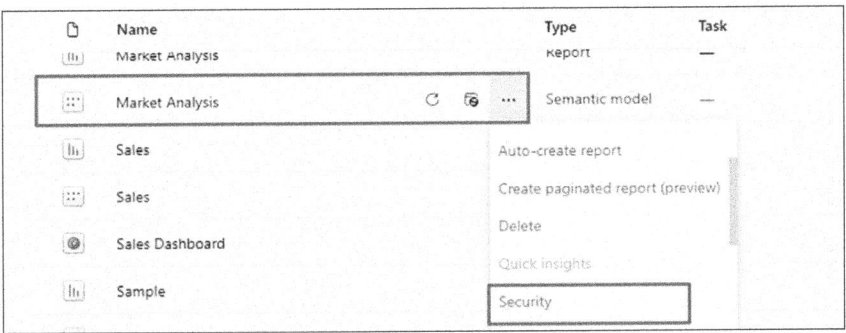

Configure row-level security in the Power BI Service.

3. Add users or groups to the role. Supported group types include

    - Microsoft Entra security groups

    - Distribution groups

    - Mail-enabled groups

When users are assigned to a role, the DAX filter defined for that role is applied to them. If at least one role exists in the dataset but a particular user is not assigned to any role, that user will receive an error when viewing the report.

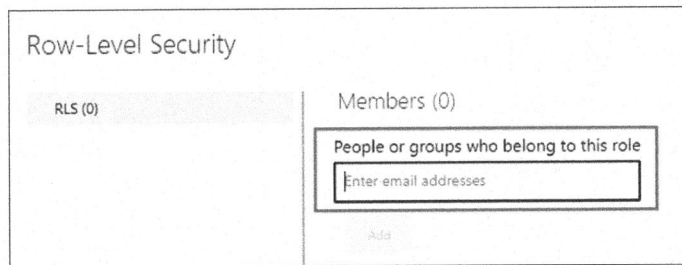

Assign users to a security role in Power BI.

 IMPORTANT Microsoft 365 groups and Power BI-created groups are not supported.

Test roles in the Power BI Service

Testing roles in the Power BI Service enables you to simulate and confirm that your RLS settings are functioning correctly.

12

To test roles in the Power BI Service

1. In the Security tab of the dataset, select **More options (...)** next to a role and then select **Test as role**.

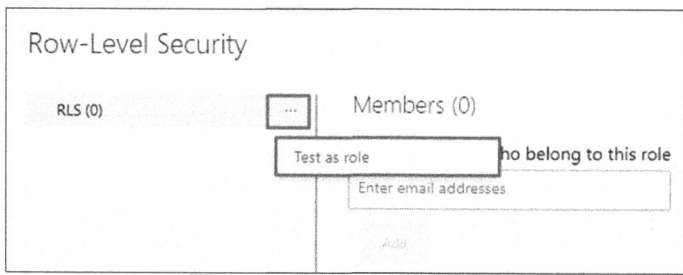

Test the RLS role.

2. The report opens in test mode with the role applied.

3. Select the **Now viewing as** option to test specific users or role combinations.

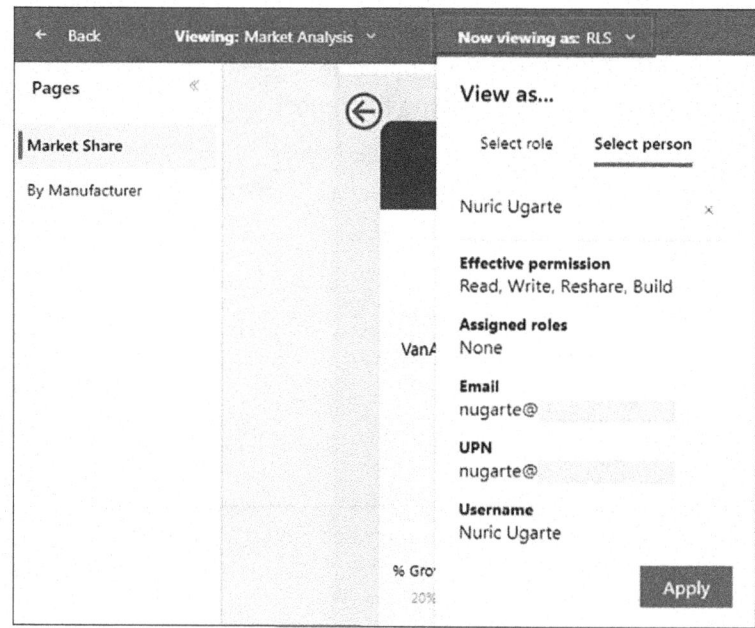

The Now viewing as option in the Power BI Service.

4. Test other reports connected to the semantic model by selecting **Viewing** in the page header.

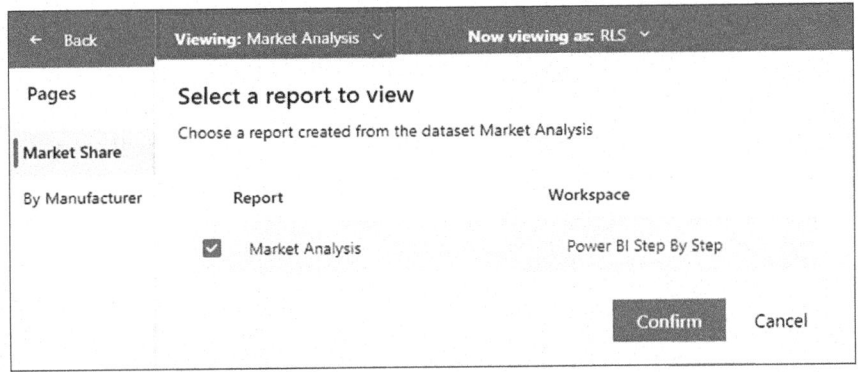

Test row-level security on reports connected to the semantic model.

5. To return to normal viewing, select **Back to Row-Level Security**.

 TIP You can test only reports that are located in the same workspace as your semantic model.

 IMPORTANT Dashboards aren't supported for testing using the Test as role option.

SSO models and some visual features (Q&A, Copilot) cannot be tested with this method.

Apply Power Query best practices

Power BI performance starts with how you connect to and prepare your data. Inefficient queries or large, unnecessary datasets can significantly slow down your reports. This section focuses on the first layer of optimization: reducing data volume, enabling query folding, and applying smart transformations.

12

Reduce data volume and granularity

By applying best practices early in the data transformation phase, you can significantly reduce the volume and complexity of your dataset before it even reaches the data model.

Load only the necessary tables in your data model

It is common practice to load extra tables just in case they might be useful later, but this approach can significantly increase memory usage and slow down your model. Include only the tables that are truly needed for analysis or reporting.

Avoid loading staging or intermediary queries into the model

In Power Query, It is common practice to create staging or intermediary queries to prepare and clean your data. However, if these queries are not needed for reporting, loading them into the model can increase memory usage and processing overhead. To keep your model efficient, disable loading for any query that serves only as a transformation step and is not required in the final dataset.

To disable loading for a staging query

1. In Power BI Desktop, open the Power Query Editor.

2. In the Queries pane, right-click the query you want to exclude from the model.

3. Deselect the option **Enable load**.

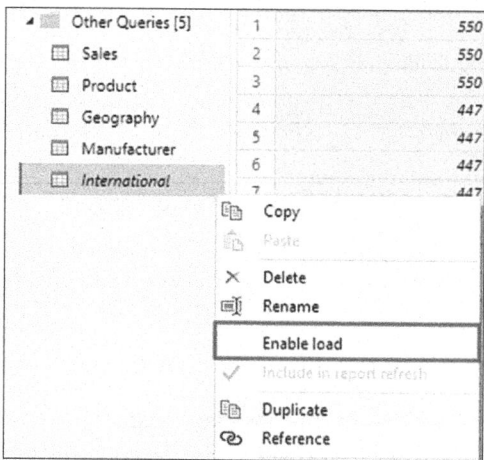

The Enable load option in Power Query.

4. Select **Close & Apply** to apply changes and return to the report view.

Include only the essential columns needed for analysis or visualization

Each column increases the processing and memory usage. Exclude columns like GUID, audit logs, or metadata that aren't required for analysis.

To exclude unnecessary columns in Power Query:

1. On the Home tab, in the Manage columns group, select **Choose columns**.

2. The Choose columns dialog opens, displaying all available fields in your table.

3. Select the fields you want to keep. Clear the check boxes for the fields you don't need.

4. Select **OK**. Your table now contains only the selected columns.

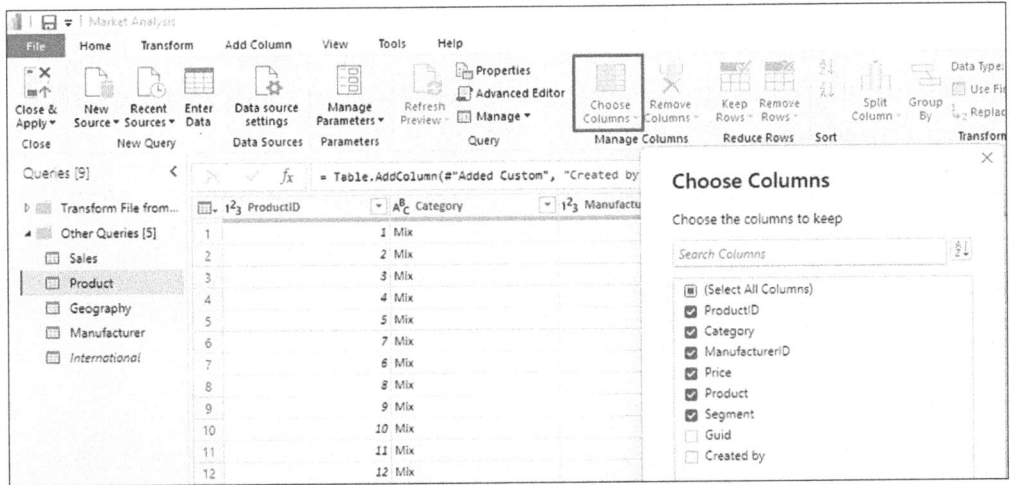

The Choose Columns option in Power Query.

> **TIP** It's easier to add a column later than to remove one that's already in use. After your model is connected to multiple reports, removing unused columns can break visuals or calculations across multiple files.

Split high cardinality columns

High cardinality (many unique values) in columns can significantly increase the size of your data model and slow down DAX calculations:

- **Split Decimal Columns:** Separate the integer and fractional parts of a decimal column into two columns.

- **Split Datetime Columns:** If both date and time are required, split datetime fields into two separate columns.

- **Split High-Cardinality IDs:** Break down unique identifiers (like TransactionID or UserID) into separate columns by extracting meaningful components (such as prefixes or regions).

Filter data early

Apply filters as early as possible in Power Query to reduce the amount of data loaded into your data model.

For example, if your report analyzes data only from the past two years, you can apply a date filter in Power Query to exclude older records before the data reaches the model. Similarly, if the report is relevant only to a specific region, filter that region during the query step rather than handling it later with DAX.

Filtering early ensures that only the data needed for analysis is processed and stored, resulting in a leaner and faster semantic model.

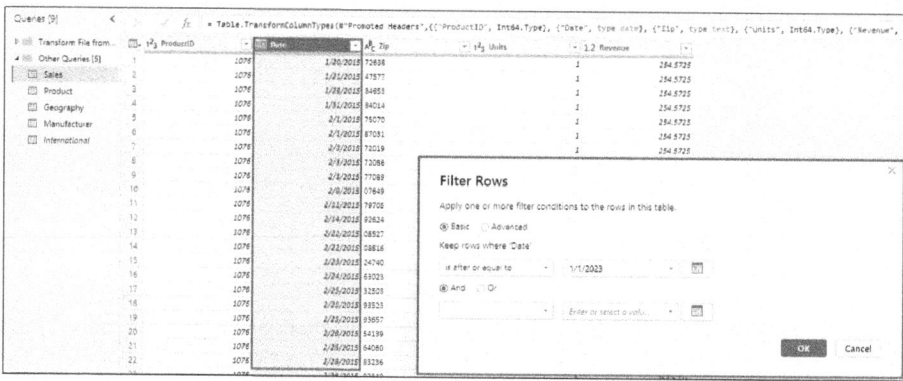

The Filter Rows dialog in Power Query.

Avoid complex transformations in Power BI

Whenever possible, offload heavy or complex data transformations to the data source using Extract, Transform, Load (ETL) tools like Data Factory, or perform the logic directly in the database using views or stored procedures.

Transformations such as joins across large tables, nested logic, pivoting/unpivoting, or custom parsing can significantly impact refresh performance when performed in Power Query. These operations are often more efficiently executed by the database engine, which is optimized for processing large volumes of data.

Rename steps and queries clearly

Use descriptive names for queries and steps to improve readability and collaboration. Avoid generic names like Changed Type1 or Renamed Columns2. Use names like Filter current year rows or Merge with region table.

Choose appropriate data types

Selecting the right data type improves performance and reduces file size.

- Use Whole Number instead of Decimal Number if decimal precision isn't needed.

- Use Fixed Decimal Number type (commonly used for currency) if four decimal places are sufficient.

- Avoid storing numeric values as text.

- Use Date instead of Date/Time when timestamps are not required.

Consolidate applied steps

When you apply multiple similar transformations, such as renaming columns one by one or removing them across separate steps, Power Query processes each of those steps sequentially. This means it reads and recalculates the query multiple times, even when the operations could have been grouped into one.

By combining these actions into a single step, you reduce the number of intermediate computations, lower the memory usage, and improve query performance, especially during a refresh.

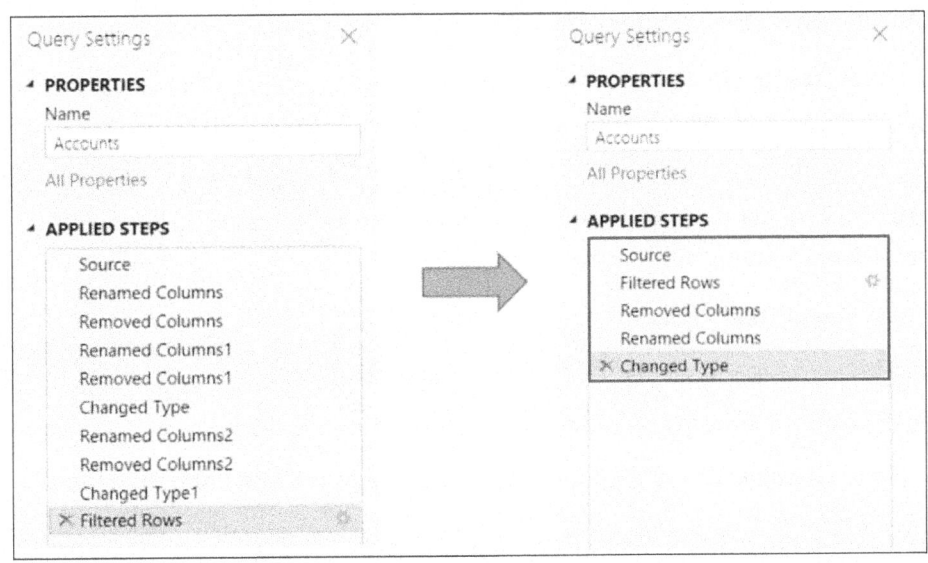

Consolidate applied steps in Power Query.

Leverage query folding

Query folding refers to the process of pushing data transformations back to the data source, allowing it to handle the computation instead of Power BI. This process improves performance by reducing the amount of data that needs to be loaded and processed locally.

Query folding is supported by most structured data sources, including

- Relational databases (such as SQL Server, Oracle, and PostgreSQL)

- Cloud-based databases (such as Snowflake and Amazon Redshift)

- OData feeds (such as SharePoint lists)

- Active Directory

 IMPORTANT Folding is not supported for flat files (such as Excel or CSV), blobs (for example, Azure Blob Storage), or web sources. In these cases, all transformations are handled locally within Power BI, which may impact refresh performance.

To check query folding

Generally, a transformation in Power Query can be folded if it has a direct equivalent in SQL. For example, operations like SELECT, WHERE, JOIN, and GROUP BY exist both in SQL and in Power Query, so they are typically folded.

However, if the transformation involves logic that cannot be expressed in SQL, such as adding custom columns with M functions, using list operations, or dynamic renaming, then query folding breaks, and the step is executed locally.

You can verify whether a transformation is being folded to the data source by using the View Native Query option in Power Query.

1. Open Power Query Editor.

2. In the Queries pane, select the query you want to inspect.

3. In the Applied Steps pane, right-click a transformation step.

   - *If View Native Query is enabled,* query folding is still occurring up to that step.

   - *If View Native Query is grayed out,* folding has probably been broken, and the step is being executed locally.

> ✓ **TIP** In some cases, View Native Query may be grayed out even though folding is still occurring in the backend. To maximize the chances of query folding, apply your transformations as early as possible and keep them simple.

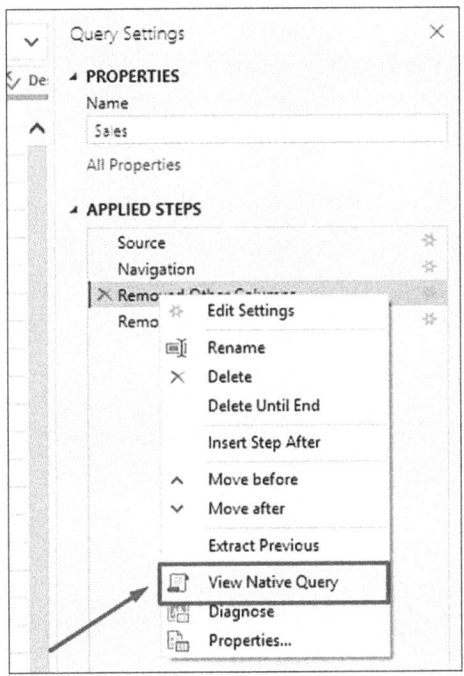

The View Native Query option in Power Query.

> ✓ **TIP** Maximize query folding for better performance.
>
> Achieve full query folding whenever possible. In scenarios where full folding is not possible, structure your query steps strategically by applying foldable transformations at the beginning of the query and moving nonfoldable steps to the end to limit local processing.
>
> If your query includes many steps that cannot be folded, consider performing those transformations outside of Power BI. You can use tools such as ETL pipelines, database views, or stored procedures to prepare the data before it reaches Power BI.

Optimize the semantic model

The semantic model is the foundation of reporting in Power BI. It serves as a centralized source of truth that enables users to build consistent, scalable, and reusable reports. As the semantic model creator, you can greatly enhance the experience for others by following best practices that improve usability, readability, and performance.

Adopt a star schema design

The recommended design pattern for Power BI is the star schema, where a central fact table connects to multiple dimension tables. This structure improves performance and enables more efficient filtering.

Avoid snowflake models with multiple layers of joins because they can slow down performance and complicate relationships.

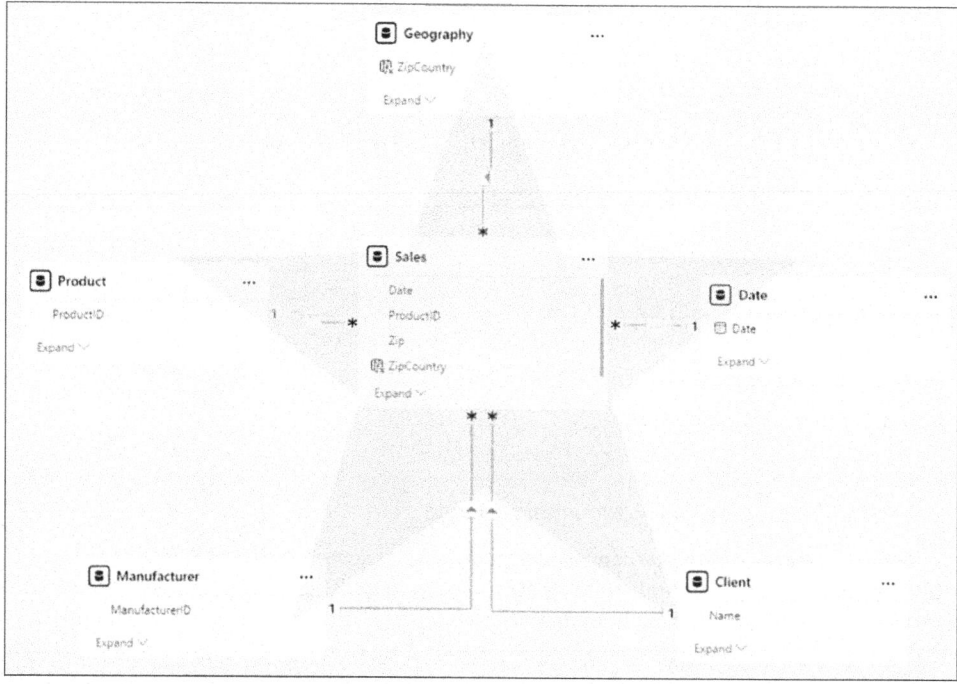

Star schema in Power BI.

Use descriptive names

Choose clear and descriptive names for tables, columns, and measures. This method of naming helps report authors understand the model without needing to explore each element in depth. For example, use Customer Orders instead of a generic name like Table1.

Add meaningful descriptions

Use the Description property on tables, columns, and measures to provide context and guidance. Describe not only what the field contains but also how it should be used in a report or calculation. These descriptions are visible as tooltips for report authors, helping them understand the purpose and usage of each element.

Hide unnecessary fields

Hide columns, tables, or measures that should not be used directly in reports:

- Hide technical columns such as foreign keys (such as CustomerID) that are needed only for relationships.

- Hide base columns if a measure already provides the preferred aggregation (for example, hide OrderQuantity and expose a Total Order measure instead).

 IMPORTANT Advanced users can still access and unhide hidden fields if needed.

Group and summarize your data

To improve performance and reduce memory usage, avoid importing overly granular data when it's not needed. Instead, group and summarize the data before loading it into the model. Doing so can reduce model size by up to 90% and simplify report building, especially when working with millions of rows.

To group data

1. In Power Query Editor, select the table you want to summarize.

2. Select the grouping columns (such as Country, Sales Channel).

3. On the Transform tab, select **Group By**.

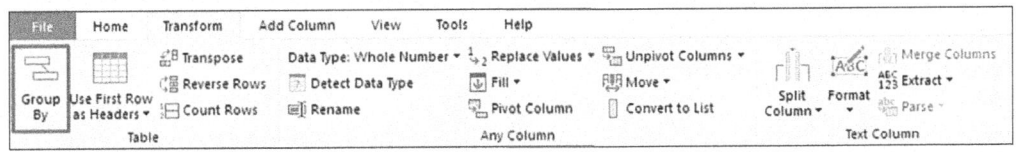

The Group By option in Power Query.

4. In the Group By dialog, choose the aggregation operations (such as Sum, Count, Average) for your value columns.

12

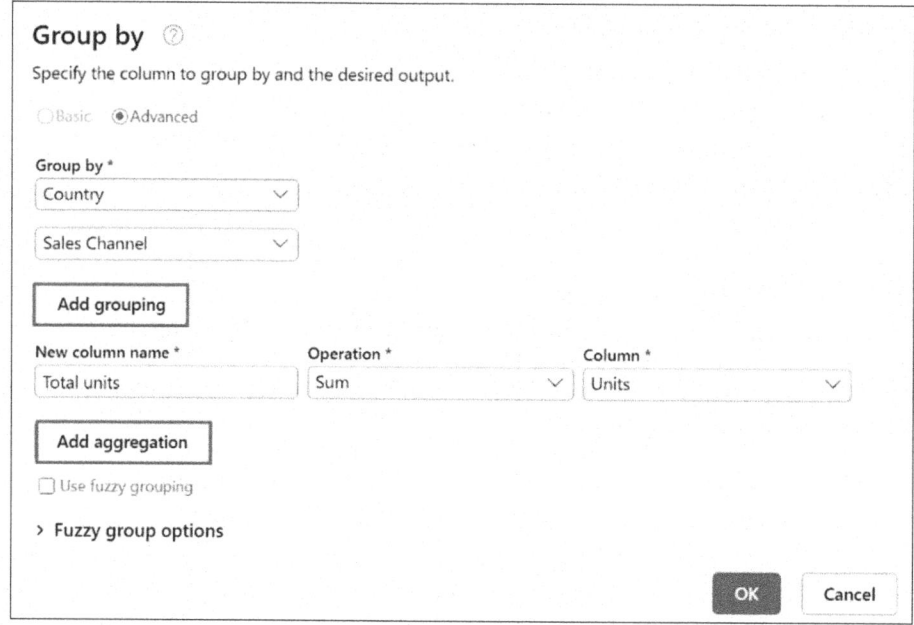

Advanced options to group by multiple columns.

5. Select **OK** to create the summarized table.

6. Rename the new table accordingly (for example, Sales Summary) and load it into the model.

> ✓ **TIP** Use a hybrid model for balanced performance and detail-level analysis.
>
> When detailed analysis is occasionally required, consider combining storage: Load summary tables in Import mode to support fast, high-level reporting. Also, keep detailed tables in DirectQuery to enable on-demand exploration of individual transactions when needed.

Optimize relationships

Efficient relationships are critical to a performant and reliable Power BI semantic model. Poor relationship design can lead to ambiguous filters, unexpected results, and performance bottlenecks.

Avoid many-to-many relationships

Although Power BI supports many-to-many relationships, you should avoid them when possible, due to the complexity they introduce in filter propagation and calculation logic.

> ✅ **TIP** A more robust approach than many-to-many relationships is to create a bridge table that contains only the distinct values shared between the related tables. Then establish one-to-many relationships from this bridge table to each of the related fact tables. This design simplifies the data model and ensures more reliable and predictable filter behavior.

Avoid bidirectional relationships

Bidirectional relationships allow filters to flow in both directions between related tables. Although useful in specific scenarios, they can significantly impact performance and introduce ambiguity in large or complex models.

> ✅ **TIP** Prefer single-direction relationships, and activate bidirectional filtering only within specific DAX expressions using the CROSSFILTER function. This approach preserves performance while maintaining control over how filters are applied.

Write efficient DAX expressions

Data Analysis Expressions (DAX) is a powerful language for creating measures and calculated columns in Power BI. Although DAX offers flexibility, poorly written expressions can slow down report performance, increase memory consumption, and make your model harder to maintain.

Use variables to improve performance and clarity

12

Variables improve both the readability and performance of your DAX formulas. When you break calculations into smaller, logical steps, they make your code easier to understand and maintain. In addition, variables are evaluated only once, even when referenced multiple times, reducing redundant computations and improving performance.

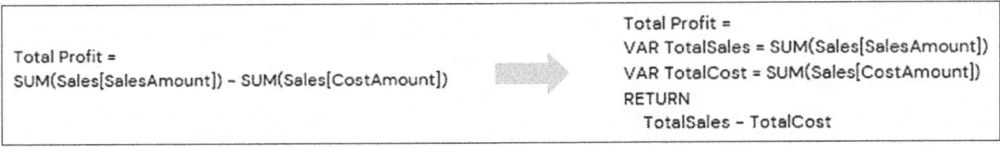

```
Total Profit =
SUM(Sales[SalesAmount]) - SUM(Sales[CostAmount])
```

```
Total Profit =
VAR TotalSales = SUM(Sales[SalesAmount])
VAR TotalCost = SUM(Sales[CostAmount])
RETURN
    TotalSales - TotalCost
```

Variables in a DAX measure.

Avoid forcing zero values in measures with no data

Displaying a zero instead of a blank might seem like a user-friendly choice, but forcing zero values in measures with no data with expressions like the following can negatively impact performance, especially on large datasets:

```
Total Sales =
IF(
    ISBLANK(SUM(Sales[Amount])),
    0,
    SUM(Sales[Amount])
)
```

Or

```
Total Sales = SUM(Sales[Amount]) + 0
```

When this logic is applied, Power BI unnecessarily recalculates the measure for every row, significantly increasing processing time and memory usage. Instead of forcing zeros, consider leaving measures blank for missing data to avoid unnecessary calculations and handle missing data visually through formatting or narrative explanations.

Use measures instead of calculated columns

Calculated columns are stored in the semantic model and evaluated during data refresh, which can increase memory usage and potentially impact performance. Instead, use measures for dynamic calculations because they are computed on demand and do not bloat your data model.

> ✅ **TIP** If you're using a calculated column only to aggregate or display results in visuals, it's a strong signal that it should be a measure instead. Ask yourself: Does this value depend on filter context? If the answer is yes, a measure is almost always the better choice.

Avoid costly and complex DAX functions

Some DAX functions are more expensive than others. Overuse or improper use of these functions can lead to performance issues. Use the following patterns with caution:

- Use DIVIDE instead of the division operator (/) with the DIVIDE function. The DIVIDE function is optimized for performance and includes built-in error handling. It prevents errors when the denominator is zero or blank.

TIP Use the third argument to define a safe fallback (such as 0) and avoid runtime errors.

- Avoid nested IF statements because they can make your DAX code complex, harder to read, and more difficult to maintain.

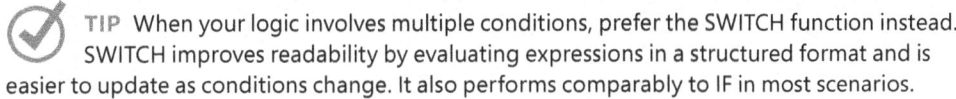 **TIP** When your logic involves multiple conditions, prefer the SWITCH function instead. SWITCH improves readability by evaluating expressions in a structured format and is easier to update as conditions change. It also performs comparably to IF in most scenarios.

- Excessive use of DISTINCTCOUNT, while useful, can be computationally heavy on large datasets.

 TIP Consider optimizing the underlying data or pre-aggregating where possible.

- Avoid using complex logic in visuals. Using highly calculated measures directly in visual filters or slicers can slow down report rendering.

 TIP Precalculate values when possible or move logic into the model.

Apply data visualization best practices

Well-designed visuals are essential for creating fast, responsive, and insightful reports. The following best practices help you build effective dashboards without compromising performance.

Simplify the layout

Avoid overcrowding report pages with too many visuals. Having many visuals increases rendering time and query complexity.

- Use fewer than 10 visuals per page when possible.
- Replace multiple cards with a multirow card or small multiples to consolidate metrics, which can also reduce the number of DAX queries generated by the visuals and improve performance.

Limit data displayed

Apply Top N filters to focus on key insights and group remaining items into an Other category.

To apply Top N

1. Select the visual where you want to apply the Top N filter.

2. In the Visualizations pane, go to the **Filters on this visual** section.

3. Drag the field you want to filter into the filter area.

4. Select the dropdown arrow for that field and choose **Top N**.

5. In the filter options, select **Top** and enter the number of items to keep.

6. Drag the numeric measure that should be used for ranking.

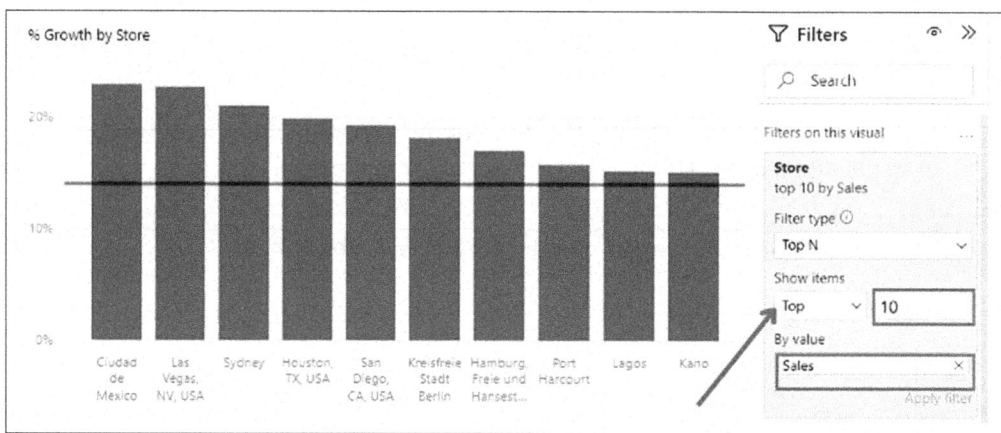

Top N filter option applied to a visual.

7. Select **Apply filter**.

> ✓ **TIP** To display the grouped Other category, you must pre-aggregate data in Power Query or model it using a DAX table if you want full control over how the remaining items are labeled.

Optimize interactions

Power BI enables cross-filtering and highlighting between visuals by default, which can lead to a smoother user experience, but also to unnecessary queries and performance issues, especially in complex reports.

Using the Edit interactions option, you can control how visuals on a page affect one another. Disabling or limiting interactions between certain visuals reduces the number of cross-filtering operations and prevents redundant or expensive queries from being triggered.

> **TIP** The Edit interactions option is especially useful when you're working with visuals based on high-cardinality fields, such as customer IDs, product SKUs, or transaction-level data. In those cases, allowing unrestricted interaction can slow down report responsiveness or even cause visuals to time out.

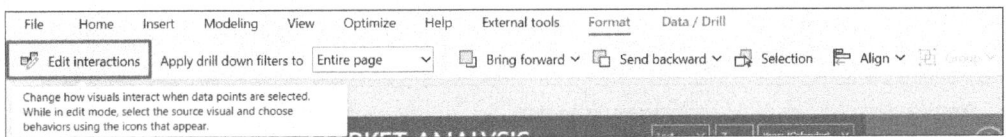

The Edit interactions option in Power BI Desktop.

Optimize slicer usage

Slicers are essential for enhancing report interactivity, but they can consume significant resources if overused or poorly configured. Follow these best practices to achieve a balance between interactivity and performance:

- Avoid adding too many slicers on a single page because they increase resource consumption, especially in large datasets. Include only the slicers that are essential for user navigation or analysis.

- Move nonessential filters to the Filter pane. These filters are more efficient than slicers, reducing interactive overhead.

- Use hierarchical slicers. Replace multiple slicers (such as Year, Quarter, Month) with a single hierarchical slicer.

- Avoid free-text slicers because they are resource-intensive, particularly in large datasets. Instead, use pre-aggregated categories, numeric fields, or IDs for faster and more efficient filtering.

12

Optimize tables and matrices

Tables and matrices are powerful, but they can become performance bottlenecks if misused. To keep your reports fast and responsive:

- Limit the number of fields displayed in the visual.

- Aggregate your data instead of showing raw rows.

- Avoid expensive calculations like Count Distinct unless strictly necessary.

- Use the Show items with no data option with caution. This option can be helpful, but it forces Power BI to render empty rows, which may impact performance, especially on large datasets. Enable it only when truly needed and with well-filtered visuals.

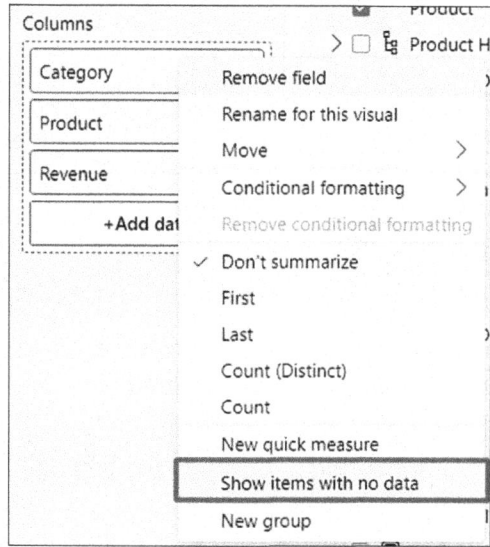

The Show items with no data option.

- Use drill-through pages to explore details on demand without overloading your visuals.

 TIP For large, detailed reports, consider using Power BI Paginated Reports.

Use certified visuals

Power BI provides a wide variety of custom visuals through AppSource. Although these visuals can extend functionality and improve report aesthetics, not all of them are optimized for performance or compliant with enterprise security standards.

Microsoft-certified visuals have been rigorously tested to meet specific performance, security, and reliability criteria. Microsoft reviews them to ensure that they behave predictably, do not access external services without permission, and integrate properly with Power BI features like exporting, filtering, and accessibility tools.

Avoid animated visuals

Although animated visuals such as Play Axis can create engaging experiences, they often come at the cost of performance and usability. These visuals continuously refresh the canvas as they animate through data points, which can place a heavy load on the rendering engine and the data model, especially when you're working with large datasets.

Animations may also interfere with accessibility features, create distractions for users, and limit the ability to analyze static data points effectively. Additionally, some animated visuals are not supported in export scenarios (to PDF or PowerPoint) or in mobile views, which can reduce their usefulness in enterprise reporting.

> **TIP** Instead of relying on animations, use alternatives such as slicers, toggle buttons, or bookmarks. These methods provide users with controlled, performant ways to explore changes over time or switch between views, without compromising report responsiveness or compatibility.

12

Use Performance Analyzer to troubleshoot slow visuals

Power BI Desktop includes a built-in Performance Analyzer that helps you identify which visuals or DAX queries are slowing down your report. It measures the time taken by each report element when users interact with the page, like changing a slicer or applying a filter, and breaks down the performance into key areas:

- **DAX query time:** Time taken to run the query against the data model
- **Visual display time:** Time needed to render the visual on-screen
- **Other:** Time spent preparing queries, waiting for other visuals, or background operations

To use Performance Analyzer

1. On the Optimize ribbon in Power BI Desktop, select **Performance Analyzer** to open the pane.

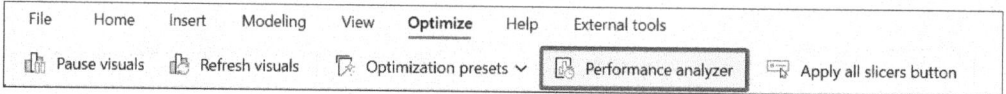

The Performance analyzer option on the Optimize tab.

2. Select **Start recording**.

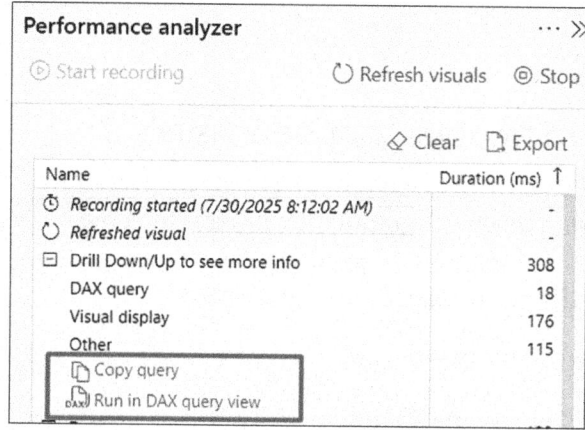

The Start recording option in Performance Analyzer.

3. Select **Refresh visuals** to reload all visuals on the page and capture their performance data.

4. Review the Duration (ms) column for each visual.

5. Select the arrow next to the Duration (ms) column to sort the visuals from highest to lowest duration. This feature helps you quickly identify which visuals are the most time-consuming and prioritize them for optimization.

The option to copy the DAX query and run it in DAX query view for performance troubleshooting.

> **TIP** If you interact with the report multiple times while recording is active, Performance Analyzer will create a separate log section for each interaction. This can make it harder to compare durations across all visuals. To simplify the analysis, select the Clear option before starting a new round of testing.

6. Select **Copy query** to paste and debug the DAX code in external tools like DAX Studio, or use **Run in DAX query view** to execute the query directly within Power BI Desktop.

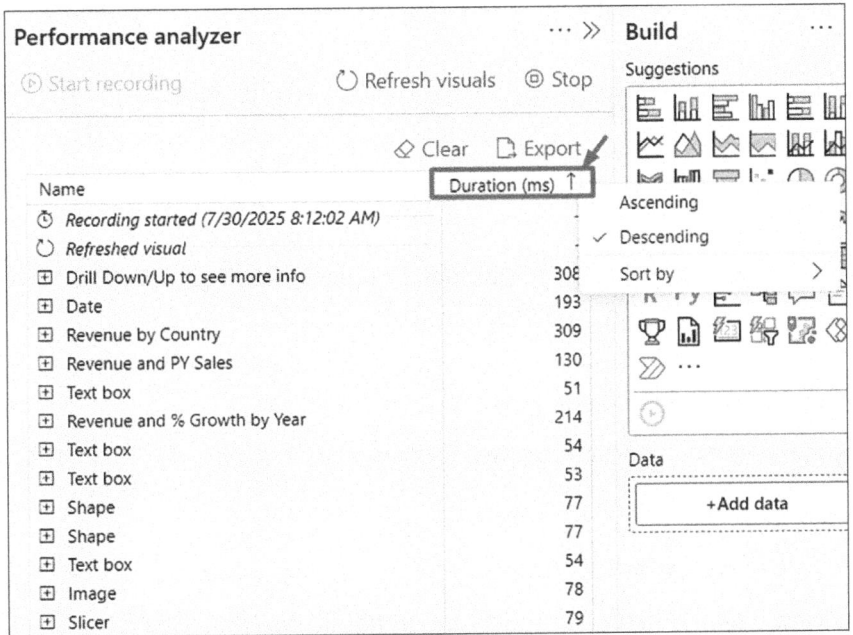

Sort visuals by duration in Performance Analyzer.

Design clean, effective dashboards

When you create a Power BI dashboard, your goal is not just to display data, but to communicate insights clearly and effectively. A well-designed dashboard helps users focus on what matters most, supports faster decision-making, and encourages meaningful interaction with the content.

In business scenarios, dashboards are often used to monitor the health of operations, track KPIs, and highlight anomalies that require attention. Unlike detailed reports, a dashboard provides a high-level snapshot, ideally on a single screen, so users can quickly assess performance without diving into every detail.

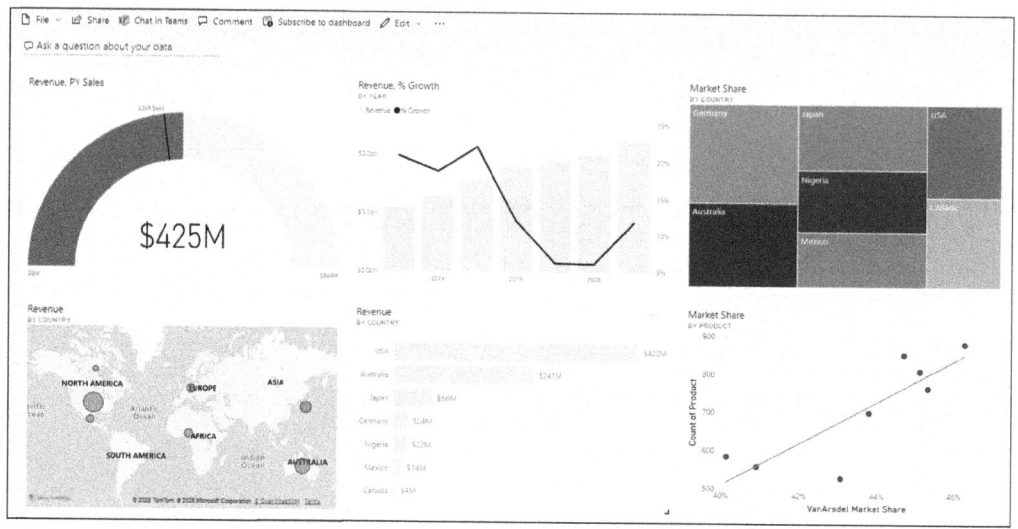

A Power BI dashboard.

Here are essential design principles to create clean, insightful, and user-friendly dashboards:

Start by understanding your audience

Include only visuals relevant to their decisions. Ask yourself:

- What decisions do they need to make?
- What KPIs are most relevant to them?
- Will they view it on a desktop, large screen, or mobile device?

Tailor the content and layout accordingly. Executives may need a summary view, whereas analysts require more detailed views.

 TIP If your dashboard will be viewed on mobile devices, design with fewer, clearer tiles, larger fonts, and minimal interactions to ensure clarity and readability.

Design for a single-screen view

Dashboards should present the most important data at a glance. Avoid requiring users to scroll, click excessively, or interpret cluttered visuals.

TIP Use full-screen mode when presenting to eliminate distractions and maximize impact.

Emphasize key metrics

Draw the user's attention to the most important metrics using visual hierarchy.

- Place key KPIs in the top-left area, where the eye naturally starts scanning.

- Use card visuals to isolate single values and apply consistent formatting for emphasis.

- Group related metrics together and avoid using bold colors for secondary information.

Choose the right visuals

Avoid visual overload. Select visuals that are intuitive, easy to interpret, and appropriate for the type of analysis. Recommended practices include

- Using bar or column charts to compare values across categories.

- Using pie or donut charts only for simple part-to-whole comparisons (fewer than eight categories).

- Using gauge charts to track progress toward a goal.

- Avoiding 3D charts because they distort comparisons and are difficult to read.

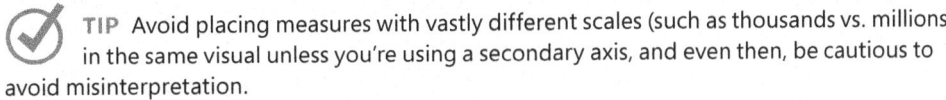 **TIP** Avoid placing measures with vastly different scales (such as thousands vs. millions) in the same visual unless you're using a secondary axis, and even then, be cautious to avoid misinterpretation.

Simplify formatting

Clarity in numerical formatting is critical. Avoid overwhelming the user with too many digits or redundant labels.

Best practices:

- Display no more than three to four digits at a time (for example, 1.5M, not 1,500,000).

12

- Use short, meaningful labels and hide axes when the context is clear.

- Align the level of precision and time frames across visuals.

- Use consistent formatting (currency, decimals, thousands separators) throughout the dashboard.

Sort and organize intuitively

Organize data in a meaningful way to guide the reader's attention:

- Sort by measure if you want to emphasize high or low values.

- Sort by axis if you want users to find specific categories quickly.

Skills review

In this chapter, you learned how to

- Recognize and apply row-level security (RLS) to restrict data access at the user level based on roles and filter logic.

- Apply best practices in Power Query to streamline transformation steps, reduce memory usage, and avoid loading unnecessary queries into the model.

- Follow performance optimization strategies in Power BI, including optimizing the semantic model structure and writing efficient DAX expressions.

- Apply effective data visualization practices to enhance readability, reduce cognitive load, and communicate insights clearly through well-designed visuals and dashboards.

- Use the Performance Analyzer tool to identify slow visuals, analyze DAX query duration, and troubleshoot performance bottlenecks in your reports.

Practice tasks

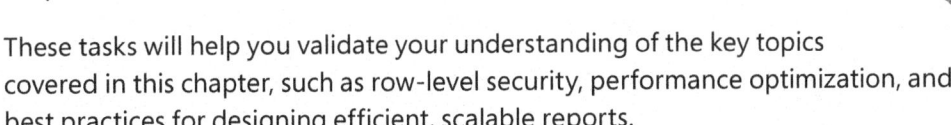

No practice files are necessary to complete the practice tasks in this chapter.

These tasks will help you validate your understanding of the key topics covered in this chapter, such as row-level security, performance optimization, and best practices for designing efficient, scalable reports.

Implement row-level security (RLS)

Reflect on the role of RLS in protecting sensitive data and delivering personalized insights to users:

1. What is the difference between static and dynamic row-level security?

2. Why is it important to test RLS rules before sharing the report?

3. What risks can arise if security roles are not configured properly?

4. How do the USERNAME() or USERPRINCIPALNAME() functions help in dynamic security scenarios?

Apply Power Query best practices

Optimizing your queries in Power Query can have a significant impact on model performance and data refresh times. Use the following questions to validate your understanding of this section:

1. How does disabling load for staging queries affect model size and performance?

2. Why is it helpful to consolidate multiple transformation steps into one?

3. What are the benefits of preserving query folding during data preparation?

4. How can you identify whether a transformation breaks query folding?

Optimize the semantic model

A well-structured semantic model is the foundation of an efficient and scalable Power BI solution. Reflect on the following questions:

1.   What is the role of star schema design in improving model efficiency?

2.   When should you use aggregations or summary tables in your model?

3.   How can many-to-many and bidirectional relationships affect performance and filter logic in a Power BI model, and what alternatives can help simplify the design?

Write efficient DAX expressions

Improve report responsiveness by applying efficient DAX coding techniques. The following questions will help you assess your understanding of DAX optimization techniques and how they contribute to better performance:

1.   What are the key differences between calculated columns and measures, and how do they impact model size and performance?

2.   What are the benefits of using variables (VAR) in DAX formulas?

3.   What are the performance implications of forcing zero values in measures with no data, and when is it better to display blanks instead?

Apply data visualization best practices

Well-designed visuals help users focus on what matters most. These questions will help you evaluate the clarity, efficiency, and impact of your data presentations:

1.   How does simplifying visuals impact user understanding and report performance?

2.   What design choices help highlight key metrics effectively?

3.   What insights does the Performance Analyzer provide about visual load times?

4.   How can you determine if a performance issue is due to the data model, DAX expression, or visual rendering?

Exploring Copilot in Power BI

13

Practice files

There are no practice files for this chapter.

The introduction of artificial intelligence in business intelligence tools has transformed how users interact with data. Traditional BI tools required users to manually prepare and transform data, build complex formulas, design visualizations from scratch, navigate through advanced interfaces, and understand intricate data models and relationships.

Microsoft Copilot in Power BI is a significant step in this evolution. It combines the power of generative AI with the flexibility of Power BI to help users, from business users to advanced creators, get the most out of their data. Instead of spending hours building visuals from scratch or navigating through multiple menus, you can describe your goal in natural language, and Copilot will generate analytics, build report pages, write DAX formulas, create relationships, and recommend visualizations.

In this final chapter, you will explore how Copilot can support every stage of your Power BI workflow, from preparing data and enhancing your semantic model to generating insights and building reports, making Power BI more intuitive, efficient, and accessible than ever before.

In this chapter

- Understand Copilot in Power BI
- Prepare semantic models for AI
- Use Copilot in Power BI Desktop
- Explore Copilot in the Power BI Service

Understand Copilot in Power BI

Copilot is an AI-powered assistant integrated into Power BI that helps users complete tasks using natural language. It's designed to support both business users and report authors by simplifying the process of building reports, analyzing data, and writing DAX formulas.

Explore the different Copilot experiences

Power BI offers two main ways to interact with Copilot, each designed for different scenarios and user needs:

The Copilot pane

The Copilot pane appears on the right side of the screen in both Power BI Desktop and the Power BI Service, focusing on the report you have open. You can

- Ask questions about the data in the current report.

- Summarize an entire report, a page, or a specific visual.

- Generate new report pages from the underlying semantic model.

- Write or explain DAX formulas.

 TIP Use the Copilot pane when you want to stay within the context of a specific report.

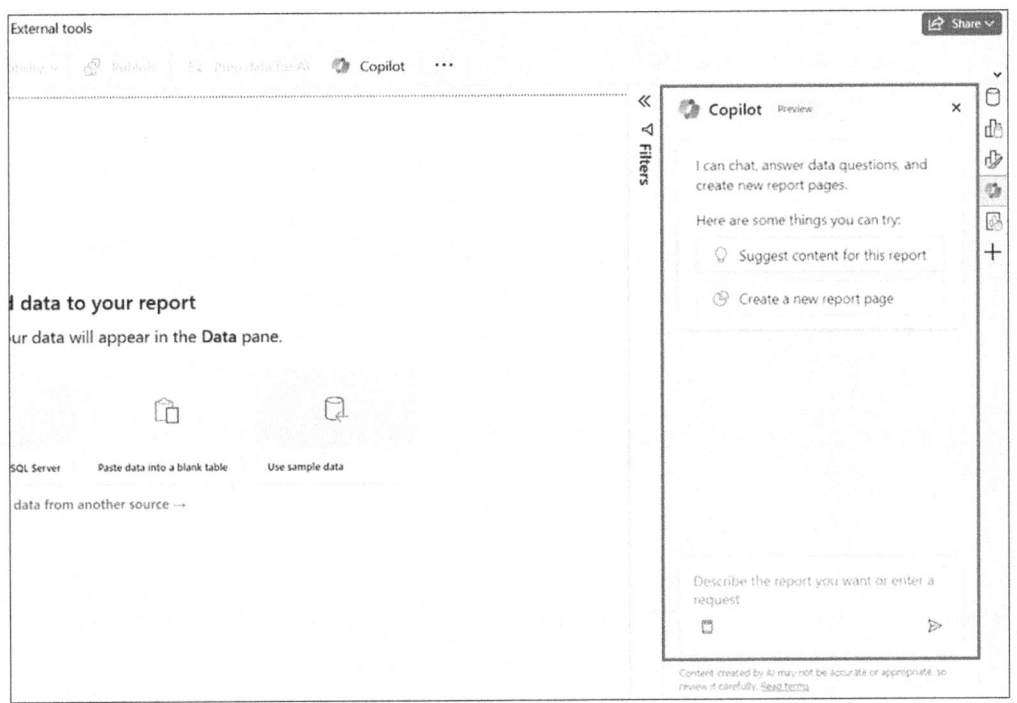

The Copilot pane in Power BI Desktop.

The standalone Copilot experience

The standalone experience opens in a full-screen window in the Power BI Service. Unlike the Copilot pane, which is limited to the report currently open, the standalone view can search and analyze across any report, semantic model, or Fabric data agent that you have permission to access. You can

- Search for and find reports or datasets across your organization.
- Summarize a report or topic without opening it first.
- Ask data questions using any accessible dataset.
- Use Fabric data agents for specialized queries.

13

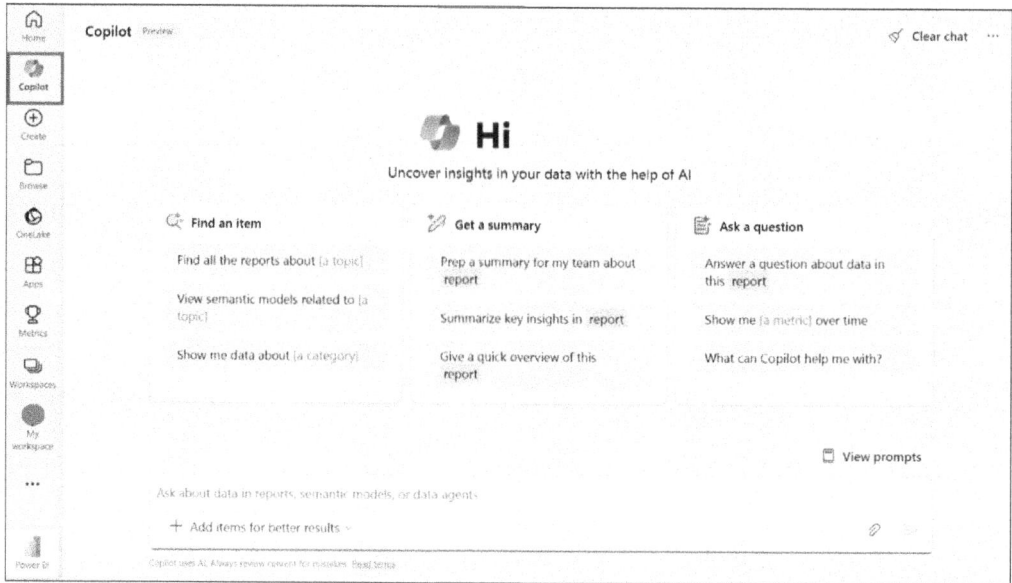

The standalone Copilot interface in the Power BI Service.

> ⚠ **IMPORTANT** At the time of writing, the standalone Copilot is in preview and may not be available in all regions. Check the Microsoft documentation for the latest availability.

> ✓ **TIP** Use the standalone Copilot to explore data across multiple sources when you don't know exactly which report contains the information. Then switch to the Copilot pane for detailed work on a specific report or calculation.

How different roles use Copilot

Copilot offers capabilities that adapt to different roles in your organization:

- **Business users:** Copilot can summarize reports, highlight key trends, or answer ad hoc questions without needing to interpret complex visuals. It's ideal for executives and analysts who need fast insights.

- **Report authors:** Copilot can generate report pages, suggest charts, write DAX measures, and summarize the semantic model to speed up development.

- **Data model owners:** Copilot can document measures and help refine model metadata, making reports easier to understand and use.

> ⚠️ **IMPORTANT** Copilot uses Microsoft Azure OpenAI and large language models (LLMs) to understand your prompts and translate them into actions. This capability allows you to spend less time writing code or building visuals manually and more time focusing on data insights.

Key capabilities overview

Copilot offers a range of capabilities designed to enhance productivity across different roles, enabling business users, report authors, and data model owners to get the maximum value from the tool. The main capabilities include the following:

- Ask questions about your data in natural language.
- Generate automated visualization based on your data and queries.
- Create complex DAX formulas using conversational descriptions.
- Clean and prepare data through natural language instructions.
- Build entire report pages based on descriptive prompts.
- Automatically identify and suggest relationships within your data model.

Configure prerequisites and enable Copilot

Before you can start using Copilot in Power BI Desktop or the Power BI Service, you must ensure that your environment meets all licensing, capacity, and configuration requirements.

Licensing and capacity requirements

The following requirements ensure that Copilot has the necessary resources and configuration to function correctly:

- Copilot is available only in paid Microsoft Fabric (F2 or higher) or Power BI Premium (P1 or higher) capacities.
- Copilot in Microsoft Fabric isn't supported on trial SKUs or Premium Per User (PPU) workspaces.
- Capacity must be in a supported region. If it is outside the United States or France, the Fabric admin must enable the setting that allows data to be processed outside your geographic region.

13

> **TIP** If the Copilot button appears grayed out, your workspace may not be in the right capacity or Copilot may not be enabled. Contact your IT administrator for assistance.

Tenant settings

Your Fabric administrator must enable several tenant settings:

- Enable **Users can use Copilot and other features powered by Azure OpenAI** in the Fabric Admin portal.

- If your capacity is outside the United States or France, enable **Data sent to Azure OpenAI can be processed outside your tenant's geographic region.**

- To use the standalone, full-screen Copilot, enable **Users can access a standalone, cross-item Power BI Copilot experience (preview).**

To enable Copilot in Power BI Desktop

1. Open Power BI Desktop and sign in to the Power BI Service.

2. On the Home ribbon, select the **Copilot** button.

3. When prompted, select a Copilot-compatible workspace from the list.

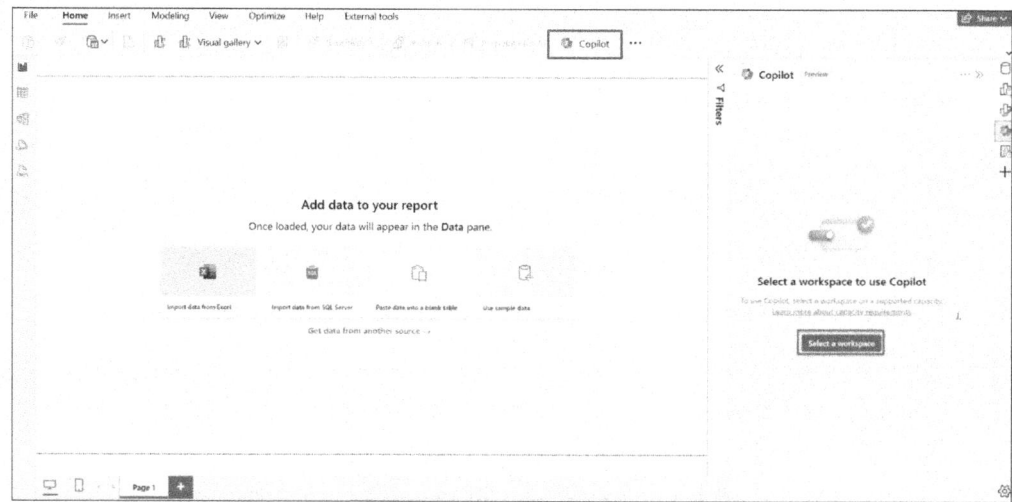

Select a workspace for Copilot in Power BI Desktop.

> **IMPORTANT** Only workspaces that support Copilot will appear in the list, and the workspace you select does not have to be the same one where you plan to publish your report.

4. To change the associated workspace later, select the **Settings** gear icon in the bottom-right corner of Power BI Desktop.

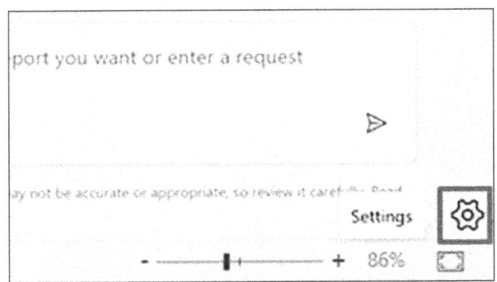

The Copilot Settings gear icon in Power BI Desktop.

5. In the Options window, navigate to **Copilot (preview) settings** to view the current workspace or select a new one.

6. If you don't have access to any compatible workspaces, you'll see the message: **Either none of your workspaces have the right capacity to use Copilot, or you don't have the right permission to use them.**

To enable Copilot in the Power BI Service

To use Copilot in the Power BI Service, the report must be in a workspace assigned to a Premium (P1 or higher) or paid Fabric (F2 or higher) capacity.

1. In the Power BI Service, open the workspace that contains your report.

2. Select **More (…)** and then select **Workspace settings**.

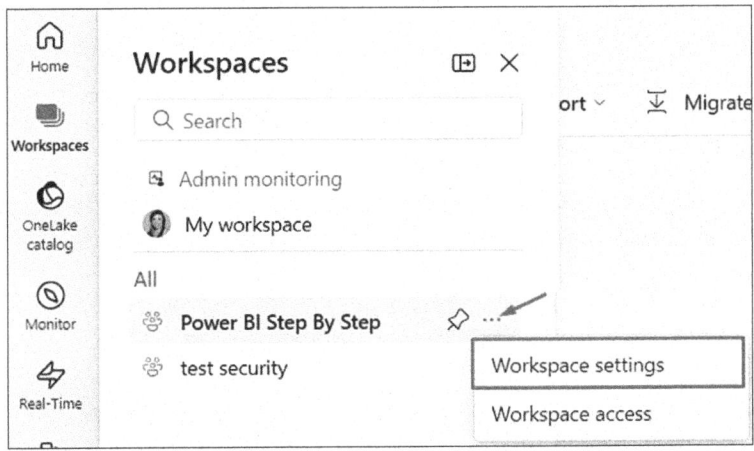

The Workspace settings option in the Power BI Service.

3. Under Premium, assign the workspace to a Premium or Fabric capacity. If the options are grayed out, the workspace does not have access to the required capacity.

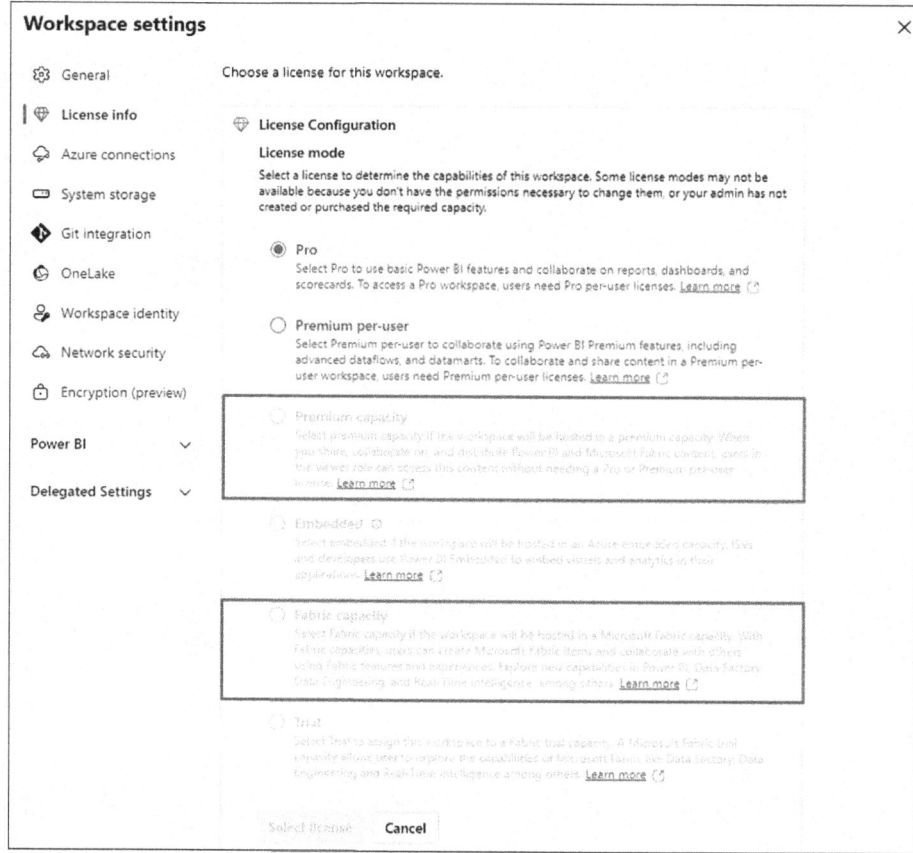

License configuration options in the workspace settings.

4. Close the settings to save your changes.

5. If you are using the standalone Copilot experience, you can select **Choose a workspace** from the Copilot screen to connect to a supported workspace.

Prepare semantic models for AI

After Copilot is enabled, the next step is to prepare your semantic models for AI. Even with the correct licensing and capacity, unoptimized models can lead to vague, incomplete, or misleading answers. A well-prepared model helps Copilot understand your business context, focus on the right information, and deliver accurate, relevant responses.

Best practices for preparing your semantic model

Follow these steps to ensure your model is ready for AI-powered analysis:

- Use clear, descriptive names for tables, columns, and measures. Avoid technical codes or abbreviations that are unfamiliar to business users. Example: **Rename tbl_Cust to Customers.**

- Create meaningful relationships that reflect your business logic. Ensure relationship directions and cardinality are correct.

- Add metadata such as field descriptions, synonyms, and business-friendly terms to improve Copilot's understanding.

- Remove unused or duplicate fields to reduce noise and improve model clarity.

Tools to prepare your data for AI

Power BI includes additional capabilities to help Copilot deliver more accurate and consistent results. These are optional but highly recommended:

- **AI data schema:** Define a dedicated schema specifically for Copilot, keeping only the most relevant tables and fields while hiding technical or administrative columns. This capability focuses Copilot's responses on meaningful business data.

 TIP Include only the fields that business users would naturally ask questions about. Hide technical or administrative columns that don't contribute to business insights.

- **Verified answers:** Allow you to link common user questions to specific visuals in your reports, ensuring that those questions always return consistent, accurate, and expert-validated responses.

- **AI instructions:** Provide Copilot with contextual information about business terminology and priorities, guiding how it interprets queries.

⚠ **IMPORTANT** You can author AI instructions and AI data schema only in Power BI Desktop. Verified answers can be authored in both Power BI Desktop and the Power BI Service. All three features can be consumed anywhere Copilot is available.

13

To prepare data for AI in Power BI Desktop

1. On the Home ribbon, select **Prep data for AI**. This selection opens a unified interface with AI data schema, Verified answers, and AI instructions.

The Prep data for AI button in Power BI Desktop.

2. To set a Verified answer, select the visual you want to link.

3. Open the (···) menu and choose **Set up a verified answer**.

4. Define one or more trigger phrases. When a user enters one of these phrases in Copilot, the linked visual will be returned as the validated answer.

 IMPORTANT All configurations made through Prep data for AI are stored in the semantic model, not in the report file (.pbix).

To Prep data for AI in the Power BI Service

1. Ensure you are working in a Copilot-enabled workspace, with edit access to the semantic model.

2. Open the semantic model from the workspace.

3. Select **Prep data for AI** in the ribbon.

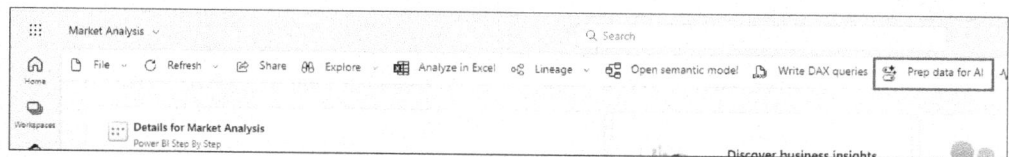

The Prep data for AI button in the Power BI Service.

4. Choose and configure:

- **AI data schema:** Keep only relevant fields.

- **Verified answers:** Link visuals to trigger phrases.

- **AI instructions:** Add business context for Copilot.

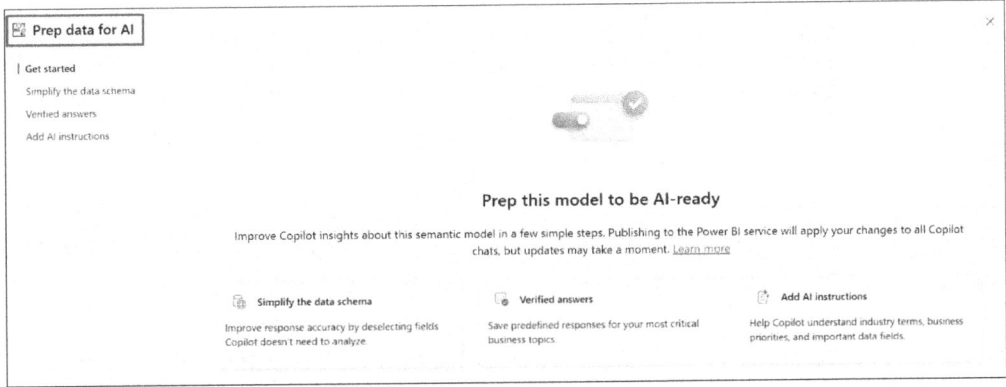

The Prep data for AI interface in Power BI Service.

5. Save changes to apply them across Copilot experiences.

Mark your model as prepped for AI

When your semantic model is fully prepared for Copilot and you've ensured it is ready for use, you can mark it as Prepped for AI so that Copilot recognizes it as optimized for AI interactions.

To mark a model as prepped for AI

1. In the Power BI Service, find your semantic model.

2. Select the **Settings** icon in the top-left corner.

3. Expand the **AI preparation** section.

4. Check the **Prepped for AI** box. Then select the **Apply** button.

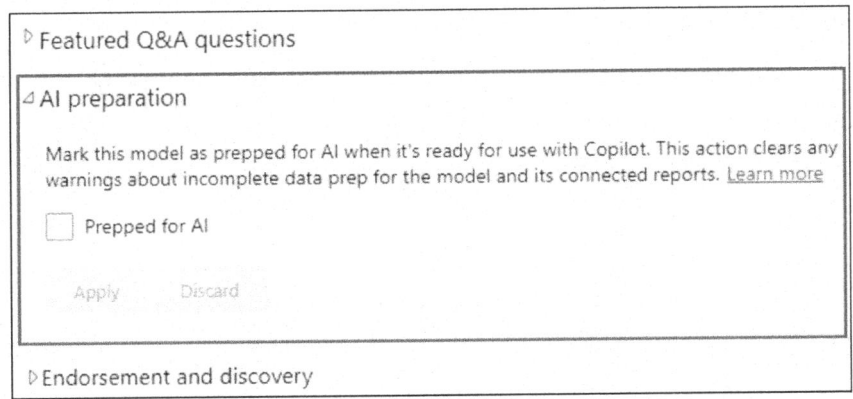

The AI preparation option in Power BI model settings.

> ⚠️ **IMPORTANT** Before marking your model as prepped for AI, thoroughly test it with Copilot by trying common questions that users might ask to ensure accurate and helpful responses.

Use Copilot in Power BI Desktop

After you review the main Copilot capabilities available in both Power BI Desktop and the Power BI Service, it is important to focus on how these features work, specifically in the Desktop environment. In Desktop, Copilot is especially valuable during the modeling and report creation phases, where you can work with your data before publishing it to the Power BI Service.

Copilot in Power BI Desktop allows you to

- Generate complete report pages from natural language prompts.
- Create visuals instantly based on your questions or requests.
- Write and explain DAX formulas to accelerate calculation creation.
- Add clear descriptions to measures, improving model documentation.

Create complete reports with Copilot

After your semantic model is prepared for AI, Copilot can help you create complete, interactive reports without starting from a blank canvas. By using natural language prompts, you can quickly generate report pages, visuals, and summaries aligned to your analysis needs.

To create a report with Copilot

1. In Power BI Desktop, connect to your data or attach an existing semantic model.

2. Select the **Copilot** button on the ribbon to display the Copilot pane in Report view.

3. Select **Create a new report page** or **Suggest content for this report** to let Copilot analyze your data. You can also type your own custom prompt.

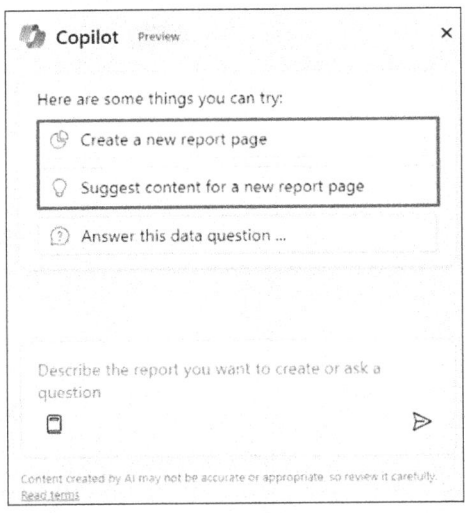

The Copilot pane in Power BI.

    4.   Select **Create** next to a suggested page or confirm your custom prompt.

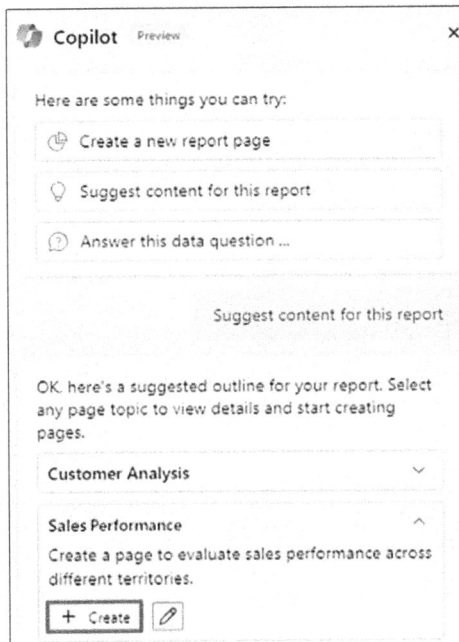

The Create button for adding a new report page.

5. Review the generated visuals and layout. Add, remove, or rearrange elements as needed.

 TIP If you want to completely restart a page, select Undo.

---

6. Save the report after all pages meet your needs.

Best practices for writing effective prompts

The quality of the report generated depends heavily on the clarity of your prompt. Here are some tips and examples:

- Be specific about metrics and dimensions: Instead of *"Show sales,"* use *"Create a report page with total sales, average order value, and number of customers, broken down by product category and month."*

- Include the type of visual you want: *"Add a line chart for monthly sales, a bar chart for top five products, and a KPI card for profit margin."*

- Add filters or scope: *"Generate a report for sales in 2025 in South America only, including a map of sales by state and a table of top customers."*

- Combine multiple insights into one request: *"Create a performance dashboard showing revenue vs. target, sales by region, and quarterly trends."*

Create a narrative visual with Copilot

Copilot can generate a text-based summary of your report, a page, or selected visuals, helping you highlight trends, comparisons, and anomalies automatically.

To create a narrative visual

1. In Power BI Desktop, select **Get Data**, then select a data source.

2. In Visualizations, select the **Narrative** icon.

3. In Choose a narrative type, select the **Copilot** button to use the new narrative visual.

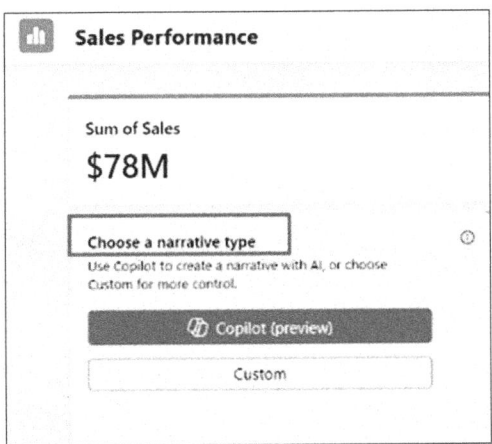

The Choose a narrative type option in Power BI.

4. In the Create a narrative with Copilot dialog, choose whether to summarize the entire report, specific pages, or selected visuals, and then select **Create**.

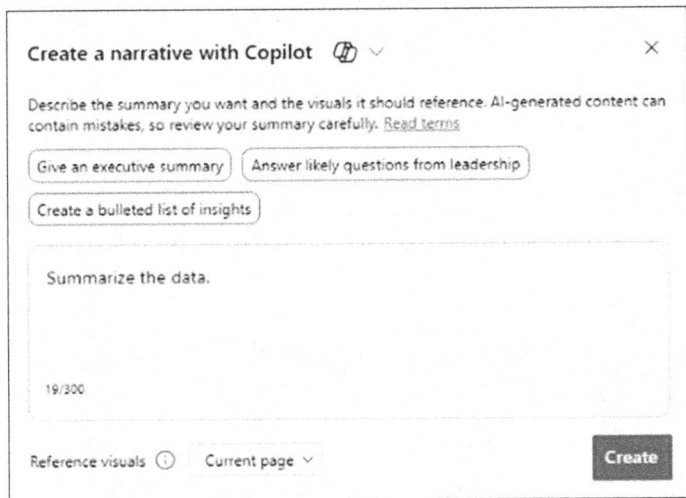

Create a narrative with Copilot.

5. Refine the summary with suggested or custom prompts such as **Provide a summary of sales performance, including total sales, costs, and profit. Describe trends over time, highlight the top and bottom products, and summarize sales by country.**

6. Copilot adds a text box containing the narrative to your page. Review the results and save the report.

TIP You cannot directly edit Copilot-generated text. If you need manual changes, copy the text into a Smart Narrative visual or adjust the prompt to regenerate it.

Best practices for writing prompts for narrative visuals

When you're creating narrative visuals, the quality of your prompt directly impacts the clarity and usefulness of the generated summary. Use these best practices to ensure Copilot delivers meaningful insights:

- Be specific about the focus. Clearly indicate the metric, dimension, or relationship you want to highlight.

- Define the scope. Tell Copilot whether the narrative should summarize the entire report, a single page, or selected visuals.

- Request a structure or format. If you want bullet points, bolded text, or a comparative tone, include that information in your prompt.

- Refine iteratively. Start with a base prompt and then improve the narrative by asking Copilot to shorten, rephrase, or emphasize certain aspects.

- Use business context. Include relevant business terms or KPIs so the narrative aligns with your goals.

 TIP Combine descriptive instructions (what to summarize) with style guidance (how to present it) for the best results.

Write and explain DAX queries with Copilot

Copilot can help you write new Data Analysis Expressions (DAX) formulas or explain existing ones, making it easier to create calculations and understand complex logic. This capability is especially useful for report authors and data model owners who want to speed up development or learn DAX concepts directly in context.

To write and explain DAX queries

1. Open an existing Power BI report or connect to a published semantic in Power BI Desktop.

2. Go to DAX Query view (the icon on the left side of Power BI Desktop).

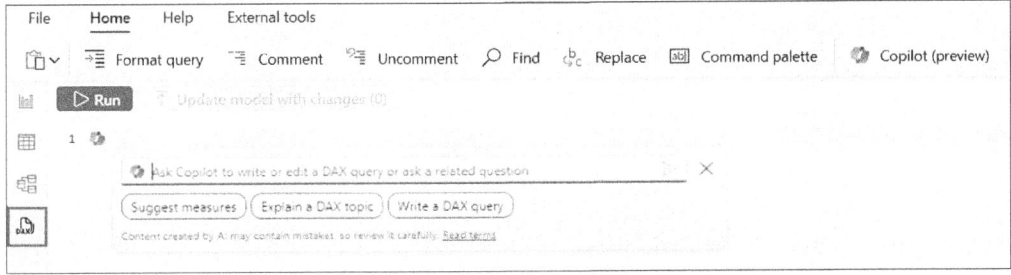

DAX Query view with Copilot in Power BI Desktop.

3. To create a new measure, type your request—for example, **Write a DAX query to show profit by products**.

4. Copilot will generate the DAX expression.

5. Run the query to verify the result before adding it to your model.

A DAX query generated by Copilot in the DAX Query view.

6. To explain a formula, select the measure, open Copilot, and type **Explain this measure**. Copilot will break down the formula in plain language.

7. For more details on a DAX function, for example, type **Explain SUMMARIZE-COLUMNS function**, and Copilot will provide a description, explanation, and example.

> ✓ **TIP** Always validate Copilot-generated DAX in your data context to ensure it returns correct results.

13

Create descriptions for DAX formulas

Copilot can help you document your semantic model by automatically generating clear, business-friendly descriptions for your measures. These descriptions improve model usability, especially for business users exploring the data or using Q&A and Copilot features.

To create descriptions for measures

1. In the Model view, select the measure you want to document.

2. Under the Description field, select **Create with Copilot (preview)**.

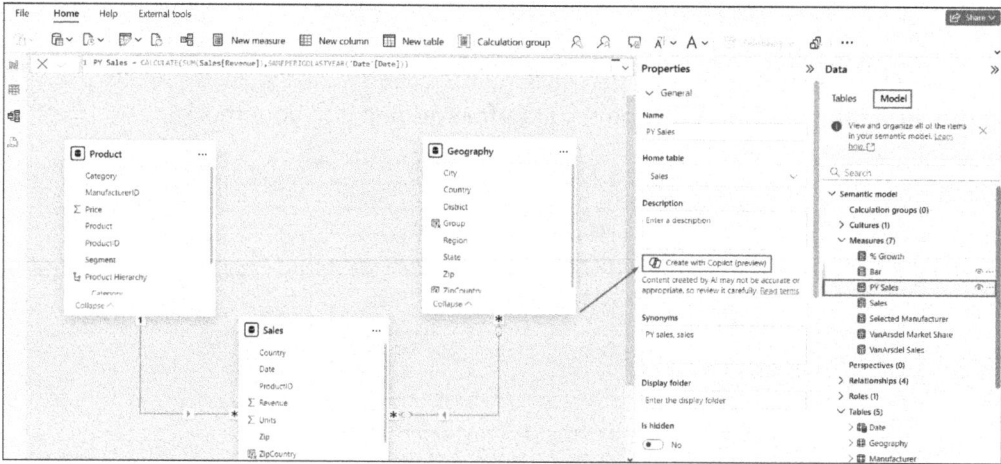

Create a measure with Copilot.

3. Review the generated description. Edit it if necessary to refine the business context.

4. Save your changes.

 TIP Focus on the business purpose of the measure. Use concise, business-friendly language that explains what it calculates and why it is important.

Explore Copilot in the Power BI Service

Although Copilot in Power BI Desktop is ideal for building and refining reports locally, the Power BI Service adds collaboration, sharing, and cloud-based AI capabilities. In the Service, you can use Copilot to

- Edit published reports without reopening them in Desktop.

- Search and analyze content across multiple workspaces.

- Add narrative summaries to pages or visuals.

- Share insights directly in Microsoft Teams, Outlook, or other channels.

 TIP Copilot can analyze only content you have permission to access. If Copilot can't access certain reports or datasets, check workspace permissions.

Find content with the standalone Copilot experience

The standalone Copilot is your organization-wide interface where you can search, explore, and interact with any accessible item in Power BI using natural language.

To explore content

1. Open Copilot from the left navigation pane in the Power BI Service (Fabric portal).

2. In the starter prompts, choose **Find an item**, or type a search such as **Find items about sales revenue**.

3. Review the results list. Each item shows its type (icon), title (hyperlink), workspace, last opened date, description (if available), matched metadata from your query, and whether it is part of an app.

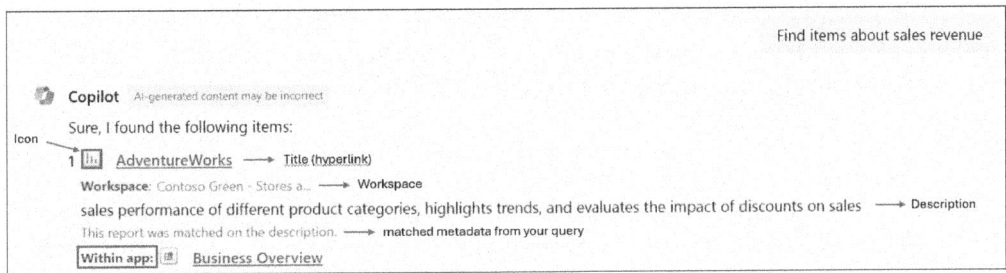

Results in the standalone Copilot.

4. Select an item's title to open it in a new tab. Your chat stays open so you can keep browsing or asking questions.

5. Refine your search with natural language filters, such as **only reports in the Sales workspace** or **items updated this quarter**.

Create a report page with Copilot in the Service

You can start from any semantic model available in the Power BI Service and let Copilot automatically draft a report page for you, based on your prompt.

To create a report page with Copilot

1. From the OneLake data hub (the central data storage in Fabric), open your semantic model and select **Create report**.

 IMPORTANT Make sure your report is stored in a workspace where you have build permissions and where Copilot is enabled.

2. In the report canvas, open Copilot.

3. Describe what you need—for example, enter **Sales by product for the last 12 months; add slicers for Region and Store**.

4. Review the generated page, fine-tune fields and visuals, and select **Save**.

 TIP After creating a report page, you can also use Copilot to enhance it—adding new visuals, slicers, or highlights—without having to rebuild anything manually.

Summarize a report with Copilot

Copilot can instantly create natural language summaries of a Power BI report's visualized data, helping you identify key trends, patterns, and anomalies without manually reviewing every visual. You can access this feature from the Copilot pane inside a report or from the standalone Copilot experience without opening the report first.

 TIP The standalone Copilot experience embeds visuals directly in the summary and allows deeper exploration via Explore buttons.

To summarize a report

1. Open the report in View or Edit mode.

2. In the right pane, select **Copilot**.

3. Choose a suggested prompt like **What is this page about?** or type a custom request such as **Summarize sales trends for the past fiscal year**.

4. Review the summary and citations; refine with follow-up prompts if needed.

5. (Optional) Add the summary as a Narrative (with Copilot) visual and save the report.

Add a narrative with Copilot (Narrative visual)

Just as in Power BI Desktop, you can create narratives in the Power BI Service. The Narrative (with Copilot) visual needs existing content to summarize, so in the Service follow these steps:

1. From the OneLake data hub, select **More options** next to a semantic model.

2. Choose **Create report**.

From this point onward, follow the same steps as described in the "Create a narrative visual with Copilot" section earlier in this chapter.

 SEE ALSO The process to create a narrative visual in Power BI Service is the same as in Power BI Desktop. Follow steps 2 through 6 in the "Create a narrative visual with Copilot" section under the "Use Copilot in Power BI Desktop" topic in this chapter.

Ask Copilot for data from your model

In the Power BI Service, Copilot can create visuals directly from the data in your semantic model, even if they are not already part of a report page. Simply describe what you need, and Copilot will query the model to return an answer in visual form.

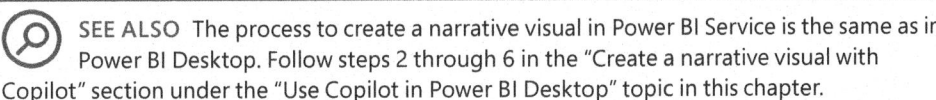

⚠ **IMPORTANT** The only supported language is English for this capability.

To ask Copilot for data from your model

1. Open the report in the Power BI Service and select **Copilot**.

2. Type your question.

3. Review the generated visual and description of the fields and measures used.

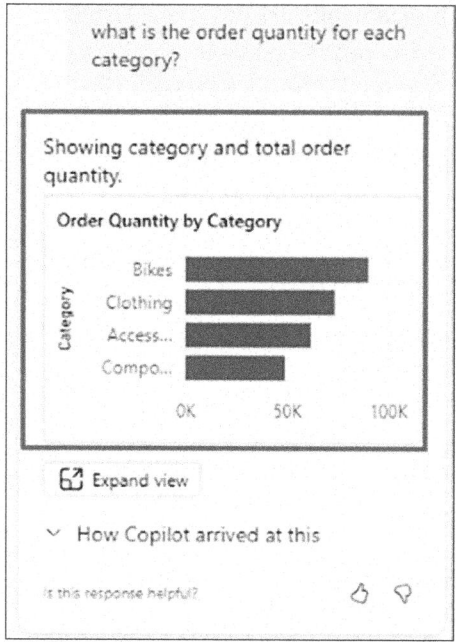

The Copilot pane in Power BI.

4. (Optional) Expand **How Copilot arrived at this** to see its reasoning and data details.

5. (Optional, authors only) Select **Add to page** to insert the visual into the report.

 TIP Authors can help Copilot understand business questions by using unique, descriptive field and measure names, following data modeling best practices, and adding synonyms for business-specific terms.

IMPORTANT Copilot cannot yet perform tasks like anomaly detection, forecasting, or key influencer analysis.

Create DAX queries with Copilot in the Power BI Service

In the Power BI Service, you can also use Copilot to help write DAX queries against a published semantic model.

To write a DAX query with Copilot in the Service

1. In a workspace, locate the published semantic model you want to query.

2. From the shortcut menu, select **Write DAX queries**.

 TIP If this option is grayed out, enable Users can edit data models in the Power BI service (preview) in the Power BI General section of the workspace settings.

3. Create a new query tab.

4. Open Copilot by selecting the **Copilot** button or pressing Ctrl+I.

Skills review

In this chapter, you learned how to

- Recognize what Copilot in Power BI is and the different ways it can be used by business users, report authors, and data model owners.

- Differentiate between the Copilot pane and the standalone Copilot experience and identify when to use each.

- Configure prerequisites to enable Copilot, including licensing, capacity, and tenant settings.

- Prepare semantic models for AI, applying best practices and using AI preparation tools such as AI data schema, Verified answers, and AI instructions.

- In Power BI Desktop, use Copilot to generate reports from natural language prompts, create narrative visuals that summarize data insights, write and explain DAX formulas, and produce descriptions for measures.

- Use the standalone Copilot experience in the Power BI Service to search and explore content, create and enhance report pages, summarize reports and visuals, ask questions, and generate visuals from a semantic model.

13

Practice tasks

No practice files are necessary to complete the practice tasks in this chapter.

These tasks will help you reinforce the concepts introduced in this chapter. You will verify prerequisites for Copilot, prepare a semantic model for AI, and explore Copilot's capabilities in both Power BI Desktop and the Power BI Service.

Understand Copilot in Power BI

Confirm that you have the right permissions, licensing, and capacity to use Copilot:

1. In the Power BI Service, open the workspace where you want to use Copilot.

2. Check that the workspace is assigned to a Premium (P1 or higher) or Fabric (F2 or higher) capacity.

3. In Workspace settings, confirm that you have build and edit permissions on the semantic model.

4. If Copilot is still unavailable, check with your Fabric admin whether Copilot and Azure OpenAI features are enabled in Tenant settings.

Reflect:

1. What happens if your workspace is in an unsupported capacity?

2. What are the key differences between the Copilot pane and the standalone experience?

Prepare semantic models for AI

Use AI preparation tools to improve Copilot's understanding of your data:

Reflect:

1. Why is it important to include synonyms in AI instructions?

2. In what scenarios would Verified answers be especially valuable?

3. Why is it important to mark a semantic model as Prepped for AI before using it with Copilot?

Use Copilot in Power BI Desktop

Practice generating reports and explaining calculations with Copilot:

1. Open a semantic model in Power BI Desktop and enable Copilot.

2. In Report view, prompt Copilot to create a report page showing three KPIs relevant to your business scenario.

3. Add a narrative visual summarizing key trends in the generated page.

4. Switch to DAX query view and ask Copilot to create a measure based on your instructions.

5. Ask Copilot to explain the measure in plain language.

6. Generate a business-friendly description for the measure and save it.

Reflect:

1. How specific did your prompt need to be to get the desired report?

2. In what ways can Copilot explanations of DAX help nontechnical users?

Explore Copilot in the Power BI Service

Explore content and create new report pages with Copilot in the Service:

1. In the Power BI Service, open Copilot from the left navigation pane to access the standalone experience.

2. Search for reports or datasets related to a topic of your choice.

3. Apply a natural language filter such as only reports in the Sales workspace.

4. Select one report from the results and ask Copilot to summarize it.

5. From a published semantic model, prompt Copilot to create a new report page with at least two visuals and one slicer.

6. Save your work and share the report link with a colleague.

Reflect:

1. How do natural language filters improve the precision of your search results?

2. What are the advantages and differences of creating report pages directly in the Service instead of in Desktop?

Index

Plug into learning at

MicrosoftPressStore.com

The Microsoft Press Store by Pearson offers:

- Free U.S. shipping

- Buy an eBook, get multiple formats – PDF and EPUB – to use on your computer, tablet, and mobile devices

- Print & eBook Best Value Packs

- eBook Deal of the Week – Save up to 60% on featured title

- Newsletter – Be the first to hear about new releases, announcements, special offers, and more

- Register your book – Find companion files, errata, and product updates, plus receive a special coupon* to save on your next purchase

 Pearson